WESTERN MUSLIMS AND
THE FUTURE OF ISLAM

Western Muslims and the Future of Islam

Tariq Ramadan

OXFORD
UNIVERSITY PRESS

OXFORD
UNIVERSITY PRESS

Oxford University Press, Inc., publishes works that further
Oxford University's objective of excellence
in research, scholarship, and education.

Oxford   New York
Auckland   Cape Town   Dar es Salaam   Hong Kong   Karachi
Kuala Lumpur   Madrid   Melbourne   Mexico City   Nairobi
New Delhi   Shanghai   Taipei   Toronto

With offices in
Argentina   Austria   Brazil   Chile   Czech Republic   France   Greece
Guatemala   Hungary   Italy   Japan   Poland   Portugal   Singapore
South Korea   Switzerland   Thailand   Turkey   Ukraine   Vietnam

First published in 2004 by Oxford University Press, Inc.
198 Madison Avenue, New York, New York 10016

First issued as an Oxford University Press paperback, 2005

www.oup.com

Oxford is a registered trademark of Oxford University Press, Inc.

Library of Congress Cataloging-in-Publication Data
Ramadan, Tariq.
[Musulmans d'Occident et l'avenir de l'islam. English]
Western Muslims and the future of Islam / Tariq Ramadan.
    p. cm.
ISBN-13 978-0-19-517111-2; 978-0-19-518356-6 (pbk.)
ISBN 0-19-517111-X; 0-19-518356-8 (pbk.)
1. Islam—Europe.   2. Muslims—Europe.   3. Islamic renewal—Europe.
4. Islamic modernism—Europe.   5. Muslims—Cultural assimilation—Europe.
6. Europe—Ethnic relations.   7. Islam—21st century.   I. Title.
BP65.A1R3613 2003
297'.09182'1—dc21   2003012908

9 8 7 6 5 4 3

Printed in the United States of America

To Aymen, my eldest brother,
always here, with love
To Muna, Shelina, Abderahman, Ibrahima,
Muneeb, and Salah as we journey together . . .
for His love, for more justice

PREFACE

Exile toward the Beginning

Someday we are bound to come back to the beginning. Even the most distant pathways always lead us inward, completely inward, into intimacy, solitude between our self and our self—in the place where there is no longer anyone but God and our self.

Paulo Coelho, in his novel *The Alchemist*, has brought in one of the most traditional and deep teachings of Sufism (Islamic mysticism). Go, travel the world, watch, look for the truth and the secret of life—every road will lead you to this sense of initiation: the light, the secret, are hidden in the place from which you set out. You are on your way not toward the end of the road but toward its beginning; to go is to return; to find is to rediscover. *Go! . . . You will return.* The apparent paradox of spiritual experience is the lesson that the constant effort, the *jihad*, that we make in order to purify, control, and liberate our heart is, in the end, a reconciliation with the deepest level of our being *(al-fitra)*—there where the spark gleams that God originally breathed into our heart, there where our conscience weds our being and gives in to peace *(salam)*. The peace of recognition, the peace of submission *(salam al-islam)*, is, deep down, a liberation.

God is "The one who created death and life to test you and to find out which of you would behave best." Death, life, experiences, ordeals, pain, solitude, as well as joy and happiness, are so many lessons along the road to reconciliation. Wounds, separations, tears, as well as smiles, "say" something: if you live in unawareness, they touch you; with God, they guide and lead you. Where to? Where to then? Toward Him, toward you, close to Him in you. Such is the most beautiful and the most difficult lesson of Islam: you find God only by rediscovering your own nature, and the essence of your nature is the only thing that can free you from its appearance. . . . "I" must set out to discover another "I": such is the meaning of life. Ordeals drive you not to your limits but to your origin, where "the need for Him" has its root. Ordeals will lead you back, whether you like it or not, to what you are, to the essence from which He has formed you. Exile will take you home.

A man once exclaimed to the mystic Rabia al-Adawiyya, "I have discovered a thousand proofs of the existence of God!" She closed the conversation by saying that she had only one proof and that was enough for her. "Which?" he asked. "If you are alone in the desert and you fall down a well, to whom will you turn?" "To God," he said. "That proof is enough for me!" A strange reply, seemingly simple, even simplistic, that a rationalist or atheist would without hesitation take as confirmation of what he had always believed: "God is the refuge of the destitute, the hope of the hopeless, a consolation, a reassuring invention!"

On the surface, on the surface only . . . suffering and the unknown seem to press the mind to look for a refuge, a consolation. This is the logic our reason proposes when it looks on the human being on the outside of its nature. The Islamic tradition says exactly the opposite: the ordeals of life, sadness, encountering the death of those we love, for example, take the human being back to its most natural state, to its most essential longing. Consciousness of limitation brings it back to the need for the Transcendent, to the need for meaning. To call on God is not to console oneself—it is to rediscover the condition God originally wanted for us—the spark of humility, the awareness of fragility.

Before your eyes is a child . . . life, dependence, fragility, and innocence. To be with God is to know how to keep this state: a humble acceptance of your fragility, a comprehension of your dependence—going back to the beginning. In fact, the temptation to pride consists in thinking that man can cut himself off from his nature and attain total intellectual autonomy to the point where he can take on his own suffering, deliberately and alone. Pride is to affirm outward independence by maintaining the illusion of liberty at the heart of one's being. Humility is to rediscover the breath of the primordial need of Him at the heart of our being, in order to live in total outward independence.

Go! . . . *You will return.*

ACKNOWLEDGMENTS

The writing of this book has not been easy. The two academic years following 11 September 2001 were full of travels, meetings, conferences, and engagements. I had long been concerned to put into writing the sum of the theoretical and practical ideas begun by and built upon *To Be a European Muslim*, and in the past few years I have received encouragement and help from a lot of people. It is impossible to name them all here one by one, but I should like to express my respect for and gratitude to all those, both near and far, who have been with me in my efforts and who have borne the difficulties of this commitment. Among my close colleagues there are those who have had to endure my daily rhythm, moods, and character more than others, and I think especially of my colleagues, Malika, who was so present for two years, and Assia, who radiates an endless generosity and reveals a constant concern to do good, along with Siham, with her ever-present energy.

I want to thank with all my heart Carol Bebawi for her excellent work on the translation and for her discreet and modest generosity—a real gift. Muna Ali, in Arizona, has spent hours and hours reading and discussing the book; our collaboration is priceless, and I thank the One for providing me with this quality of spiritual and human companionship. A sense of fraternity unites the very generous and good traveling companions Shelina, Abd al-Rahman, Ibrahima, Salah, and Muneeb: they accompany me, support me, offer me their love. To all of them, and to those close to them, I say, "Thank you for being there and giving me so much."

I do not have words sufficiently illuminating and deep to thank Maryam, Sami, Moussa, Najma, and Iman. I shall never forget the very favorable conditions in which I have been able to write this book. May the Light be with you, protect you, and love you.

To Khadija and Tariq I acknowledge my special gratitude for help, sunshine, and home.

I should also like to thank those who supported me when I was facing difficulties and criticism and who sustained my profound optimism. It is thanks to God and to their love, affection, and loyalty that I still find the strength to pursue these efforts and to continue on this path. Thank you for not doubting my sincerity in spite of my faults and mistakes.

CONTENTS

WESTERN MUSLIMS AND
THE FUTURE OF ISLAM

INTRODUCTION

In Practice...

When I wrote *To Be a European Muslim: A Study of the Islamic Sources in the Light of the European Context* in 1997,[1] many readers were surprised and challenged by the approach to the Islamic textual sources (the Qur'an and the Sunna) that I was proposing, and by the propositions I was trying to articulate with regard to rereading our sources. Their questions were usually aimed in the same direction: where would it lead *in practice*? For I had said that this was only a first step and that more work would have to follow to formulate the vision of the whole and to apply these reflections in practical terms on the ground. These past years have been fed by a constant threefold work of deepening my reflection on the sources, bringing them face to face with the realities on the ground, and analyzing the local dynamics in accordance with meetings and exchanges with Muslim association groups (and consequently a number of partners) in Europe and North America (not forgetting the very Western circumstances of Mauritius, Reunion, or Singapore). This has made it possible for me to take up the work begun five years ago and to synthesize it into a more global and coherent vision of Islamic principles, the available juridical instruments, and the means of employing them. This work makes up the whole of the first part of this present volume. I have not included all the elements of the reflection contained in *To Be a European Muslim*, but I have restricted myself to those that had a direct link with my purpose here: to understand the universality of the message of Islam and to highlight the means we are given to help us live in our own time, in the West, with respect for ourselves and for others. The approach I propose is anchored in the Islamic tradition and amplified from within it: in this sense it is both deeply classical and radically new. Beginning with the Qur'an and the Sunna and the methodologies set down by the ulama throughout the history of the Islamic sciences,[2] I have tried to immerse myself again in reading these sources in the light of our new Western context; even though the methodology I have adopted is classical, I have not hesitated sometimes to question certain definitions and categorizations and to suggest others. It is especially in my suggestions and my replies that one will doubtless find some new perspectives, which I hope may be useful. My conviction in elaborating on this work is that the movement toward reform, which was once intrinsic to the juridical compass of Islam, can take place effectively only from within, in and through a rigorous faithfulness to the sources and the norms of reading them. This is the requirement I have laid upon myself.

The second part of my study concentrates on the practical application of these reflections in Western society.[3] Questions as essential as the spiritual life, or education in industrialized, more or less postmodern, more or less secularized societies, are studied with an attempt, whenever possible, to approach the subject from three perspectives: the principles to respect, the reality of the situation, and the reforms that seem to me necessary to face the challenges of life in Europe or in North America. I have tried to follow the same stages in each chapter. Following on from spirituality and education, social engagement and political participation, economic resistance, interreligious dialogue, and the cultural equivalent are some of the subjects I have felt needed to be addressed at this precise juncture of our history in the West.

We are currently living through a veritable silent revolution in Muslim communities in the West: more and more young people and intellectuals are actively looking for a way to live in harmony with their faith while participating in the societies that are their societies, whether they like it or not. French, English, German, Canadian, and American Muslims, women as well as men, are constructing a "Muslim personality" that will soon surprise many of their fellow citizens. Far from media attention, going through the risks of a process of maturation that is necessarily slow, they are drawing the shape of European and American Islam: faithful to the principles of Islam, dressed in European and American cultures, and definitively rooted in Western societies. This grassroots movement will soon exert considerable influence over worldwide Islam: in view of globalization and the Westernization of the world, these are the same questions as those already being raised from Morocco to Indonesia.

Globalization contains the paradox that at the same time that it causes the old traditional points of reference to disappear, it reawakens passionate affirmations of identity that often verge on withdrawal and self-exclusion. The Muslim world is not exempt from such phenomena: from Africa to Asia, via America and Europe, this kind of discourse is multiplied. It is about self-protection, self-preservation, and sometimes even self-definition over and against the "Western megamachine," to use the formulation of Serge Latouche: "Whatever is Western is anti-Islamic" or "Islam has nothing in common with the West." This bipolar vision is widespread and gives some Muslims a sense of power, might, and legitimacy in Otherness. But not only is this bipolar and simplistic vision a decoy (and the claims that justify it are untruths), but the power it bestows is a pure illusion: in practice, the Muslims who maintain these theses only isolate themselves, marginalize themselves, and sometimes, by their excessive emotional, intellectual, and social isolation, even strengthen the logic of the dominant system whose power, by contrast, lies in always appearing open, pluralistic, and rational.

The approach I propose here is the exact opposite of this attitude. Beginning with the message of Islam and its universal principles, I have investigated the tools that can give an impetus, from the inside, to a movement of reform and integration into the new environments. The power and effectiveness of the "principle of integration," which is the foundation upon which all the juridical instruments for adaptation must depend, lie in the fact that it comes with an entirely opposite perspective; instead of being sensitive, obsessed by self-protection and withdrawal and attempts to integrate *oneself* by "the little door," on the margin, or "as a minority," it is, on the contrary, a matter of *integrating*, making one's own all that people have produced that is good, just, humane—intellectually, scientifically, socially, politically, economically, culturally, and so on. While our fellow-citizens speak of this "integration" of Muslims "among us," the question for the Muslims presents itself differently: their universal principles teach them that wherever the law respects their integrity and their freedom of conscience and worship, they are at home and must consider the attainments of these societies as their own and must involve themselves, with their fellow-citizens, in making it good and better. No withdrawal, no obsession with identity—on the contrary, it is a question of entering into an authentic dialogue, as between equals, with all our fellow-citizens with respect for the identical universality of our respective values, willingly open to mutual enrichment and eventually to becoming true partners in action.

I know that these ideas are frightening and that they appear new and "offensive," to use the expression of a questioner who heard them at one of my lectures in the United Kingdom. Let me say that my reading of the scriptural sources and the study of our Western environment have led me to lay down two fundamental theses that involve the determined rejection of certain intellectual positions. First, for me it is not a question of relativizing the universal principles of Islam in order to give the impression that we are integrating ourselves into the rational order. In my view, the issue is to find out how the Islamic universal accepts and respects pluralism and the belief of the Other: it is one thing to relativize what I believe and another to respect fully the convictions of the Other. The post-modernist spirit would like to lead us unconsciously to confuse the second proposition with the first. I refuse: it is in the very name of the universality of my principles that my conscience is summoned to respect diversity and the relative, and that is why, even in the West (especially in the West), we have not to think of our presence in terms of "minority." What seems to be a given of our thinking: "the Muslim minority," "the law of minorities" (*fiqh al-aqalliyyat*), must, I believe, be rethought. We shall do a little of this in the following pages. Second, I defend fiercely the idea that Western Muslims must be intellectually, politically, and financially independent. Of course, this does not imply that exchanges and discussions with Muslim countries should cease—rather the contrary. We have more need than ever to maintain spaces for meeting and debate (especially since there are not yet any ulama we can refer to who were born and formed in the West). In this period of transition, links between Muslims of West and East are essential. What I mean exactly by the idea of "independence" is that West-ern citizens of the Muslim faith must think for themselves, develop theses appropriate to their situation, and put forward new and concrete ideas. They must refuse to remain dependent, either on the intellectual level or, more damagingly, on the political and financial levels. These types of de-pendences are the worst because they prevent the acquisition of respon-sibility and the reform and liberation of hearts and minds.[4] In the same way, as a citizen, I refuse to support the colonialist reaction found among certain governments and commentators that consists of wanting to keep Muslims in these old (or other new) dependences and in wanting to "speak for them," as we reject the insidious "paternalism" of some who "help" "young" Muslims eternally destined in their spirits never to become adults.

These two positions of principle are ultimately nothing but the reflection of the dynamics that are slowly coming into place in the West. I have consciously decided not to deal specifically with the problems of political security faced by European and American states, or with Islamophobia or social discrimination—not because I think these problems are secondary but because my thinking is based at a higher level. It is by acquiring the conviction that they can be faithful to their principles while being totally involved in the life of their society that Muslims will find the means to confront these difficulties and act to resolve them. It is an established and unacceptable fact that the governments of the United States (particularly after the outrages of 11 September 2001) and Europe maintain relations that are sometimes disrespectful of and even clearly discriminatory against citizens and residents of their countries who are of the Muslim faith. It is no less true that they apply a security policy including constant surveil-lance: distrust is maintained, and the image of the "Muslim" often remains suspect. The general picture conceived by the Western population in general is so negative that one could call it Islamophobia, and this is a fact that many Muslims have lived with on a daily basis. One could extend the list of difficulties, complaints, and criticisms at will. My response to all these phenomena is to insist to Muslims that they stay in the higher reaches, in awareness of their principles, values, and responsibilities. By developing a global vision of their points of reference and their objectives, by studying their situation and being reconciled with themselves, they have the responsibility to become engaged in all the areas we shall study in the second part of this book. Muslims will get what they deserve: if, as watchful and participating citizens, they study the machinery of their society, demand their rights to equality with others, struggle against all kinds of discrimination and injustice, establish real partnerships beyond their own community and what concerns themselves alone, it will be an achievement that will make political security measures, discrimination, Islamophobic behavior, and so on drift away downstream. In the end, the ball is in their court . . . unless they are determined to remain forever on the margins.

This book is only one step more toward the building of the Muslim personality in the West and doubtless in the modern era, too. It will not be the last. Other works, *in sha Allah*, must continue to trace the path back to the beginning. I have humbly tried to draw the theoretical and practical outlines of a vision for the future, full on. I want to engage with this in practice, and already, across all the countries of the West, this vision is being accomplished. The road is still long, but indwelt by this humble "need of Him," one must not be afraid or apologize for needing time.

Part I

A Universe of Reference

Whether they are Western or Eastern, the Muslims of the world refer to a universe of meaning elaborated and constructed around a certain number of fundamental principles. Above and beyond the diversity of their national cultures, the essence of their faith, their identity, their being in the world, is the same; they define themselves on the basis of points of reference that explain their sense of belonging to the same community of faith and at the same time, more profoundly, root them in the universe of Islam. The often complex connection between the common principles and the diverse ways of life that one quickly notices if one visits the Muslim countries of Black Africa, North Africa, or Asia has led some orientalists and sociologists to speak of various "Islams" to take account of this plurality of cultures. Only an in-depth study of the sources and the Islamic sciences can enable us to understand how, across various geographical areas, the oneness of the points of reference and the diversity of their lived manifestations become concrete and overlap. There is one Islam, and the fundamental principles that define it are those to which all Muslims adhere, even though there may be, clothed in Islamic principles, an important margin allowed for evolution, transformation, and adaptation to various social and cultural environments. Western Muslims, because they are undergoing the experience of becoming established in new societies, have no choice but to go back to the beginning and study their points of reference in order to delineate and distinguish what, in their religion, is unchangeable (*thabit*) from what is subject to change (*mutaghayyir*), and to measure, from the inside, what they have achieved and what they have lost by being in the West.

It is a long, difficult, and sometimes dangerous journey, demanding deep immersion in the heart of the sources and the Islamic sciences and at the same time having a knowledge of the West, its history, and the social, cultural, political, and economic dynamics that constitute what one may call its specificity. But it is a journey nonetheless imperative for those spirits who, while wanting to remain loyal to the principles of their faith and ethic, are no less conscious that they must confront the challenges of their time and their society.

This first part is an essentially theoretical study of the fundamental principles of "universal Islam" and the tools that Muslims have available to confront diversity and change, whether historical, geographical, or cultural. This research, by establishing a corpus of reference, will enable us to suggest in the second part a number of concrete responses to questions asked by Western Muslims in the various areas of their daily lives.

1

ENCOUNTER WITH THE UNIVERSAL

The word "Islam" has often been translated as "submission" to God, or "entering into the peace" of God, for these are indeed the two senses provided by the declension of the root "*s—l—m*." But what is missing from this approach, which relies on simple translation, is the understanding of the fundamental conceptions of Creator, human being, and universe that underpin this conceptualization. It is assumed that the meaning is obvious, understood, and immediately accessible, whereas one cannot truly apprehend the meaning of "submission" or of "peace" in the Islamic universe of reference if one does not study, even if only a little, what is meant at the heart of the Muslim tradition by the realities of "God," the "human being," and "Revelation." If the "act of faith" is in itself *simple*, and considered, in Islam, as *natural*, it is because it is born in the depths of time and mind and is considered an *essential* dimension of the human being, or, more precisely, the being that is becoming human.

It is very precisely at this point that the most perfect expression of the universal, and the possibility of an encounter with it that is spiritual as well as intellectual, is expressed in the Islamic consciousness. Flowing from it is the development of a conception of existence, of the human, of society, and of death that accompanies the Muslim wherever he may be: so the central question is to know whether this conception is exclusive and closed or, on the contrary, open and respectful of Otherness and difference.[1]

The Transcendent and His Names

There is no "Islamic theology." It is meaningless, and in actual fact wrong, to compare the often peripheral discussions that took place among Muslim scholars (particularly from the tenth century) with the radical reflections that gave birth to "Christian theology." Admittedly, some debates were lively, and in the course of history in the Islamic Schools the meaning and significance of the names of God and of His attributes, and the status of Revelation have been discussed, but the boundaries of these controversies, in contrast to the history of Catholic dogma, for example, have remained circumscribed and have never gone as far as to open to question three fundamental principles: *the absolute oneness of the Creator, the impossibility of there being a representation of Him, and the truth of His word revealed in the Qur'an.*[2]

An authentic "theology" would first and foremost have discussed these three principles. But a careful study of the history of the debates among the Schools shows that the disputes took place mainly in separation from these three principles, which, at the heart of the Muslim understanding, are the basis of what is called "*tawhid.*" Islam begins just here: to understand Islam is to grasp the meaning and significance of the multiple dimensions of *tawhid.*

The concept of *tawhid* expresses first and essentially the fact of the absolute oneness of God: the first Principle, Creator of all, eternally present in history and at each moment, He is the Most High (*al-Ali*), beyond all that is (*al-Kabir, al-Wasi, al-Jami*), infinitely near (*al-Qarib*), closer to each of us than his jugular vein.[3] He is the One (*al-Wahid*), the Only One (*la ilaha illa Hu*), the Absolute (*al-Samad*), Justice (*al-Adl*), Truth (*al-Haqq*), and Light (*al-Nur*).

The whole of creation, in its most natural state, is the most immediate expression of the order intended by the Transcendent. Here, in the universe of the "laws of nature" and "rule of instinct," everything is in itself already and eternally "Islamic"—submissive to and at peace with the Living One (*al-Hayy*), the Eternal (*al-Qayyum*), who grants life (*al-Muhyi*) and brings death (*al-Mumit*). Nature is a book abounding in signs (*ayat*) of this essential link with the divine, this "natural faith," this "faith within nature" that is chanted by the mountain and the desert, the tree and the bird: "Art thou not aware that it is God whose limitless glory all [creatures] that are in the heavens and on earth extol, even the birds as they spread out their wings? Each [of them] knows indeed how to pray unto Him and to glorify Him; and God has full knowledge of all that they do";[4] "The seven heavens extol His limitless glory, and the earth, and all they contain; and there is not a single thing but extols His limitless glory and praise: but you [O men] fail to grasp the manner of their glorifying Him!"[5]

"You" refers here to human beings, beings endowed with consciousness and freedom,[6] yet who "do not see" and "do not understand" the celebration that the creation, simply by being what it is, addresses to God. With consciousness and freedom, another dimension is opened up, a dimension of faith, nature, submission, and peace, where one must listen, hear, understand, search, begin, resist, reform. Here we must learn to celebrate, learn to pray.

Humans are beings that have knowledge as well as ignorance, memory as well as forgetfulness. In contrast with the rest of creation, they have to live with dignity, risk, and freedom, all at once. What the Transcendent demands of their consciousness is to know Him or, more precisely, to recognize Him, and He has given them the means by which they can meet His demands. The idea that an intelligent being may find itself alone, abandoned, a prey to doubt with no landmarks in the midst of the "tragedy of life" is alien to Islam: God always makes available to humankind tools and signs on the road that leads to recognizing Him.[7]

The first space that welcomes human beings in their quest is creation itself. It is a book, as we have said, and all the elements that form part of it are signs that should remind the human consciousness that there exists that which is "beyond" them. This Revelation in and through space is wedded to Revelations in time, which, at irregular intervals, came as reminders of the origin and end of the universe and of humanity. The Qur'an, the last of these Revelations in the Muslim view, has as its main purpose to remind and to direct—to recall to memory the presence of the Only One, to direct the intelligence toward the knowledge of Him.

In the natural order, distinct from all the other creatures by virtue of consciousness, intelligence, and free will, human beings express needs according to the measure of their qualities and nature. With regard to the latter, the most natural of human quests is, when all is said and done, to know the source of the power and energy that give life to the world—in fact, it is the search for the divine. The first teaching we may draw from Revelation is to understand the absolute necessity for the Revelation itself. Basically, we learn from this that we can say of God only what He says of Himself. In other words, we must be listening for what He has said and communicated to humankind throughout history about recognizing and approaching Him. By this means, the Being has offered His names to human intelligence in order to direct it toward the knowledge of Him, but never toward the definition of Him. "Nothing is like Him, and He is the All-Hearing, the All-Seeing":[8] all the divine names,[9] of which we have mentioned some, make it possible to meditate and gain access to His Transcendence, His closeness, His kindness, and His mercy, but all reveal, in the human heart, human insufficiency, dependence, and "need of Him."

The second teaching of the Revelation is to invite individuals to a deep study of their own inner lives. The search for God and the sense of "the need of Him" may also arise from the indefinable work of looking inward that is required of each of us. The knowledge of God leads us to our self, as the knowledge of our self leads to God. What is uncovered through the two Revelations, the written Book (*al-Kitab al-mastur*) and the Book that is spread out (*al-Kitab al-manshur*—the universe), is a profoundly harmonious conception of the human being. With the turning of the pages and the passage of time, it takes shape and allows us better to find an order in divine commandments, human characteristics, and the meaning of the effort toward bringing about harmony and justice, which is required of humankind.

The encounter with the Only One, the "full and natural faith" of the created universe, the "need of Him" as the essence of being human, are, I suggest, the three fundamentals of the universal at the heart of Islamic civilization. Flowing from our observations about the Transcendent and His names, we find a special concept of humankind.

The Humanity of the Being

The notion of *tawhid*, the oneness of God (*tawhid al-rububiyya*), of His names and His attributes (*tawhid al-asma wa-al-sifat*), determines that the conception of human nature will be "a mirror image" and "*a contrario*," one may say. If God is one, everything in creation is in pairs, double, seeking union. Oneness, for the Transcendent, is an expression of the essence of being; union, for created beings, is achieved through marriage, fusion, movement. Created by the One, humans must go in search of the unity of their own being—their heart, their soul, their mind, and their body.

Put thus, it may give the impression that there is nothing to differentiate this from the Greek, Jewish, or Christian traditions. We well know the approach whose most familiar expression is the opposition between the soul and the body.[10] But a careful reading of the scriptural sources reveals that there is nothing in the Islamic tradition that can serve as a basis for the dualistic approach that opposes two constituent elements of humankind, each characterized by a positive or negative ethical quality: the soul would be the expression (explicitly or implicitly) of good, the body the expression (explicitly or implicitly) of evil. Never does the Qur'anic Revelation or the Prophetic tradition suggest anything of the sort. The ethical crux is not in the opposition of two elements that are separate and ethically fixed (which would represent the two poles of morality) but rather in controlling and guiding them toward their necessary merger, their inevitable union. From the beginning, the Islamic tradition rejects this kind of antithetical dualism and bases the measurement of moral categories on the ability of human consciousness to take responsibility for finding balance, establishing harmony, making peace. The human being is, essentially, responsible; awareness of *tawhid* invites humanity to set out on the quest, along the divine path (*sabil Allah*), to control, in the midst of the fluctuations of life, the contradictions within its being, its weaknesses, and its deficiencies. This exercise of responsible control is an education that makes the human being truly human at the heart of a search which is like a virtuous and ascending circle; union, which is at the center of being, brings us toward the oneness of the Being. The opposite here would be an absence of boundaries and morality, a lack of constraint, that would drag the conscience into sleep, into the vicious circle of excess, which may even extend to bestiality.[11]

Thus, there is no moral quality good "in itself" attached to "the soul in the body" *(al-nafs)*, the heart, or the spirit, and there is no moral quality bad "in itself" attached to the body, the senses, or the emotions. It is the human ability to control, to combine, and to guide that determines the ethical quality of individuals, their *nafs*, their hearts, their bodies, feelings, each of their emotions, as well as each of their actions. This perception is the basis of the relationship that Muslims are invited to have with the world, which is not evil in itself (as opposed to the next world, which is presumed to be absolute good). Conversely, motherhood and fatherhood are not good in themselves (as opposed to the solitary life, which is presumed to be evil). Knowledge is not always positive in itself (in contrast to ignorance, which is by nature negative). Nothing like this is to be found in the Islamic universe of reference. Sexuality may be a prayer[12] and motherhood may be hell, depending on the moral intention that motivates the person. In other words, the ethical quality of the elements of which we are constituted (*nafs*, heart, body, and so on), the faculties by which we are characterized (such as perception, intelligence, and imagination) and, of course, the actions we produce are determined only by the guidance our conscience gives them. This teaching reveals a perception of the human that is at once very demanding and very optimistic—demanding because the human conscience must acquire alone ("No one can bear another's burden"[13]) responsible control in a world where evil is neither an indelible mark on the being-in-the-world (like original sin) nor *in itself* a constituent part of the being (like the body or the imagination). It is above all optimistic, for it requires us not to reject any part of our being, encouraging in us the confidence that the Only One will give us in every situation the means to meet this ethical challenge. "God only imposes on each soul [human being] what it is able to bear,"[14] and along the way He provides numerous signs, invitations, and supports. Thus, a relationship of obligation and trust is established with the divine that is fully achieved only when we cross the threshold of the realm of inner peace.

It remains to discover how to discern the guidance we have spoken of. The Islamic tradition also offers an original conception of humankind that the Sufis (Muslim mystics) have very much emphasized. It contains the idea of movement and dynamism that, as we have seen, characterizes Islamic thought. Awareness of the divine, far from the dualist thinking which opposes "faith" to "reason," sets in motion, as we shall see, a quest for the original breath that cannot dispense with reason in order successfully to bring to birth a faith that is both confirmation and reconciliation.

The story of creation, as it is told in the Qur'an, is remarkable. It all began, one may say, with a *testimony* and a *covenant*. Indeed, Revelation tells us that in the first stage of creation the Only One brought together the whole of mankind and made them bear witness: "And when your Sustainer took the offspring of Adam from his loins to bear witness about themselves: 'Am I not your Lord?,' they replied, 'Assuredly, yes. We bear witness to it.' This is a reminder lest on the day of judgment you say: 'We did not know!' "[15] This original testimony is of fundamental importance for the formation of the Islamic conception of humanity. It teaches us that in the heart and consciousness of each individual there exists an essential and profound intuitive awareness and recognition of the presence of the Transcendent. Just as the sun, the clouds, the winds, the birds, and all the animals express their natural submission, as we have seen, the human being has within it an almost instinctive longing for a dimension that is "beyond." This is the idea of the *fitra*, which has given rise to numerous exegetical, mystical, and philosophical commentaries, so central is it to the Islamic conception of the human being, faith, and the sacred. We find it mentioned in the following verse: "Surrender your whole being as a true believer and in accordance with the nature [natural desire] which God gave to human beings when He created them. There is no change in God's creation. This is the unchangeable religion, but most people do not know,"[16] and confirmed by a Prophetic tradition: "Every newborn child is born in *fitra*: it is his parents who make of him a Jew, a Christian, or a Zoroastrian."[17]

So this "original testimony" has impressed each person's heart with a mark, which is a memory, a spark, a quest for transcendence in a sense very close to Mircea Eliade's insight when he affirms that religions "play a part in the structure of human consciousness." This statement from the first age, in which human beings declared their recognition of the Creator, fashions their relationship with God: they are bound by a sort *of original covenant* to which their consciousness presses them to stay faithful. There is no original sin in Islam: every being is born innocent and then becomes responsible for his or her faithfulness to the covenant. Those who do not believe, the *un*-faithful (*kafir*),[18] are those who are not faithful to the original covenant, whose memory is faint and whose sight is veiled. In the notion of *kufr* in Arabic there is the idea of a veiling that leads to the denial of the Truth. Only God decides whether human beings will be enlightened or veiled. Their responsibility consists in their constant action and personal effort to keep the memory alive.

Little by little, we feel that the outlines of an Islamic conception of human nature are emerging. If none of the elements that make up the human being has, in itself, a positive or negative moral quality, if, on the contrary, it is the awakened, responsible conscience that exerts, through the exercise of control, ethical guidance on one's way of being in the world, one is naturally entitled to wonder how to comply with the way this guidance is leading, how, in short, to be with God. We find the answer in the second part of the analysis we have just presented: all of us are required to return to ourselves and to rediscover the original breath, to revive it and confirm it. In order for this to be achieved, the Creator has made available to human beings two kinds of Revelation. One is spread out before us in space—the whole universe. The other stands out in history at points in time. These two kinds of Revelation "remind" and send the conscious back to itself: "We will show them our signs on the horizons and in themselves so that it will be clear to them that [this message] is the truth."[19] This quest for the Transcendent cannot be undertaken without the mind. There is absolutely no contradiction here between the realm of faith and the realm of reason. On the contrary, the spark of faith, born in the original testimony, needs intellect to confirm that testimony and to be capable of being faithful to the original covenant. The realm of faith necessarily calls on intellect, which, by accepting the two types of Revelation, allows faith to be confirmed, deepened, and rooted and to grow to fullness in the heart and in human consciousness. Here again the two must be wedded, and each has a part to play: a living faith makes it possible for the intellect to accept signs beyond simple elements of nature, and active reason makes it possible for faith to understand and also to acquire more self-understanding, and in that way to draw closer to the divine: "Of all the servants, those who know are those who are [fully] open to the intimate awareness of God."[20] Blaise Pascal had an apt expression: "The heart has reasons that reason does not know," thus differentiating the two realms of faith and reason (even though this formula has often been [wrongly] reduced to an opposition between the emotional and the rational). From an Islamic point of view, the relationship of the heart (where the first longing, the first breath toward faith takes place) and the intellect (which responds to the call of this breath and takes up the quest) might rather be expressed this way: the heart has reasons that reason will recognize. Apart from the expression, the difference is profound.

At the conclusion of these reflections on the human being, we may sketch two fundamental teachings that clearly have consequences for the lives of Muslims wherever they are, for they are the basic factors that constitute how to be in the world, which is what Muslims have to manage, whether in the West or in the East. The first teaching tells us that humans are not made up of morally antithetical elements: the spirit, the breath (al-ruh) breathed into the body, which becomes al-nafs, the heart, the reason, the body where the emotions live, are, so to speak, "neutral elements" that invite individuals to the awareness of their responsibilities. One enters into this intimate awareness only by turning back to oneself, looking for the original spark, which is the most immediate expression of the search for meaning. The universe, like the revealed books, calls on reason to find a way to meaning and to try to bring about, through awareness of responsibility and the exercise of control, ethical concords and moral harmonies of being. When all is said and done, it is wending one's way toward one's self, a "going" to make a better returning, as all the mystical traditions teach us simply: we are on our way to the beginning.[21] We come upon the knowledge of God close to our heart "and know that [the knowledge of] God dwells between the human being and his heart."[22]

The second teaching concerns the different states of human life. In the beginning, one's innocence is absolute: one is, indwelt by the breath, and is soon inevitably searching. Becoming aware of this state immediately makes one a responsible and in fact free being. Before God, and before their own consciouses, all people must take charge of themselves, knowing that the Only One is expecting them to know Him, to liberate themselves from all objects of adoration and idols (tawhid al-uluhiyya) that would not be He, and to recognize Him, intimately. To accomplish this, He has implanted, with the first spark, "the need of Him" and for "signs" of His presence. It is for humankind to learn to read these signs and to try to satisfy this need: such is the first dimension of human responsibility. In this perspective, the most serious deficiency in a free and responsible being is not moral error as such, but pride—to suffocate the "need of Him" and to think that one's intellect alone can know and read the universe. By marrying the two states of innocence and responsibility, humility is the state that allows the human being to enter into its humanity. Humility is the source of ethics.

These two teachings are fundamental and have extraordinarily important consequences for the daily life of Muslims. With the awareness of the divine, facing the universe, individuals think of themselves above all as beings with responsibility. The faith and humility that surround this last idea carry persons to an understanding of the meaning of their obligations before any affirmation of their rights. This is the first meaning of the vicegerency in Islam: "It is He who has made you His vicegerents [khalaifa] on earth."[23] It is the role of humankind to manage the world on the basis of an ethic of respect for creation not only because people do not own it but, more deeply and spiritually, because it is in itself an eternal and continual praise addressed to the Most High. We are speaking here of a true spiritual ecology, an ecology that existed before ecology,[24] which imposes on persons the awareness of limitations so that they may have dignified access to the meaning of their freedom and their rights.[25]

We could pursue reflection on the conception of human rights. Although a statement of the universality of human rights may pose no basic problem, it is rather the way they are formulated and the structure of the statement that is open to discussion. The Muslim consciousness would, of course, add, before the proclamation of universal rights, a series of relevant and constraining articles on the responsibilities and obligations of human beings.

Revelation: Principles and Tools

A fundamental aspect of the Islamic tradition is the recognition of the accomplished cycle of prophecy and all the prophets who preceded Muhammad. And one can only understand their meaning and function in human history if one has a clear idea of the Islamic conception of humankind. Revelations come, all through time, to reawaken the original breath, to make it possible for humankind to stay faithful to the original covenant, and to respect the divine commandments that ensure that they will live in His light and walk in His path in a way appropriate to the time in which they live. It is in this context, according to Islamic teaching, that the Qur'an, confirming the essential message of the Revelations that came earlier, goes back to the sources of *fitra* and confirms it, reviving the original impulse in humans and making them live by recalling it. To reveal, in fact, is to recall the closeness of the faith of Eve, Adam, Noah, Abraham, Moses, Mary, Jesus, and all the prophets; to reveal is to revive the light that is dormant in the heart of each of us and that forgetfulness often dims or stifles.

The first function of Revelation is to recall and confirm what went before, which, according to Islamic tradition, may be summed up in four fundamental principles: (1) There is one God who has no associates (*tawhid al-rububiyya*); (2) human beings are linked with the Creator by an original testimony and covenant; (3) the Transcendent has sent Revelations and prophets throughout history to call humankind back to the testimony and the covenant and to tell them about the requirements of religious ritual and morality that are laid upon them; (4) to be *with* God is to be *for* Him and to free oneself of all idols—material, fantasy, and even emotional[26]—in order to live in His presence and respect His commandments (*tawhid al-uluhiyya*).

From the revealed Pages of Noah (*suhuf*), to the Psalms of David, to the Torah of Moses, to the Gospel of Jesus, and up to the Qur'an of Muhammad, each Revelation has as its first purpose to confirm these four fundamental principles. The second purpose of each of the Books has been to put right what was forgotten, modified, and sometimes corrupted by human interventions in the previous Revelation. These two first functions are on the level of general principles. The last function has then been to reveal to humankind the religious practices they should follow from then on, the specifics of moral teaching that were relevant to them, and, finally, the patterns of interpersonal and social relations that they should establish and respect. The second level determines the newness or uniqueness of the religion in question.

In the consciousness of Muslims, the Qur'an is clearly active at these two levels. Considered by them to be the final Revelation, Islam presents itself at the first level of general principles as a natural religion that goes back to the source of all the messages. The terminology itself carries an echo of the "return to the source": the last of the monotheisms is called *islam*, expressing the natural act of recognizing the order created by the Only One and surrendering to His peace. To be a Muslim is to pronounce the declaration, *al-shahada*, which recalls the original testimony of which we have spoken, while the path of faithfulness, the way to the source, *al-sharia*, expresses the requirement to be faithful to the original covenant. As for the second level, concerning religious practices and specific judgments, we find a series of verses directly referring to this and in fact defining and circumscribing Islamic practice as well as Islamic ethics regarding individual and collective behavior more generally.

The status of the Qur'an is, for Muslims, a question of greatest importance. Here there are a great number of misunderstandings and narrow ideas expressed even by some Muslim faithful. The Qur'an is the word of God revealed in small parts over a period of about twenty-three years. It is a text, revealed at a given moment in history, in a certain context, and presented first to the intelligence of women and men of faith. It must be said over and over again that the Revelation of a Book, of a Text, would have no meaning if intelligence, human reason capable of grasping its meaning, were not taken for granted. There can be no revealed Text unless there is human intellect up to the task of reading and interpreting it. One must also add that recourse to reason, though essential, is not the only and sufficient approach to be adopted in the realm of faith. The Book must also be approached in awareness of that "need of Him" of which we have already spoken, with that state of humility that opens up the meaning, the spiritual power, and dimension of the Text more extensively and deeply than the lights of rational understanding alone. This is how one can understand the very beginning of the story of the Qur'anic Revelation: when invited to read and recite, the Prophet three times declared himself unable to do it because he was not "one who could read." Being illiterate, he expressed a logical inability. He could read only when the spiritual nature of it—"in the name of your Lord"—gave him access to other lights and another dimension of knowledge. Which is not nothing.

The Qur'an includes various kinds of teaching. Full of oft-repeated stories from the accomplished cycle of prophecy, the Text makes it possible for the heart and mind to deduce, almost naturally, universal principles and truths on the human and ethical levels: faith in the Only One, the shared origin and destiny of humanity, the demand for truth and justice, essential diversity and its consequent necessary respect, the constant presence of adversity and deceit, the duty to resist and to reform. There is no need for contextualization here, or when it comes to the verses that explicitly lay down Muslim rites and practice: prayer, fasting, and so on.[27] The Text calls the mind to look further than accidents of space and time and to set these teachings beyond all contingency.

But there are verses that are quite different in nature, particularly most of those that deal with social matters (al-muamalat). In this area, the Text almost never allows itself, alone, to lay down a universal principle: it is the human mind that derives both absolute and relative principles, as appropriate, from the Text and from the reality of the context in which it was revealed. In setting out the specificity of these verses, we understand better the importance of remembering that the Revelation was elaborated in time and space, over twenty-three years, in a certain context, expressed in pronouncements affected by circumstance, open to evolution, accessible to reason in a historical setting.

Being fully conscious of the difference in nature among these teachings, the ulama have gradually established a categorization of verses, precise rules for deducing norms, and various methodologies to deal with different subjects of study (e.g., religious practices, social matters, morality). This is a work of rational analysis a posteriori necessitated by the different levels of expression in the Qur'an and with the aim of determining clearly the extent of the latitude permitted for interpretation. It is out of this work that the "Islamic sciences" were born,[28] as classically defined from the tenth century, particularly in the area of law and jurisprudence. The multiple rules elaborated in the "science of the fundamentals of law" (ilm usul al-fiqh) have as their objective to lay down rules of interpretation and distinct methodological principles and to fix a clear framework for the exercise of critical interpretation (al-ijtihad). We must be clear that this work has not been done arbitrarily: a logical series of objective guidelines explain the proposed categorizations, norms, and methodologies worked out (including the Text itself; the Prophetic tradition; the grammar, semantics, and morphology of the Arabic language; and logic) and makes transparent the internal coherence of the Islamic universe of reference on the ethical and legal planes.

Certain verses (actually a minority) leave no scope for interpretation, or at least only a very narrow one. But the great majority demand real interpretive effort, and that on several levels: the meaning of the words, the general meaning of the instruction, the context in which it was revealed, the universal aspect of the principle (and consequently the temporal aspect of the manner of its application), its logical setting within the global meaning of the Qur'anic message and the Prophetic traditions (*Sunna*), and so on. It goes without saying that such work requires that the interpreter, the scholar (especially the specialist), not only be equipped with religious knowledge, but also that he have the ability to transfer these teachings into a new context, in a new era, and with a meticulous concern to stay faithful to the universal and general principles while studying how rules may be modified and adapted to the contingent, the contextual, or, even more broadly, the cultural situation.[29]

In fact, it is human intelligence that deduces and determines the universal at the heart of the scriptural source. Guided and sometimes limited by the Text itself and by the objective parameters of its mode of expression (the believer remains aware that it is the final Revelation to which respect and faithfulness are due), reason has the task of establishing rules and methods of reading the Text to identify and distinguish the essential principles (*al-usul*) from secondary injunctions (*al-furu*), the explicit from the implicit, the general from the particular, and so on. The final purpose of this critical work *on the Text itself* (and on the Sunna in the same way) is to determine how much room is available for critical work *based on the Text* (*al-ijtihad*) to reply to new questions raised in the course of history and to new social realities. Reason functioning in time thus acquires the means to gain access to the eternity of the revealed Text.[30]

It is appropriate to mention that it is essentially the ways of reading the Qur'an that distinguish the various trends of thought among Muslims, both Sunnis and Shiis. Beyond the dualistic and simplistic divisions set up between the "moderates" and the "fundamentalists" (and one never knows very well whether these reflect strictly religious or more generally political positions, or both indescribably confused), we find a diversity of readings of the Qur'an that can be attributed principally to the greater or lesser role the human intellect is allowed to play and, consequently, to the scope for interpretation that is permitted as an integral part of the Islamic field of reference. Here we have a key that allows us, on the basis of the internal logic of the Islamic system, and on a strictly religious plane,[31] better to understand the differences, the justifications, and the possible points of convergence among the various lines of thought.

A Typology of Trends of Thought

The various tendencies we analyze here are evident throughout the world, in the West as well as in Muslim-majority countries. They exist, admittedly with circumstantial divergences, across the Sunni as well as the Shii traditions, and they are more or less representative and entrenched depending on the continent, region, or country studied. The typology I propose is based on principles that are precise without being detailed and that do not aim to bring out the specificities of particular groups in particular locations. With this in mind, it will be useful to outline the method used to distinguish the trends.

Trends of Analysis

It is important to remember that, for these trends of thought as a whole, the points of reference are the same and that the essential principles that form the basis of the Muslim religion are, with rare exceptions, unanimously recognized. So, in this sense, as we have said, *Islam is one* and presents a body of opinion whose essential axes are identifiable and accepted by the various trends or schools of thought, in spite of their great diversity. To explain this diversity it is not enough simply to use the plural, as has been done in some recent studies: faced with the apparent impossibility of putting forward a legal, political, or ideological analysis, the matter is simplified by speaking of diverse "Islams." The use of the plural, which is intended principally for clarification, is more problematic than truly practical: by signaling diversity, it blurs the reading of explicit points of convergence and, more important, says nothing about the exact and often precise areas of divergence of opinion. A phrase applied with the sole purpose of pointing out that there are divisions neither justifies nor explains their causes and expressions and indeed misleads the observer about the very nature of the various positions. This approach is therefore anything but scientific.[32]

It is essential here to lay down a clear principle on the basis of which a study of the various tendencies may really make sense. If it is accepted unanimously that the scriptural points of reference for Islam are the Qur'an and the Sunna (these two fundamental sources are not disputed by any of the schools of thought), it seems legitimate to investigate the way in which the various trends actually make reference to these Texts. This approach, as we shall see, gives a clearer result because it investigates the attitudes that lie behind religious, social, and political expressions and actions. It does not cast doubt upon the fundamental adherence of one group or another to Islam but seeks to uncover their respective approaches to reading the sources: the status of the Text, the scope allowed for interpretation, the admissibility of a contextualized reading, the role of reason, and the strength of the literalist position are some of the factors that explain the various and differentiated approaches. Clearly, Islam is one, but its textual references allow plural readings (even if, in order to be recognized, they must respect certain normative criteria, as we have shown).

We cannot study here all the trends of thought one by one. They are many and are called by different names from one country to another, so that the same title may represent diametrically opposed tendencies, depending on the continent in which the group is found. Each country would therefore require a different treatment, which would present a very complicated and daunting prospect. We shall therefore limit ourselves here to sketching the distinctive characteristics of specific broad tendencies represented across the world by groups that may have different names but that nevertheless, to a large extent, have adopted an identical reading of the Texts, along with the doctrinal and often social attitudes that follow as a consequence.

Six Major Tendencies

The six major tendencies refer here to the different tendencies among those for whom Islam is the reference point for their thinking, their discourse, and their engagement. So-called sociological or cultural Muslims, even if we legitimately consider them Muslims, do not enter into this typology, for their reference to Islam, by their own reckoning, does not play a particular role in their reflections and actions.

Scholastic Traditionalism. Scholastic traditionalism refers to a tendency that has attracted followers in the West and is found in various regions of the Muslim world. Adherents of this line of thought have a distinctive way of referring to scriptural Texts, the Qur'an and the Sunna, characterized by a strict and sometimes even exclusive reference to one or other of the Schools of jurisprudence (the Hanafi, Maliki, Shafii, Hanbali, Zaydi, Jafari, among others), thus allowing no criticism of the legal opinions established in the School in question. The Qur'an and the Sunna are references considered through the filter of the meaning and application stipulated by the recognized scholars of a given School. The scope for interpretation of Texts is very limited and does not realistically allow development. Many trends, in one way or another, come under this mediated and scholastic approach to reading source texts: whether we look at the Deobandis, the Barelwis, the Ahl al-Sunna, the Taliban in Afghanistan, or the Tabligh-i Jamaat,[33] we find a traditionalism that insists on the essential aspects of worship, on dress codes, and on rules for applying Islam, that rely on the opinions of scholars that usually were codified between the eighth and eleventh centuries. There is no room here for *ijtihad* or for a rereading, which are taken to be baseless and unacceptable liberties and modernizations.

Scholastic traditionalism movements are present in the West, notably in the United States and Great Britain among Indo-Pakistani groups and in Germany among the Turks. Small communities of this type are also found scattered in other countries. They are concerned mostly with religious practice and in the West do not envisage social, civil, or political involvement. Their reading of the Texts and the priority they give to the protection of strict traditional practice makes them uninterested in and even rejecting of any connection with the Western social milieu, in which they simply cannot conceive that they have any way of participating. The discourse they propound and the education they provide are based on a religious foundation perceived through the prism of their traditional reading of the legal principles of a given or recognized school.[34]

Salafi *Literalism.*   *Salafi* literalism is often confused with the traditional one just described, although their differences are significant. In contrast with the scholastic traditionalists, the *salafi* literalists reject the mediation of the juridical Schools and their scholars when it comes to approaching and reading the Texts. They call themselves *salafis* because they are concerned to follow the *salaf*, which is the title given to the Companions of the Prophet and pious Muslims of the first three generations of Islam. The Qur'an and the Sunna are therefore interpreted in an immediate way, without scholarly conclaves. The literalist character of this approach gives this trend an equally traditionalist character that insists on reference to the Texts but forbids any interpretive reading. This school of thought is a direct descendant of those that very early on were called *ahl al-hadith* and that opposed interpretations based on the search for the objective (*qasd*) of an injunction or prescription, which is the attitude that characterized the *ahl al-ray.*

The *salafis* insist, in all circumstances, on the necessity of reference to and on the authenticity of the Texts quoted to justify a certain attitude or action, whether in the area of religious practice, dress code, or social behavior. Only the Text in its literal form has constraining force, and it cannot be subjected to interpretations that, by definition, must contain error or innovation (*bida*).[35] The doctrinal position of the *salafi* literalists and their groups in the West, which are in constant communication with scholars based primarily in Saudi Arabia, Jordan, Egypt, or Syria (mostly through former students of their respective educational institutions), refuses any kind of involvement in a space that is considered non-Islamic. The concepts of *dar al-kufr* and *dar al-harb* [36] are still operational and continue to explain the relationship of the *salafis* with the social environment, which is characterized primarily by isolation and by a literally applied religious practice protected from Western cultural influences.

Salafi *Reformism.* *Salafi* reformists share with *salafi* literalists a concern to bypass the boundaries marked out by the juridical Schools in order to rediscover the pristine energy of an unmediated reading of the Qur'an and the Sunna. They too, therefore, refer back to the *salafs*, the Muslims of the first generations, with the aim of avoiding the commentaries of the eighth-, ninth-, or tenth-century scholars who have been accorded sole authority to interpret the Texts. However, in contrast with the literalists, although the Texts remain for them unavoidable, their approach is to adopt a reading based on the purposes and intentions of the law and jurisprudence (*fiqh*). In this they are closer to *alh al-ray*, and they believe that the practice of *ijtihad* is an objective, necessary, and constant factor in the application of *fiqh* in every time and place.

Most groups within the *salafi* reformist trend that exists in the West grew out of the influence of reformist thinkers of the late nineteenth and early twentieth centuries, who found a wide audience in the Muslim world. These included the well-known names of al-Afghani, Abduh, Rida, al-Nursi, Iqbal, Ibn Badis, al-Banna, al-Fasi, Bennabi, Mawdudi, Qutb, and Shariati, in addition to the many others whose influence was or is restricted to a national level. All these reformists held somewhat divergent ideas, and the extent to which they were reformists varied. It is impossible to set out here their sometimes significant divergences of opinion. But what does clearly unite them is a very dynamic relation to the scriptural sources and a constant desire to use reason in the treatment of the Texts in order to deal with the new challenges of their age and the social, economic, and political evolution of societies.

The arrival of *salafi* reformist intellectuals in the West followed repressive measures imposed after national independence, as in Egypt and Syria regarding the Muslim Brothers (in 1960 and 1966), or grew out of later political situations such as those in Tunisia vis-à-vis the Nahda movement, in Morocco vis-à-vis al-Adl wal-Ihsan, and in Algeria vis-à-vis the Jazara supporters. These influences gave birth, as elsewhere in the Muslim world at large, to two different trends. The first, in the line of the legalist tradition of the most famous *salafi* reformists, pursued and adapted the application of reformism to the Western context. The original school of thought remained a reference point in that the methodology of approaching the Texts remained open to interpretation and necessarily applied *ijtihad* in response to contexts of social life. However, fidelity to reformist thought and methodology, while henceforth very broad, did not necessarily require adherence to any sort of structure; thinking had gone beyond the authority, as a frame of reference, of any group or organization. In the West, reflection has evolved extensively and it is, moreover, in this that it has remained faithful to the original reformist ideal. The aim is to protect the Muslim identity and religious practice, to recognize the Western constitutional structure, to become involved as a citizen at the social level, and to live with true loyalty to the country to which one belongs. *Salafi* reformist thought is very widespread in the West, and a large number of associations are influenced by this way of reading the Texts, which they adopted and adapt in keeping with their needs and actions.[37]

Political Literalist Salafism. This is the second trend referred to earlier, and it was essentially born of the repression that has ravaged the Muslim world. Scholars and intellectuals originally attached to the legalist reformist school went over to strictly political activism (while they were still based in the Muslim world). All they retained of reformism was the idea of social and political action, which they wedded to a literalist reading of Texts with a political connotation concerning the management of power, the caliphate, authority, law, and so on. The whole constitutes a complex blend that tends toward radical revolutionary action: it is about opposing the ruling powers, even in the West, and struggling for the institution of the "Islamic state" in the form of the caliphate.

The discourse is trenchant, politicized, radical, and opposed to any idea of involvement or collaboration with Western societies, which is seen as akin to open treason. The Hizb al-Tahrir and Al-Muhajirun movements are the best known in Europe, and they call for *jihad* and opposition to the West (always considered as *dar al-harb*, the realm of war) by all means. These trends, which attract a lot of public attention, are represented only by structures and factional networks.[38]

"Liberal" or "Rationalist" Reformism. Essentially born out of the influence of Western thought during the colonial period, the reformist school, presenting itself as *liberal* or *rationalist*, has supported the application in the Muslim world of the social and political system that resulted from the process of secularization in Europe.[39] The liberals were the defenders of Mustafa Kemal Ataturk's secularization project in Turkey, for example, and of the complete separation of the religious arena from the ordering of public and political life. In the West, supporters of liberal reformism preach the integration/assimilation of Muslims, from whom they expect a complete adaptation to the Western way of life. They do not insist on the daily practice of religion and hold essentially only to its spiritual dimension, lived on an individual and private basis, or else the maintenance of an attachment to the culture of origin.

The majority of liberals are opposed to any display of distinctive clothing that might be synonymous with seclusion or even fundamentalism.

With social evolution in mind, they believe that the Qur'an and the Sunna cannot be the point of reference when it comes to norms of behavior and that it is applied reason that must now set the criteria for social conduct. Thus, the term *liberal* is here used in the same sense the word has acquired meaning in the West, which elevates reason and is based on the primacy of the individual.[40]

Sufism. We must not forget the Sufi trend in the Western landscape. Sufis are in fact numerous and very diversified. Whether Naqshbandis, Qadiris, Shadhilis, or any of the many other *turuq* (plural of *tariqa*), Sufi circles are essentially oriented toward the spiritual life and mystical experience. This is not to say that Sufi disciples (*murids*) have no community or social involvement; the contrary is often the case. In the end, it is first and foremost a matter of priorities, which are determined differently: the scriptural Texts have a deep meaning that, according to Sufi teachings, requires time for meditation and understanding. This is a call to the inner life, away from disturbance and disharmony. Here the Text is the ultimate point of reference, because it is the way to remembrance (*dhikr*) and nearness (*taqarub*): it is the only path to the experience of closeness to God. The *turuq* are kinds of circles of initiation organized internally, with a specific hierarchy from disciples to guide (*shaykh*). Each order has its own mode of operation. We should also note that there are highly structured brotherhoods in the West that are directly linked with networks of orders in Asia and in North and West Africa. We know, for example, about the organizational capability of the Murids and the Tijanes of Senegal, who operate most of the time in a closed circle but who maintain a very effective internal fabric of support and solidarity, both in Europe and in North America.[41]

This presentation of broad trends in contemporary Islam is far from exhaustive, but it is made in the hope that it will at least have the merit of bringing out some nuances to counteract the dualistic simplistic readings of the situation that set the liberals over and against all the rest—the radicals and the fundamentalists. The situation is much more complex than that, and the boundaries are more subtle: their roots go back deep into history, it is true, but above all originate in particular ways of understanding the source Texts. The scholastic traditionalists, the literalist *salafis*, and the politicized and radicalized *salafis*, despite their divergences, agree on the fact that the Texts, whether the Qur'an or the Sunna (or even the views of the great scholars), can admit of no interpretation or distortion. Reason is useful for understanding the Text, but not, by extension, for determining its purpose. The Qur'anic Text is the obligatory route to initiation for the Sufi traditions. For the reformist *salafis*, the Text still remains the source, but reason, applied according to the rules of deduction and inference (*qawaid al-istinbat*), enjoys significant latitude for interpretation and elaboration through the exercise of *ijtihad*.[42] At the other extreme of doctrinally fixed positions, liberal reformism gives priority to rational elaboration, while the scriptural Texts have a prime role in spiritual guidance and broad moral instruction, but always directed toward the individual, reflecting the way religious texts have come to be seen in the West in relation to the social and political life.

The distinctions we have described, based on the mode of reference to "Texts/Reason," can be represented diagrammatically as shown in figure 1.1.

At the end of this brief presentation, it is important to note that there are other, minor trends of thought in the West that are usually offshoots of or similar to sects (*firaq*). Their specific points of difference are based on certain very precise articles of doctrine that make them want to see themselves as distinct from all other Muslims, even to the extent of issuing general anathemas against them. There are varieties of these groups in the United States, Great Britain, France, Germany, and Spain, as well as in other countries. It is impossible to make an exhaustive list of them here, but we may mention the sectarian group, the Ahbash, which originated in Lebanon and has its European base in Switzerland (Lausanne), while being active in Europe, the United States, and Africa. Often calling themselves the "Islamic Benevolent Association," adherents carry on a permanent double discourse: to Western questioners, they claim to support the

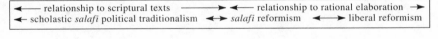

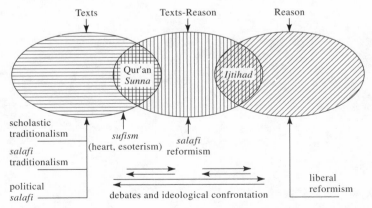

Figure 1.1. The Principal Islamic Tendencies and Their Relationships to Texts and Reason

emancipation of women and laicism and to oppose the "fundamentalists" (all the issues they know are sensitive and useful for getting them recognized). However, within Muslim communities, they carry on an extremely intransigent and closed discourse, usually treating most of the principal Muslim ulama as *kuffar* (by which they mean "unbelievers," "impious people"). They base their teachings on interpretations recognized as deviant by all other schools of thought and all other scholars of note (for example, their singular understanding of the meaning of the names of God, or their assertion that the Qur'anic Text was interpreted by the angel Gabriel, or the practice of praying to the dead).[43] Their approach on very specific points of doctrine (such as those we have referred to) is hostile and usually violent.[44]

2

THE WAY (AL-SHARIA)

In the West, the idea of *Sharia* calls up all the darkest images of Islam: repression of women, physical punishments, stoning, and all other such things. It has reached the extent that many Muslim intellectuals do not dare even to refer to the concept for fear of frightening people or arousing suspicion of all their work by the mere mention of the word.

It is true that scholars of law and jurisprudence have almost naturally restricted the meaning to their own field of study, that dictators have used it for repressive and cruel purposes, and that the ideal of the *Sharia* has been most betrayed by Muslims themselves, but this should not prevent us from studying this central notion in the Islamic universe of reference and trying to understand in what ways it has remained fundamental and active in the Muslim consciousness through the ages.[1]

If the idea of "establishing rules" is indeed contained in the notion of *Sharia* (from the root *sha-ra-a*), this translation does not convey the fullness of the way it is understood, unless its more general and fundamental meaning is referred to: "the path that leads to the spring." We have pointed out the tone of Islamic terminology, which systematically reflects a corpus of reference that sets a certain way of speaking of God, of defining the human being and of understanding the relationship between them by means of Revelation. We have seen that this corpus of reference is, for the Muslim consciousness, where the universal is formulated: God, human nature, which makes itself human by turning in on itself and recognizing the "need of Him," reason, active and fed by humility, and, finally, Revelation, which confirms, corrects, and exerts a guiding influence.

Just as the *shahada* is the expression, in the here and now, of individual faithfulness to the original covenant by means of a testimony that is a "return to oneself" (a return to the *fitra*, to the original breath breathed into us by God), so the *Sharia* is the expression of individual and collective faithfulness, in time, for those who are trying in awareness to draw near to the ideal of the Source that is God. In other words, and in light of all that has been said in the first chapter, the *shahada* translates the idea of "being Muslim," and the *Sharia* shows us "how to be and remain Muslim." This means, to put it in yet another way and extend our reflection, that the *Sharia* is not only the expression of the universal principles of Islam but the framework and the thinking that makes for their actualization in human history. There can be no *Sharia* without a corpus of fundamental principles that set, beyond the contingencies of time, a point of reference for faithfulness to the divine will. This corpus of principles, as we have seen, is a fundamental given of the Islamic universe of reference, which asserts, in the midst of postmodernism, that all is not relative, that there does indeed exist a universal, for it is a God, an only God, who has revealed timeless principles, which, while not preventing reason from being active and creative, protect it from getting bogged down in the contradictions and incoherences of the absolute relativity of everything.

By inviting Muslims to accept pluralism by a purely rationalistic approach, to express their faithfulness in a purely private way, or to define themselves in terms of minorities, some commentators have thought to ward off the danger of Islamic universality, which they perceive as inevitably totalitarian. Is this not how the West understands the quasi summons to have to affirm one's "faith" in the autonomy of reason in order to prove one's open-mindedness or one's firm support for the "universal values of the West";[2] or the new fashion of apologetic for a Sufism so interior that it has become disincarnated, almost invisible, or a façade with only blurred links to Islam; or, again, stigmatization and the exercise of constant pressure on Muslims driven to adopt the monochrome reaction of minorities on the defensive, obsessed with their only right—to be—and with their differentness? This is all happening as if, in order to ward off the "necessarily expansionist" universality of Islam, either Islam must be refused its claim to universality or Muslims must be pressed to accept this exercise in wholesale relativization.

Some Muslim intellectuals have accepted the imposition of these game rules. Others have opposed it and continue to oppose it by rejecting the West per se, with all it has produced, because it has forgotten God or because all that takes place there is Promethean, if not "satanic." Between these two extremes, there is a way, I believe, to change the terms of the debate: if, for Muslims, it is a matter of rejecting the insidious process of the relativization of their universal values, it is also incumbent on them to explain clearly in what sense, and how, those values respect diversity and relativity. If the Way to faithfulness, the *Sharia*, is the corpus of reference in which Islamic universality is written down, it is urgent and imperative to say how it is structured and how it expresses the absolute, and rationality, and the relation to time, progress, the Other, and, more broadly, difference. At a deeper level, the intuition that must feed this refusal of relativization and this presentation of the fundamental principles of Islam in the heart of the Western world is the conviction that this is the only true way to produce an authentic dialogue of civilizations and that this is now more necessary than ever. With globalization at hand, the fear is that the West—helped by an intangible Westernization of the world—will engage in a "dialogical monologue" or an "interactive monologue" with civilizations different only in name but so denatured or so exotic that their members are reduced, taking the good years with the bad, to discussing their survival and not the richness of their otherness. Muslims have the means to enter into this debate on an equal footing, and they should do so, and find debating partners ready for this worthy, enriching, and essential confrontation of ideas and ideals.

Comprehensiveness, the Absolute, and the Evolution

Wherever they find themselves, Muslim women and men[3] try, in their practice and daily lives, to conform as much as possible to Islamic teachings. In this they follow the path of faithfulness, "the path towards the spring," of which we have just spoken. In other words, in the West as in the East, they try to actualize the *Sharia* as we have defined it beyond its merely legalistic form. In Europe and in North America, as soon as one pronounces the *shahada*, as soon as one "is Muslim" and tries to remain so by practicing the daily prayers, giving alms, and fasting, for example, or even simply by trying to respect Muslim ethics, one is already in the process of applying the *Sharia*, not in any peripheral way but in its most essential aspects.

This practice and moral awareness are the source and heart of the *Sharia*, which is personal, faithful commitment. Beyond that, the Way itself exerts its own influence more comprehensively, with regard to the guidance that marks the elements or the actions. It touches all the aspects of existence, even if not in the same way, and we must mention this essential factor here, with regard to the methodologies, norms, and details of application of various regulations. This characteristic of Islam is contained within the concept of *shumuliyyat al-islam*, the comprehensiveness of Islam, which we could translate in a more immediately expressive form as "the comprehensive character of Islamic teaching." We certainly find in the sources regulations that touch on the intimate personal dimension (with regard to spiritual practices whose culmination is mystical experience)[4] and religious practice, but there are also directions concerning individuals' behavior with regard to the self, the family, and others, and again general principles pertaining to the management of interpersonal relations and of the community. It seems difficult to draw a line of demarcation here between the private and the public spheres, between the realms of faith and reason, between the religious and the political, so interconnected and mingled do these areas appear under the sole transcendent authority of the Book and the Prophetic traditions. Many Muslims have continued down through the ages to say formulaically, as if they were presenting evidence: "There is no difference, for us, between private and public, religion and politics: Islam encompasses all areas." Many orientalists have fallen into step with them and affirmed, and still affirm, that Islam does not think in distinct categories and that all areas are governed by the same authority. Moreover, often, because of this kind of approach, it is assumed that Muslims are by definition "not capable of integration" into secularized societies because their religion prevents them from accepting modern demarcations between the categories we have mentioned.

But one has the right to ask whether these statements are based on sound evidence. Islamic teaching certainly has "a comprehensive quality" that one cannot fail to notice even upon one reading of the Qur'an, but can it be so easily asserted that no distinction exists between the various realms of human activity? In other words, does the fact that there is one source necessarily require a similarity of approaches? Nothing is less certain, and Muslim scholars such as Abu Hanifa and al-Shafii, who in the earliest times tried to set the norms for reading and deducing rules, were deeply intuitive. For it must be said and remembered that the formulation of universal principles and the elaboration of a basic frame of reference, which give "the way to faithfulness" its meaning, were produced by human intelligence. It is from the reading of the scriptural sources, with the internal limitations this imposed (e.g., the Arabic language, grammar, the practice of the Prophet), that they decided upon the normative parameters from which it was possible to extrapolate principles, formulate regulations, and elaborate rules of morality faithful to the guidance of the Qur'an and the Sunna. It is human intelligence that formulates the universal and elaborate methodologies, which vary according to the object of study to which they are applied (e.g., religious practice, social affairs, sciences), by working on the Qur'an and the Sunna. In other words, the *Sharia*, insofar as it is the expression of the "the way to faithfulness," deduced and constructed a posteriori, is the work of human intellect. The Source and undisputed reference is the Book and then the Prophetic traditions: we have already said that these texts touch upon every area of life in ways both general and diverse and summon human intelligence to discern the difference between the categories, as well as the logic that underpins religious regulations, and to try to bring the whole of the message into harmony and make its guidance more accessible. This harmonization is rational, and, insofar as it tries to be faithful to the wisdom of Revelation, it does its utmost also to be reasonable.

The work of categorization left by scholars through the ages is phenomenal. Specialists in the foundations of law and jurisprudence (*usul al-fiqh*), who labored at this exercise of extrapolating and categorizing rules on the basis of a reading that was both careful to be faithful to the norm and profoundly rational, have bequeathed to us an unparalleled heritage. A careful reading of these works reveals that very precise modes of grasping the sources were set down very early. Consideration of the language was supported by a double process of distinguishing on the one hand between the unequivocal and the equivocal and on the other between the presence (explicit or implicit) or absence of a causal link (*illa*) in the pronouncement of rules. The other essential side of this work was the elaboration of methodologies differentiated according to the area being studied. Thus, in the area of religious practice (*al-ibadat*), it was determined that it was the texts that were the only ultimate reference because the revealed rites are fixed and not subject to human reason: here one can do only what is based on a text, and the margin for interpretation is virtually nil. In the wider area of human and social affairs, the established methodology is the exact opposite: bearing in mind the positive and trusting attitude of the Qur'anic message, as we have seen, toward the universe and human beings, everything is permitted except that which is explicitly forbidden by a text (or recognized as such by the specialists). Thus, the scope for the exercise of reason and creativity is huge, in contrast with the situation in matters to do with religious practice, and people have complete discretion to experiment, progress, and reform as long as they avoid what is forbidden.[5] So the fact that the fundamental principles of Islam, and its prohibitions, are stated can never allow Muslims to dispense with a study of the context and the societies in which they live. This is the price they must pay for their faithfulness.

It is on the basis of these same logical categorizations that it has been possible to differentiate, through reading the scriptural sources, between the universal principles to which the Muslim consciousness must seek to be faithful through the ages and the practice of those principles, which is necessarily relative, at a given moment in human history. We are here confronting the fundamental distinction that should be established between timeless principles and contingent models, a distinction that is a direct consequence of a normative reading of the sources and, as such, is in itself fundamental. So, a distinction should be made, in the case of the society of Medina, for example, between the fundamental principles on which it was established (e.g., the rule of law, equality, freedom of conscience and worship) and the form in which that society historically appeared. Faithfulness to principles cannot involve faithfulness to the historical model because times change, societies and political and economic systems become more complex, and in every age it is in fact necessary to think of a model appropriate to each social and cultural reality.[6]

For example, one could investigate further the areas of custom and culture, because these concern Western Muslims very directly. The methodological distinction between religious practice and social affairs, like the difference in nature, as far as the basis of reference is concerned, between universal principles and historical, temporal models, brings out another demarcation—that which distinguishes between the religious judgment and its cultural garb. *Al-urf*, custom, has been considered one of the sources of law in the sense that all that is recognized as "established for the good" (*maruf*) in a given culture (and that is not in contradiction with any prohibition) is, in practice, integrated into the local Islamic sphere of reference. In fact, as we have seen, even if the forms of religious practice do not change with changes in time and space, some religious commands related to the affairs of the world naturally take on the color of the culture of various countries: the principles remain the same, but the ways of being faithful to them are diverse.[7] So the concern should not be to dress as the Prophet dressed but to dress according to the principles (of decency, cleanliness, simplicity, aesthetics, and modesty) that underlay his choice of clothes.[8]

We have now moved beyond the pronouncement of slogans that, because they relied on one source (the Qur'an and the Sunna) ended in a necessary similarity in commandments, methodologies, and, finally, rules of behavior. All this assumed that the absolute origin of the scriptural sources embraced all areas of life in one logic to the point of denying development, rationality, and diversity in human societies. But we have just seen that this is not so, and the situation is clearly very different: the Revelation and the Sunna call on human intellect to determine the categories, methodologies, and rules for reading and deduction, allowing it to identify first the absolute and universal at the heart of them, to establish the specifics of religious practice, and to open up a vast area to rational investigation, which, in order to remain faithful, must be creative in the matter of relations with the societies and cultures within which and upon which it is working.

For there is indeed a difference in Islam between creed and rationality, the private and the public, the religious and the political: it is true that the Transcendent One through His Revelation refers to all the areas of life and shows "the Way," but the scriptural verses and the Prophetic traditions, which are very precise and compelling (insofar as they refer to our relationship with God and to religious practice), are distinct from those that fix universal and general principles concerning the affairs of the world and the ultimate ideals that the believer must try to achieve, as well as he can, in the future. Sustained by faith, strong in reasoning ability, and guided by ethical injunctions, a believing consciousness must live within his own time, at the heart of his society, among other human beings, and put his energy into this constant dialectical movement between the essential principles determined by Revelation and actual circumstances. In practice, the "Way to faithfulness" teaches us that Islam rests on three sources: the Qur'an, the Sunna, and the state of the world, or of our society (al-waqi). It is through a study of the Texts and the deep understanding of the context that all the pairings and unions of which we spoke in the first chapter come into being and are fulfilled—those between oneself and one's self, oneself and the Other, and, more broadly, with the whole of humankind. The "way to the source" is never confused with the Source itself: the latter declares the absolute and the universal outside of time, but everything along the way must consider itself in time, in change, in imperfection, immersed in the reality of humankind—their rich humanity as well as their disturbing deceits. It really is a way, a way toward the ideal, and anyone traveling along it is invited to make a constant effort to reform in the light of the universal, without ever claiming that one has attained the Truth of the universal. The three sources, the Texts as well as the universe, teach one this humility.[9]

Maslaha, Ijtihad, and Fatwa

Among the tools listed by the classical ulama who specialized in the fundamentals of law and jurisprudence (usul al-fiqh), we find three basic notions that provide a way of making a connection between universal principles and social realities that change with the passage of time and cultures. A study shows that they present a significant amount of leeway for proposing new readings of the sources, finding new responses or thinking of innovative models of social and even economic organization. It is Muslim thinking that is stalled these days: the tools are available, and the work to be done is the double task of reading the sources and interpreting the world. It must also be remembered that it is not a question of understanding the world better in order to adapt to it, but, at a much deeper level, through this contact with the changing realities of the world (scientific, social, political, and economic), it is a question of rereading the scriptural sources themselves with a new eye. In doing this, it is essential to remember that the corpus of the Sharia is a human construction, and some aspects of it may evolve just as human thought evolves and just as some aspects of the Qur'an and the Sunna were revealed over time. This is precisely the meaning of the Prophetic tradition that "God sends to this community, every hundred years, someone to renew its religion." This renewal is not a modification of the sources but a transformation of the mind and eyes that read them, which are indeed naturally influenced by the new social, political, and scientific environment in which they live. A new context changes the horizon of the text, renews it, and sometimes gives it an original purport, providing responses never before imagined.

The three notions in the heading act exactly in this way. Beginning from the state of society, they invite the mind to reread the sources and give it the means either to find a response that has already been given (for example, in another similar case), or to think of a new legal development (when the texts say nothing that applies to the case in question), or to state a specific legal opinion allowing some adaptation (more or less restricted to circumstance and time). This is an essential process for Muslims living in the West, even if, as we shall see in the next section, these tools must be used with a certain number of necessary conditions if one is to avoid falling into the trap of "racing into adaptation," which is either timid or risky, and never wholly reliable.

Al-Maslaha *(The Common Good)*

The notion of *maslaha*, as a legal term, has given rise to numerous debates since it was first used, principally by the ulama of the Maliki school, against the firm opposition displayed by the Zahiri school, and in particular by Ibn Hazm. These quarrels were very often ill founded, and it seems that very often it was, more than anything, a question of defining relations to the sources and to the corpus of the *Sharia*.

In more recent times, this notion has been used to justify all sorts of new *fatawa* (plural of *fatwa*), even some that were manifestly in contradiction with obvious proofs from the Qur'an and the Sunna, as in the case of rules concerning interest (*riba*) and inheritance.

It is therefore important to recall briefly the early researches and studies carried out in this area, not only in order to understand the scope of *maslaha* but also to evaluate the advantages to be derived from applying it in the light of developments over time and from the diversity of contexts. The Imam Malik referred to the notion of *istislah*,[10] which meant "to seek the good." In his legal research, he therefore used the example of the Companions—who formulated numerous legal decisions in the light of the common good while respecting the corpus of the sources—to justify the fact that "to seek the good" (*istislah*) is one of the fundamentals of the *Sharia* and so is part of it. After the work of codification carried out by al-Shafii, the ulama, as we have recalled, began to set out distinctions between what were actually the sources and their areas of legal application, the hierarchy of values among the regulations, and so on.

Numerous ulama, such as al-Juwayni, in his *Al-burhan*, and the Mutazila Abu al-Husayn al-Basri, in *Al-mutamad fi usul al-fiqh* (both ulama lived in the eleventh century), refer to this notion in one way or another. At that time, the polemic had already begun concerning the definition of the exact meaning of this notion and its status within the Islamic legal apparatus. It is Abu Hamid al-Ghazali who, with his strict codification, provided the clearest framework for tackling this question from that time to the present. In his *Al-mustasfa min ilm al-usul*,[11] he states very precisely: "In its essential meaning, *al-maslaha* is a term which means to seek something beneficial [*manfaa*] or avoid something harmful [*madarra*]. But this is not what we mean, because to seek the beneficial and avoid what is bad are the objectives [*maqasid*] intended by creation, and good [*sahah*] in the creation of humanity consists in the attaining of these objectives [*maqasid*]. What we mean by *maslaha* is the preservation of the objective [*maqasid*] of the Law [*shar*], which consists in five things: the protection of religion, life, intellect, lineage, and property. Whatever ensures the protection of these five principles [*usul*] is *maslaha*; whatever goes against their protection is *mafsada*, and to avoid it is *maslaha*."[12]

This general definition defines a structure on which almost all later ulama were to agree,[13] for he refers implicitly to the sources without making a distinction between the objective of the good, which is found in the Qur'an and the Sunna, and how it is humanly stipulated when nothing is clearly stated in the sources. In fact, with this definition al-Ghazali placed himself above the disputes of the ulama, and when this light was shed on the subject, a more detailed codification in the nature of things opened the way for a precise understanding of *maslaha* and what was at stake in the legal argument; his contribution was therefore immense and central.

Al-Ghazali, still referring to the broad meaning of *maslaha*, mentions three different types: *al-daruriyyat* (the imperative), a category which has to do with the five elements of *maqasid al-sharia* (here in the sense of the objectives of the Law) listed earlier, that is, the protection of religion, life, reason, lineage, and property;[14] *al-hajiyyat* (the necessary, the complementary), which has to do with the prevention of anything that could be a source of difficulty in the life of the community, without leading to death or destruction;[15] and finally *al-tahsiniyyat* and *al-kamaliyyat* (the enhancing and the perfecting), which concern anything that may bring about an improvement in religious practice.[16] These three levels cover all that can be considered as the *masali* (common good) of the human being considered as a person and as a worshipper of God, and this categorization was hardly ever questioned in debate and polemic.

What did give rise to disagreements and conflicts in the legal field was the question of discovering whether there was a real need for this notion within the Islamic legal framework[17] or whether *al-maslaha* should be considered an independent source, though supplementary, of *Sharia* (and thus a part of the latter, and whose scope should be limited),[18] or, finally, whether it should simply be seen as part of another source, such as *qiyas* (analogy).[19] These various positions also rely on another qualification that distinguishes three types of *masali* (this time differentiated according to their classification, not according to their hierarchical importance), by which the ulama established a typology based on the degree of proximity of *al-maslaha* to the sources. If *al-maslaha* is based on textual evidence (i.e., a quotation from the Qur'an or the Sunna), it is called *maslaha mutabara* (accredited), and it must necessarily be taken into account. If, on the other hand, the *maslaha* invoked is contradictory to an undisputed text (*nass qati*), it is called *mulgha* (discredited) and cannot be taken into account. The third type occurs when there is no text: the Qur'an and the Sunna do not confirm but neither do they reject a *maslaha* that became apparent after the age of Revelation. A *maslaha* of this type is call *mursala* (undetermined),[20] for it allows the "ulama" to use their own analysis and personal reasoning in order to formulate a legal decision in the light of the historical and geographical context, using their best efforts to remain faithful to the commandments and to the "spirit" of the Islamic legal corpus where no text, no "letter" of the Law, is declared.

It is this last type that has given rise to much debate and polemic (the analysis is beyond the scope of this study). Suffice it to say here that the main cause of disagreement was the fear, on the part of those opposed to the very concept of *al-maslaha al-mursala*, that such a notion, with such broad scope, might then allow the ulama to formulate regulations without reference to the Qur'an and the Sunna on the basis of exclusively rational and completely free reasoning, all in the name of a remote hardship or "an anticipated difficulty." These were the main arguments of the Zahirite school, as well as numerous Shafii and even Maliki ulama who did not recognize *al-maslaha al-mursala*—not referring back to the sources—as a legal proof; they saw in it a specious (*wahmiyya*) proof, not valid for legislation. This was the same instinctive fear of an approach that was purely rational and not connected with the Law that pushed al-Ghazali to restrict work on *al-maslaha* to the area of the application of *qiyas* (analogy), which, of its nature, requires a close link with the text for the deduction of the cause (*illa*) on which analogical reasoning rests.

Some ulama in the course of history have formulated judgments in the name of *al-maslaha* and sometimes completely changed and disturbed the manner and conditions of the use of legal instruments within the Islamic framework. The particularly interesting example of the famous fourteenth-century Hanbali jurist Najm al-Din al-Tufi seems to have partly given them just reason to be fearful: al-Tufi ended up giving *al-maslaha* priority over texts from the Qur'an and the Sunna, which, according to him, should be applied, according to Mahmasani, only "to the extent that the common good does not require anything else."[21] Moreover, in our own times, we see very strange "modern Islamic legal decisions" based on "modern *maslaha*" that are clearly contradictory to the sources. The notion of *al-maslaha al-mursala* thus sometimes seems to justify the strangest behavior, as well as the most obscure commercial dealings, financial commitments, and banking investments, under the pretext that they protect, or could or should protect, "the common good."

But this kind of excess was not typical among those who supported taking *al-maslaha al-mursala* into account as an authentic and legitimate source of legislation. They believed that the formulation of Islamic legal decisions should take place in the light of the Qur'an and the Sunna and in agreement with them and, moreover, upon certain demanding conditions (even if *al-maslaha al-mursala* should be considered as an independent source in the absence of any text). A careful study of the various opinions (for and against *al-maslaha al-mursala*) shows that the ulama are in agreement on numerous important points, even considering the conditions stipulated by supporters of the concept, among the first of whom was the *alim* of Grenada, al-Shatibi (fourteenth century). We find in his works a series of conditions and precise definitions regarding recognition of the "common good" as a reliable juridical source, which restrict its application and prevent the ulama from having recourse to *al-maslaha* without justification. Without going into too much detail, we may summarize the three generally recognized main conditions for situations when it is sure that no text has been enunciated:

1. The analysis and identification must be made with serious attention so that we may be sure that we have before us an authentic (*haqiqiyya*) and not an apparent or spurious (*wahmiyya*) *maslaha*. The scholar must reach a high degree of certainty that the formulation of an injunction will avoid a difficulty and not do the opposite and increase problems in the context of the Islamic legal structure.
2. The *maslaha* must be general (*kulliyya*) and be beneficial to the population and to society as a whole, and not only to one group or class or individual.
3. The *maslaha* must not be in contradiction to or in conflict with an authentic text from the Qur'an or the Sunna. If it were, it would no longer be a *maslaha mursala* but would be a *maslaha mulgha*.[22]

These three conditions[23] give us broad guidelines by which we can understand the concept of *maslaha*, the common good, in the Islamic frame of reference. What is clear above all is the supremacy of the Qur'an and the Sunna over all other references and legal instruments. Yusuf al-Qaradawi[24] rightly recalls, taking up the ideas of al-Ghazali, Ibn al-Qayyim, and al-Shatibi, that everything found in the Qur'an and the Sunna is, in itself, in harmony with "the good of humankind" in general, for the Creator knows and wants what is best for human beings, and He shows them what they must do to achieve it. We find in the Qur'an, referring to the revealed message: "[the Prophet] who will enjoin upon them the doing of what is right and forbid them the doing of what is wrong, and make lawful to them the good things of life and forbid them the bad things, and lift from them their burdens and the shackles that were upon them [aforetime]";[25] "O human beings! An exhortation has come to you from your Lord, a healing for what is in your hearts, a guidance and a mercy for the believers."[26] We find the preference for the good of humanity in the first revelation (of the three that led to their eventual prohibition) concerning intoxicating drinks: "They ask you about intoxicating drinks and games of chance. Say: 'These two things contain great harm for men as well as benefits; but the harm found in them is greater than the benefit.' "[27]

Ibn al-Qayyim al-Jawziyya summarized the position as follows: "The principles and fundamentals of the *Sharia* concerning the injunctions and the good of humankind in this life and the next are all based on justice, mercy, the good of man, and wisdom. Every situation in which justice succumbs to tyranny, mercy to cruelty, goodness to corruption, wisdom to foolishness, has nothing in common with the *Sharia*, even if it is the result of an allegorical interpretation [*tawill*]. For the *Sharia* is the justice of God among His servants, the mercy of God among His creatures, His shadow upon His earth, and His wisdom, which is both the proof of His own existence and the best witness to the authenticity of His Prophet."[28]

To seek for the good (*maslaha*) of man, in this life and the next, is the very essence of Islamic commandments and prohibitions. If the latter are clearly proclaimed (*qati al-thubut wa-qati al-dalala*)[29] in the Qur'an and/or the Sunna, they must be respected and applied in the light of an understanding of the whole body of the objectives of Islamic teaching, *maqasid al-Sharia*:[30] they are, and represent, the revealed good (*maslaha*) granted by the Creator to His creature to guide him toward the good.

Nevertheless, the sources are sometimes silent. When facing new situations and problems, the ulama cannot find specific responses in the Qur'an and the Sunna; so, guided by the light of Revelation and the example of the Prophet, they have to formulate judgments such as will protect the best interests of people without betraying the frame of reference. These interests are called *masalih mursala* and require the total and constant commitment of the ulama if they are to make it possible for individuals to live as Muslims in all times and places and prevent them from carrying too heavy a burden, for God said: "God wants things to be easy for you, He does not want it to be difficult for you."[31]

So this is the framework within which we must consider the notion of *maslaha*, which has been a controversial concept, often because there has been a lack of clarity in the way it is defined and because of the strict and demanding conditions required for its application. It has sometimes suffered from excessive use by some ulama and scholars when they have tried to justify some "modern judgment" or "progress" in the name of *al-maslaha*. We have seen that it is a very specific concept—in its definition, its levels, its types, and its conditions—and requires that the ulama constantly refer back to the sources so that they are able to formulate judgments in conformity with the revealed Message, even when there is no specifically relevant text. They must try—by carrying out a deep, thorough, and detailed study—to provide the Muslim community with new rational judgments guided by Revelation. This is the meaning of *ijtihad*, which is both the source and the legal instrument that allows a dynamism to be set in motion at the heart of Islamic law and jurisprudence.

Al-Ijtihad

Definition and Classification.   When the Prophet sent Muadh to Yemen, he asked him about the sources on which he would base his judgments and approved of his intention of "putting all his energy into formulating his own judgment" in cases where he could find no guidance in the Qur'an and the Sunna. This personal effort undertaken by the jurist in order to understand the source and deduce the rules or, in the absence of a clear textual guidance, formulate independent judgments is what is called *ijtihad* in the field of Islamic law and jurisprudence. Hashim Kamali proposes the following definition: "*Ijtihad* is defined as the total expenditure of effort made by a jurist in order to infer, with a degree of probability, the rules of *Sharia* from their detailed evidence in the sources. Some ulama have defined *ijtihad* as the application by a jurist of all his faculties either in inferring the rules of *Sharia* from their sources or in implementing such rules and applying them to particular issues. *Ijtihad* essentially consists of an inference [*istinbat*] that amounts to a probability [*zann*], thereby excluding the extraction of a ruling from a clear text."[32]

Like *al-maslaha*, the legal instrument of *ijtihad* has been used to justify all kinds of new judgments. So Hashim Kamali quite rightly recalls the general principle (about which the ulama are unanimous), according to which there can be no *ijtihad* when an explicit text exists in the sources (*la ijtihada maa al-nass*). This means that if there is an explicit Qur'anic verse whose meaning is obvious and leaves no room for any hypothesis or interpretation (*qati al-dalala*), no *ijtihad* is possible. Similarly, if the jurist finds an authenticated hadith (*mutawatir, qati al-thubut*) whose content is also completely explicit and unambiguous (*qati al-dalala*), he must use that as his reference and there is no room for the exercise of *ijtihad*.

Indeed, clear texts that are both authenticated and explicit, even though they are not very numerous, constitute the unalterable foundation, the fixed principles, on which the *Sharia* is based—principles to which the jurist must refer, from which he must analyze, comment on, and explain texts that contain some conjecture (*zanni*), and on the basis of which he should also formulate new judgments through a dynamic process when his community faces new situations. The laws and judgments provided by these clear texts together constitute a specific corpus, which the ulama *al-usul* call *al-malum min al-din bil-darura*, which means that they bring out the fundamental essence of Islamic law and that to reject them leads to the negation of Islam (*kufr*).

But the great majority of the verses in the Qur'an and the traditions of the Prophet are not of both a strict and compelling nature. The Qur'an is authenticated in itself (*qati al-thubut*, of indisputable origin), but most of the verses containing legal judgments (*ayat al-ahkam*) are open to analysis, commentary, and interpretation (*zanni al-dalala*), and this is also the case with the *ahadith*, most of which leave some scope for speculation as much concerning their authenticity (*thubut*) as concerning their meaning (*dalala*). This means that the *fuqaha* (jurists) had, and still have, an important and essential function in the formulation of laws that may be called Islamic. They fulfill this function particularly through their *ijtihad*, applied at various levels: to understand a specific text (in the light of the whole Islamic legal corpus); to classify texts on the basis of their clarity or their nature (e.g., *qati* [indisputable] or *zanni* [conjectural]; *zahir* [obvious] or *nass* [explicit]; *khass* [specific] or *amm* [general]); or to formulate judgments where no text exists. *Ijtihad* taken as a whole (as both source and legal instrument) has in fact been considered by numerous ulama as the third principal source of *Sharia*, encompassing *al-ijma* (*ijtihad jamai*), *al-istislah*, and *al-istihsan*, as well as other subdivisions recognized among what are called the supplementary sources of the *Sharia*. As Muhammad Hashim Kamali has emphasized: "The various sources of Islamic law that feature next to the Qur'an and *Sunnah* are all manifestations of *ijtihad*, albeit with differences that are largely procedural in character. In this way, consensus of opinion, analogy, juristic preference, considerations of public interest [*maslahah*], etc., are all interrelated not only under the main heading of *ijtihad*, but via the Qur'an and the Sunnah."[33]

Al-Ghazali, al-Shatibi, Ibn al-Qayyim al-Jawziyya, and, more recently, al-Khallaf and Abu Zahra have referred to this type of classification, underlining the importance of *ijtihad* as the third source of Islamic jurisprudence, for *ijtihad* includes all the instruments used to form judgments through human reasoning and personal effort. *Ijtihad* is, in fact, the rational elaboration of laws either on the basis of the sources or formulated in the light of them. Thus, even *ijma* (consensus) is the product of a collective human, rational discussion, and so one can conceive—even if it would be very unlikely and rare—that a legal decision made by *ijma* might eventually become unsuitable and be referred again for debate. As Professor Hamidullah has said in connection with the Hanafi school of law: "The opinion of a jurist can, however, be rejected by another jurist who can offer his own opinion instead. This applies not only to individual opinion or an inference but also covers collective opinion. At least the Hanafi school of law accepts that a new consensus can cancel an old consensus. Suppose there is a consensus on a certain issue. We accept its authority, but it does not mean that no one can oppose it till eternity. If someone has the courage to oppose it with due respect and reason, and if he can persuade the jurist to accept his point of view, a new consensus comes into being. The new consensus abrogates the old one. This principle has been propounded by the famous Hanafi jurist Abu al-Yusr al-Bazdawi in his book *Usul al-Fiqh* [Principles of Jurisprudence]. Al-Bazdawi belongs to the fourth and fifth century of the Hijrah. This work is a great contribution to Islamic jurisprudence. It is on account of his statement that we can say that consensus cannot become a source of difficulty for us. If a consensus is reached on some issue and it is found subsequently to be unsuitable the possibility remains that we may change it through reasoning and create a new one canceling the old consensus."[34]

This analysis recalls an important principle from the realm of *usul al-fiqh*, which is that the Qur'an and the Sunna are the only two indisputable sources, sources at whose core the prescriptive verses and *ahadith* (*ayat wa-ahadith al-ahkam*)[35] are divided into two main levels: the *qati* (indisputable), which is clear in itself, and the *zanni* (conjectural, open to hypotheses and interpretations), which requires on the part of the ulama an attentive study of the texts in question before they can deduce appropriate judgments on passages taken from the sources. The aim of this type of *ijtihad* (applied to *zanni* texts)—sometimes called *bayani* (explanatory *ijtihad*)—is to analyze the text (*nass*) in order to draw from it a ruling and its *illa* (the effective cause of this specific ruling); this allows both an adequate understanding of the text and consequent analogical reasoning (*qiyas*) in the light of the historical context. This type of *ijtihad* has given rise to numerous and diverse subdivisions following the various opinions of the ulama.

There is another type of *ijtihad* that is applied when there is no scriptural reference. Here, too, we find numerous subdivisions because of the diversity of opinion among the ulama and the collections of writings and commentaries that have been made in the course of history. At least three types stand out:

1. *Ijtihad qiyasi* works by analogical reasoning, taking into consideration the effective cause (*illa*) of a ruling drawn from the sources.
2. *Ijtihad zanni* comes in when it is impossible to refer to an effective cause; this type is often linked with *ijtihad istislahi*.
3. *Ijtihad istislahi* is based on *al-maslaha* and seeks to deduce rulings in the light of the general objective of the *Sharia*.

But the ulama are not unanimous about the specific classification of *ijtihad*, because they do not even agree on its definition and methods of application.

Another distinction has to do with the degree of *ijtihad*, which may be absolute (*mutlaq*) or limited (*muqayyad*). The first type, also called *ijtihad fi al-shar*, is based on the ability of the *mujtahid* (a scholar qualified to practice *ijtihad*) to extrapolate and formulate his or her own judgments on the basis of a direct study of the sources. The second, also called *ijtihad madhhabi* (pertaining to a school), is, by contrast, limited to a particular school of law and the *mujtahid* must formulate his judgments according to the rules of a given juridical school.

The Conditions (*Shurut*) of Ijtihad

The framework we have just presented, with the definition and classification of *ijtihad*, has been taken into account by the ulama when determining the conditions for *ijtihad*.[36] In order to analyze and classify, they have focused on the qualities a scholar must possess in order to practice an authentic and reliable *ijtihad*, in order to become a *mujtahid*. As with other classifications, the conditions formulated by the ulama have been numerous and divergent because of their various opinions about legal instruments, the applicability of laws, or, simply, the priority allotted to their implementation.

Before going further in setting out the requirements for being a *mujtahid*, it may be useful to refer here to the concise opinion of al-Shatibi, who differentiated between the very nature of *ijtihad* and its instruments. His overall view, in this sense, is simple and edifying, for he brings together all the conditions under two main rubrics. Thus, according to him, "the level of *ijtihad* is attained when two qualities are present:

1. A deep understanding of the objectives (*maqasid*) of the *Sharia*.
2. A real mastery of the various methods of deduction and extraction (*istinbat*) based on knowledge and understanding."[37]

The "five essential principles" (*al-daruriyyat al-khamsa*) that we have already mentioned (religion, life, intellect, lineage, and property), as well as the necessary distinctions between the indispensable (*daruri*), the necessary or complementary (*haji*), and the embellishments or improvements (*tahsini*), constitute the framework provided by the Lawgiver to guide the research of the *mujtahid* and so represent the fundamental terms of reference. The *mujtahid* must also know which instruments[38] he may resort to among the general maxims of *fiqh, qiyas, istihsan*, and so on.

From Abu al-Husayn al-Basri and his work *Mutamad fi usul al-fiqh* (eleventh century) to Ibn al-Qayyim al-Jawziyya with his *Ilam al-muwaqqiin an rabb al-alamin* (fourteenth century), numerous ulama have proposed various classifications of the qualities required and the conditions to be met in order for a scholar to be considered a *mujtahid*. Some believed that the first condition was knowledge of the Arabic language;[39] others thought that what mattered above all was knowledge of the verses and *ahadith* that had legal significance. In spite of these divergences, which are in fact essentially procedural, since their respective conditions overlap, we may summarize the efforts of the ulama in this area in the following seven points: The *mujtahid* must possess:

1. A knowledge of Arabic, which enables him to understand the Qur'an and Sunna correctly and particularly the verses and *ahadith* that contain rulings (*ayat wa-ahadith al-ahkam*)
2. A knowledge of the sciences of the Qur'an and *hadith*, which enables him to understand and identify the evidence (*adilla*) contained in the texts and, what is more, to deduce and extract judgments from them
3. A thorough knowledge of the objectives (*maqasid*) of the *Sharia*, their classification, and the priorities they imply
4. Knowledge of questions on which there was *ijma*; this requires knowledge of the works on secondary issues (*furu*)
5. Knowledge of the principle of analogical reasoning (*qiyas*) and its methodology (the causes [*ilal*] and circumstances [*asbab*] of a specific judgment, conditions, e.g., *shurut*)
6. Knowledge of his historical, social, and political context, that is to say, the situation of the people living around him (*ahwal al-nas*), the state of their affairs, traditions and customs, and so on
7. Recognition of his own competence, honesty, reliability, and uprightness.[40]

As we have already mentioned, numerous other conditions, in different orders, have been proposed, but these seven points more or less cover the most important qualities needed by a *mujtahid*.[41] Some ulama believe that these conditions and qualifications are so advanced and demanding that it has not been possible to reach this standard since the time of the great ulama in about the ninth century. This is how they justify the pronouncement that forever closed the "doors of *ijtihad*" after this very rich period. Other ulama, the great majority, are of the opinion that the practice of *ijtihad* has been partly abandoned for historical reasons that have pressed either the political leaders or the ulama to declare that it was no longer necessary to practice *ijtihad*.[42] Consequently, the doors of *ijtihad* have never been closed; no scholar would have had the right to make such a decision in the name of Islam because a declaration such as this is, by its very nature, against Islam. In fact, *ijtihad*, as the third source of Islamic law and jurisprudence, is *fard kifaya*, a collective responsibility. Everyone recognizes that these conditions are demanding and that they are required for a qualified *ijtihad*, but they also say that these qualifications have never been beyond the reach of the ulama in recent times and up to the present. The progress that has been made in authenticating *ahadith*, easier access to reference works, and computer-aided classification make the work of the *mujtahid* easier and more effective. Consequently, the Muslim community, through its ulama, should still be fulfilling this fundamental duty today, even though it will be necessary to find a way to apply it appropriately in our contemporary context because of the new complexity of many sciences, such as medicine, technology, economics, the social sciences, and so on.[43] *Ijtihad* remains the most important instrument the ulama have at their disposal to fulfil the universal vocation of Islam, through a constant dynamic of adaptation in response to the time and the context.

What Is a *Fatwa*?

To understand what a *fatwa* is, we should keep in mind the whole substance of the preceding analysis, for a *fatwa* is a part, an element, and, more precisely, a legal instrument, which must be understood in the light of the corpus of Islamic law and jurisprudence. *Fatwa* (plural *fatawa*) means, literally, "legal decision," "verdict," or, following the definition of al-Shatibi, "A reply to a legal question given by an expert (*mufti*) in the form of words, action, or approval."[44] A *fatwa* has two essential aspects: it must, first and above all, be founded on the sources and on the juridical inferences and extractions arrived at by the *mujtahidin*[45] who practice *ijtihad* when the sources are not clear or explicit (that is, when they are *zanni*) or when there is no relevant text. It must also be formulated in the light of the context of life, the environment, and the specific situation that justifies its being made—and which is in fact its cause.

The place of the *mujtahid* and the *mufti* is of prime importance. As al-Shatibi said: "The *mufti*,[46] within the community, plays the part of the Prophet. Numerous evidences support his assertion. First there is the proof of *hadith*: 'Truly the scholars are the heirs of the prophets, and what one inherits from prophets is not money [*la dinaran wa-la dirham*], but knowledge [*ilm*].' Second, he [the *mufti*] is the source of transmitting rulings [*ahkam*] in conformity with the words of the Prophet: 'Let the one among you who is witness transmit [that to which he is witness] to those who are absent' and 'Transmit from me, even if it is only one verse.' If this is the case, it means that he [the *mufti*] stands in for the Prophet.

In fact, the *mufti* is a kind of legislator, for the *Sharia* that he conveys is either taken [insofar as it has already been stipulated] from the Lawgiver [by way of the Revelation and the Sunna] or inferred or extracted from the sources. In the first case, he is simply a transmitter, while in the second he stands in for the Prophet in that he stipulates rulings. To formulate judgments is the function of the legislator. So, if the function of the *mujtahid* is to formulate judgments on the basis of his opinion and efforts, it is possible to say that he is therefore a legislator who should be respected and followed: we should act according to the rulings he formulates and this is vicegerency [*Khilafa*] in its genuine implementation."[47]

Al-Shatibi underlines the importance of the *mujtahid* who stands in for the Prophet in the Muslim community after the death of Muhammad. In this way, the *mujtahid* or the *mufti* represents the continuity of knowledge (*ilm*) guided by the two sources, so that it may be rightly applied throughout history. Al-Shatibi made a distinction between clear and explicit evidence (that stipulated in the sources) and that which requires the exercise of deduction and inference and puts the *mujtahid* in the position of legislator (even though he must seek the guidance of God, the supreme Legislator, and follow the example of the Prophet). The distinction drawn by al-Shatibi has the great advantage of setting out the two different levels of *fatwa*: when questioned on legal issues, the *mujtahid* will sometimes find a clear answer in the Qur'an and the Sunna because there is an explicit text. Then the *fatwa* consists of a quotation and a restatement of the authoritative proof. If there is a text that is open to interpretation, or if there is no relevant text, the *mufti* must give a specific response in the light of both the objectives of the *Sharia* and the situation of the questioner. Al-Shatibi underlines that the *mufti* really does play the role of vicegerent who must come up with a legal judgment for the one who calls on him. The more the issue is related to an individual or a particular case, the more precise, clear, and specific it must be. Consequently, a *fatwa* is rarely transferable, because it is a legal judgment pronounced (in the light of the sources, of the *maslaha*, and of the context) in response to a clear question arising from a precise context. In the field of law, this is in fact the exact meaning of "jurisprudence."

Many questions have been raised in the course of history about the diversity of *fatawa*. If Islam is one, how could there be differing legal judgments on the same legal question? The ulama have unanimously affirmed that if geographical or historical contexts differ, it is no longer the same question, for it must be considered in the light of a new environment. Thus, properly considered responses should naturally differ, as is shown by the example of al-Shafii, who modified some of his legal judgments after traveling from Baghdad to Cairo. So, even though Islam is one, the *fatawa*, with all their diversity, and sometimes contradiction, still remain Islamic and authoritative.

This kind of diversity was understood, accepted, and respected, while the problem of disagreement between ulama faced with an identical legal question has given rise to endless debates. Is this possible in the area of religious affairs, and if so, how can Islam be a unifying force for Muslims? Two essential points have been emphasized by the vast majority of ulama.

1. There is no divergence of opinion on the principles, the fundamentals (*usul*) of Islamic law. There is a consensus among the jurists on the fact that these principles constitute the essence, the frame of reference, and the benchmark of the juridical corpus of Islamic law and jurisprudence (*fiqh*). However, it is impossible to avoid differences of opinion on points related to secondary issues (*furu*), for a legal judgment on these points is dependent on and influenced by many factors, such as the knowledge and understanding of the ulama and their ability to deduce and extrapolate judgments. The natural diversity in their levels of competence inevitably gives rise to divergent interpretations and opinions. This even happened among the Companions at the time of the Prophet, and, according to the ulama, such divergences should be recognized and respected, within their limits, as based upon the fundamentals of Islam.

2. A question naturally arises from this consensus: even if there are various "acceptable" legal opinions on one and the same problem (even a secondary problem [*far*]), does this mean that all the *fatawa* have the same value; in other words, are they all correct? If that were the case, it would lead to the conclusion that two divergent opinions could both be true at the same time, in the same place, and in respect of the same person, which is rationally unacceptable. The majority of ulama, including the four principal imams of the Sunni schools of law, are of the view that only one of the divergent opinions pronounced on a precise question can be considered correct. This is indicated in the passage in the Qur'an that relates the story of David and Solomon, where it is clear that, although they had made judgments on the same case and although both of them had received the gift of judgment and knowledge, only Solomon's opinion was correct: "We made it understood to Solomon."[48] This position is also confirmed by the *hadith* already cited about the *mujtahid*'s reward: he will

receive two rewards if he is right but only one if he is wrong, because his effort and sincere research will be taken into account by God.

So, to accept that there may be a diversity of legal opinions on precise questions (formulated in the same context, at the same time, and for the same community or individual) does not in the least lead to the assumption that there are several "truths" and that all these opinions have the same value and correctness. There is only "one truth," which all the ulama should try to discover, and they will be rewarded for the effort they make toward this. As long as there is no indisputable proof applicable to the problem in question, each Muslim should, after consideration and analysis, follow the opinion whose evidence and worth seem to him the clearest and most convincing.

Guided by the Qur'an and the example of the Prophet, which are for Muslims the sources of truth, the ulama should do their best to discover the truth when the texts are not clear or simply do not exist. In fact, the meaning and content of the delegation granted by God to humankind reaches its peak and is fulfilled when the ulama struggle constantly and tirelessly to arrive at the most correct judgment, or that which is closest to what is correct and true. So these ulama, both *mujtahids* and *muftis*, must be determined, demanding, and confident in their own judgments, while remaining humble and calm to face and accept the fact that there will necessarily and inevitably be a plurality of opinions. The imam al-Shafii aptly said, concerning the state of mind that should characterize the attitude of the ulama: "[As we see it] our opinion is right though it may turn out to be wrong, while we consider the opinion of our opponents to be wrong though it may turn out to be right."[49]

The Principle of Integration

A study of the three notions of *al-maslaha*, *ijtihad*, and *fatwa*, though rather technical, is unavoidable if we are to think from the inside about the presence of Muslims in the West, with their legitimate hope of remaining faithful to their religion and its scriptural sources. What emerges first from this presentation is a clear confirmation of what we brought out earlier: we are dealing with codifications and legal instruments thought up and elaborated by human intelligence on the basis of work on the Qur'an and the Sunna. There are numerous differences among scholars, who are sometimes not even in agreement on the existence of some of these tools or how to define and apply them. It nevertheless remains true that, beyond these disagreements, a true frame of reference has been drawn up that has become, over time, the universe through which Muslim ulama have been given the means to think in terms of evolution and faithfulness at the same time.

It is nevertheless appropriate, particularly when we speak of the new realities that face us in the West, to stay within the spirit of the whole landscape at whose core are set the legal principles and instruments referred to earlier. And it is imperative to remember the meaning of these principles, their interactivity, and their hierarchy. There is a great temptation to use these notions incoherently, chaotically, or only selectively, without fully grasping the whole philosophical legal corpus and consequently to become detached from global progress. As a result, we hear in the West of intellectuals and scholars calling for a new *ijtihad* or for the formulation of innovative *fatawa* without integrating or even connecting this demand with the more general fundamentals of Islam concerning *tawhid*, the concept of the human being and the *Sharia* (with the universal principles it contains). This approach, which almost naturally tries to resolve the problems of integration faced by Muslims through attempts at legal adaptation that are based on circumstance, could soon prove to have serious limitations. First of all, because it is built on a dualistic vision of two universes that do not mingle and that make compromises at their boundaries, or in the limited area where they intersect, it assumes that it is Muslims, being in the numerical minority, who must adapt by force of circumstances. This approach also implicitly carries the idea (even if the discourse says the complete opposite) that Muslims must think of themselves as a minority, on the margin, in their societies, which will continue to be the societies of "the Other" and in which they will live somewhat as strangers, their belonging at best being confined to symbolic "acts": expressions of solidarity, voting, for example. And finally, and perhaps most serious, the vision that undergirds this approach is clearly the concern only that Muslims should integrate into their new environment, and not that they should contribute.

It is certainly quite normal that, during the first decades of their new presence in the West, Muslims should have sought principally to protect themselves; they had no choice, and it was as much about the survival of their religious identity as about the preservation of the richness of their culture. This is how all the initial steps toward adaptation undergone by all immigrant populations should be understood. For Muslims, the process went from the building of mosques to the establishment of Islamic associations via the elaboration of a way of thinking, a discourse, and, little by little, a legal reference framework in the various continents and countries. The various meetings of ulama in the West (from the 1980s in the United States to the beginning of the 1990s in Europe), which tried to address the new questions faced by Muslims in industrialized societies, were part of this trend. The institutionalization of this dynamic with the establishment of the Fiqh Council (Council of Islamic Law and Jurisprudence) in the United States and the European Council for Research and Fatwas, in 1997, made possible the formulation of a series of legal opinions in step with Western societies and available to the public.[50] There was then talk of a "*fiqh al-aqalliyyat*"[51] (law and jurisprudence of minorities), which was to allow Muslims in the West to live their faith and religion more peacefully.

These achievements were, without a shadow of doubt, fundamental and particularly necessary; they constituted a new and important stage in the establishment of Muslims in the West. We must nevertheless be aware that it was just a stage and that we should rethink our presence in the West more comprehensively. Indeed, our own sources come to our aid and press us to go beyond three staging posts, which are in the long term to be considered as traps: the dualist approach, minority thinking, and integration thought of only in terms of adaptation. Doubtless the coming generations will be better equipped to understand and take up these challenges, but the need to reformulate from the inside is already being felt. To think of our belonging to Islam in the West in terms of Otherness, adaptation to limitations, and authorized compromise (*rukhas*) cannot be enough and gives the impression of structural adjustments that make it possible to survive in a sort of imagined borderland but that do not provide the means really to flourish, participate in, and fully engage in our societies. In his book *On Law and the Jurisprudence of Muslim Minorities*, Yusuf al-Qardawi adds a telling subtitle: *The Life of Muslims in Other Societies*. In his mind, Western societies are "other societies" because the societies normal for Muslims are Muslim-majority societies.[52] But this is no longer the case, and what were once thought of as some kind of "diasporas" are so no longer. There is no longer a place of origin from which Muslims are "exiled" or "distanced," and "naturalized," "converted" Muslims—"Western Muslims"—are at home, and should not only say so but feel so.

It will also be necessary to change the way we look at our societies. As we have been saying, our sources help us in this if we can only try hard to reappropriate for ourselves the universality of the message of Islam, along with its vast horizon. This reappropriation should be of a depth that will enable it to produce a true "intellectual revolution" in the sense intended by Kant when he spoke of the "Copernican revolution." Well before the tools that allow us to interact with the world, the Only One established a threefold relation with human beings—exactingness, trust, and humility. If the use of reason is essential for the return to self and the confirmation of the original breath, it also holds the key to applying the revealed books. We must engage with the world armed with faith, the scriptural sources, and an active intellect; in the course of the intellectual development of our universe of reference, we have learned to distinguish methodologies, grasp the religious rites (within the strict limits of its codification based on the texts), and observe the universe (with the methodology appropriate to social affairs) with assurance and confidence. In this we know that everything a society or culture produces and accepts that is not in opposition to a clearly stipulated prohibition is in fact integrated and considered part of the Islamic universe of reference.

It is precisely in this that the intellectual revolution for which we long must live. "The way of faithfulness," "the path to the spring," the *Sharia*, teaches us to integrate everything that is not against an established principle and to consider it as our own. This is, after all, the true universality of Islam: it consists in this principle of integrating the good, from wherever it may come, which has made it possible for Muslims to settle in, and make their own, without contradiction, almost all the cultures of the countries in which they have established themselves, from South America to Asia, through West and North Africa. It should not be otherwise in the West. Here, too, it is a matter of integrating all the dimensions of life that are not in opposition to our terms of reference and to consider them completely our own (legally, socially, and culturally). We must clearly overcome the dualistic vision and reject our sense of being eternal foreigners, living in parallel, on the margins or as reclusive minorities, in order to make way for the global vision of universal Islam that integrates and allows the Other to flourish confidently.[53]

Does this mean that this attitude will by itself make it possible for us to overcome all the problems and that there will then be no contradictions in the Islamic consciousness between the need to remain Muslim and the realities of life in the West? Of course not—but this is nevertheless the way to set the terms of the equation, which must change entirely. To begin by distinguishing all the dimensions of Western life that are already "Islamically based" and thus completely appropriated is to be already equipped with the means to understand this universe from the inside and to consider it truly our own. The next stage is to engage in a systematic work of selection, at several levels, in order to delineate from within the West the limits of the public good (*maslaha*) and to identify the margins available for maneuver between the situations in which we are free to act in accordance with our conscience and the more rare situations where we must find possible legal adaptations (through *ijtihad* and *fatwa*). These legal instruments must not be used only in the perilous area at the limits but must also find their place in a global vision that integrates and makes the West into an acquired territory, a land for Muslims: it is only this vision that will allow us to avoid the kind of adaptation that resembles a hodge-podge of *fatawa* thought up like so many accommodations largely in response to arguments from necessity (*darura*) in order to justify a number of legal exemptions (*rukhas*) to make life less difficult. It all happens as if

Muslims should ghettoize themselves and become spectators in a society where they were once marginalized. The universality of the message of Islam and the principle of integration that is at its heart invite us to integrate everything that is positive, to move forward selectively, and to act from within, as full members in our society, in order to promote what is good, to work against injustices and discrimination, and to develop alternatives that do not restrict *fiqh* in the West to thinking of itself as on the defensive, moving in a protective fashion, giving the name of "exemptions" (*rukhas*) to what in the long term could take on the color of surrender.[54] The intellectual revolution we are referring to here is extremely demanding, as we shall see in part II: it compels us, from within, as free citizens in societies under the rule of law, to strengthen our faith and to use our intelligence to find solutions and alternatives to the problems of our societies—to move from integration to contribution, from adaptation to reform and transformation.

Faith, Science, and Ethics

The whole of the analysis we have proposed in the preceding sections will help us to deal with a question that is basic for the contemporary Muslim intellect.[55] We often recall the extraordinary contribution Muslims have made historically to scientific development and progress and emphasize the fact that they—more than any other civilization—have advanced the sciences to a higher level. If these facts prove that the current backwardness and difficulties in the area of science in Muslim countries are not intrinsic to Islam, it is nonetheless true that although they may comfort our hearts, they do not provide solutions to contemporary problems. In industrialized and technologically advanced countries, Muslims seem to suffer from a malaise, wedged between their particular ethics and science, which sometimes seems to contradict, or more often to jostle, their faith and convictions. What sort of relationship can be maintained among faith, the scriptural sources, ethics, and the human or hard sciences? Most Muslims ask themselves this question without always providing a clear answer. Are there aspects of the study of the sciences, or at least some of them, that have become "non-Islamic" under the pressure of modernity? How can we speak of the "comprehensive character" and the universality of Islam and at the same time feel ill at ease in the world of knowledge and progress? What is the source of the problem, and how can this apparent contradiction be resolved?

We have seen how necessary and crucial was the work of categorization undertaken by scholars in their reading of the sources. When they were carrying out this work, the sources themselves, as much as the demands of their studies and the vicissitudes of history, at the same time forced them to differentiate between the specific areas of religious study:[56] thus were born the sciences of the Qur'an (*ulum al-Qur'an*), the sciences of Prophetic tradition (*ulum al-hadith*), the science of creed (*ilm al-aqida*), the science of the fundamentals of law and jurisprudence (*ilm usul al-fiqh*), and others.

Between approximately the tenth and eleventh centuries, the corpus of these sciences was formed according to a design represented in figure 2.1. This was a stimulating typology appropriate for the clarification of the limits and objectives of each area. Moreover, it naturally lent itself to encouraging research in all the other sciences for at least three reasons: first, because the Qur'an and the traditions invited the human spirit to study and understand the world; second, because the religious sciences themselves very often referred to scientific discoveries (in medicine or astronomy, for example) to work out an aspect of practice; and third, because the framework of reference was so nourished by religion that the connection between ethics and science was immediate and natural and necessarily less at risk at that time because few situations were recognized as delimited.

When the Renaissance, humanism, and the Reformation—all deeply influenced and enriched by Islamic civilization—worked together in the West, although differently, to start the process of secularization and to set free the power of reason that has become more and more autonomous and scientific, Islamic civilization seemed to freeze. The natural and once coherent interaction between the "Islamic sciences" and other areas of knowledge—and some ulama had mastery of both—now seems defunct. The naturally ethical approach to the sciences that had characterized the Muslim stance till now seemed to suffer as, in the West, the successes of science took shape—a science that was becoming more and more distant from moral norms and also seemed to draw its power from a liberation from religious authority. Gripped by the ethical teaching of Islam, increasingly incapable of renewing the dynamic link between the moral frame of reference and the autonomy of reason, and feeling that they are in danger vis-à-vis the dynamism and expansion of Europe, the ulama were bound to the supreme authority of the religious sciences and preferred to sacrifice "the other knowledge," rather than the norms of religion. For more than six centuries, no Muslim scholar has spoken out against science; rather, they all much prefer to recall the glorious past of Islam regarding the subject and the constant invitation of the religious sources to move science forward. Behind this sustained nostalgia and idealized dream, a deep malaise lies hidden, because we do not know, we no longer know, how to reestablish the connection between religion and science such that religion's ethical teachings give science a dignified finality without perverting its implementation or impeding its advances.

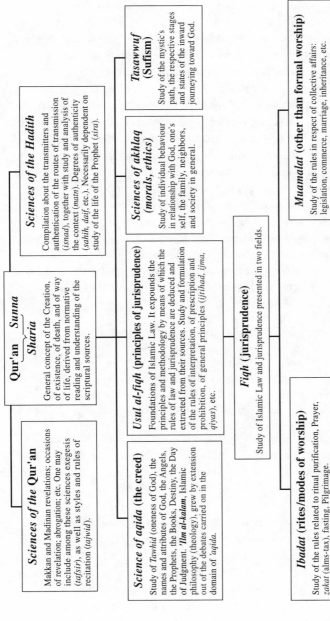

Qur'an ‿ **Sunna**

Sharia

General concept of the Creation, of existence, of death, and of way of life, derived from normative reading and understanding of the scriptural sources.

Sciences of the Qur'an

Makkan and Madinan revelations; occasions of revelation; abrogation; etc. One may include among these sciences exegesis (*tafsir*), as well as styles and rules of recitation (*tajwid*).

Sciences of the Hadith

Compilation about the transmitters and authentication of the routes of transmission (*isnad*), together with study and analysis of the context (*matn*). Degrees of authenticity (*sahih*, *daif*, etc.). Necessarily dependent on study of the life of the Prophet (*sira*).

Science of aqida (the creed)

Study of *Tawhid* (oneness of God), the names and attributes of God, the Angels, the Prophets, the Books, Destiny, the Day of Judgment. '*Ilm al-kalam*, Islamic philosophy (theology), grew by extension out of the debates carried on in the domain of *aqida*.

Usul al-fiqh (principles of jurisprudence)

Foundations of Islamic Law. It expounds the principles and methodology by means of which the rules of law and jurisprudence are deduced and extracted from their sources. Study and formulation of the rules of interpretation, of prescription and prohibition, of general principles (*ijtihad*, *ijma*, *qiyas*), etc.

Sciences of akhlaq (morals, ethics)

Study of individual behaviour in relationship with God, one's self, the family, neighbors, and society in general.

Tasawwuf (Sufism)

Study of the mystic's path, the respective stages and states of the inward journeying toward God.

Fiqh (jurisprudence)

Study of Islamic Law and jurisprudence presented in two fields.

Ibadat (rites/modes of worship)

Study of the rules related to ritual purification, Prayer, *zakat* (alms-tax), fasting, Pilgrimage.

Muamalat (other than formal worship)

Study of the rules in respect of collective affairs: legislation, commerce, marriage, inheritance, etc.

Fiqh al-waqi (events, cases) and **Fiqh al-awlawiyyat (priorities)**

Study of the determination of priorities in the application of the Islamic laws and regulations in the light of period and context.

Fiqh al-dawa (communicating Islam to others)

Study of the methods of explaining and transmitting the Message of Islam according to period and context.

Figure 2.1.   Typology and Classification of the Islamic Sciences

The overall sense is that the categorization of the Islamic sciences that was so useful in the context of the Middle Ages has become a stumbling block because it still retains a dualistic—and essentially very "Greek"—perception of the hierarchy of knowledge. For the Muslim spirit, the problem remains the same: the "all-comprehensive character of the message" comes face to face with a diametrically opposed reality whose terms of reference are apparently irreconcilable with its own. One of the solutions seems to be a wholehearted rush into activity, consisting of showing how the Qur'an contains scientific truths; but this collecting of scientific discoveries in the text, this "harmonization," which too easily turns Revelation into a scientific textbook,[57] ill conceals an inability to engage with the scientific world while treating the Texts with integrity. Another response, interesting in itself, has been suggested by the eminent Muslim intellectual Ismail al-Faruqi, who lived in the United States until his death and who was one of the founders of the International Institute of Islamic Thought (IIIT). He suggested the idea of an "Islamization of knowledge" and proposed discussion of the paradigms that underlay the various so-called profane sciences. This development has now revealed its limitations and has not met the hopes of its proponents. The question facing the Muslim mind remains: how can the connection be reestablished?

Once again it is a return to the scriptural sources that will make it possible for us to sketch the outlines of a solution. What they have taught us may be presented as two major theses:

1. The unity of the Source (God as revealed in the Texts), which is where ethics finds its coherent foundation, never implies a similarity of approaches or a uniformity of methodologies.
2. Varieties of methodologies are constructed rationally, taking as the starting point the object of study,[58] not the relation to the Transcendent or to a system of knowledge that He has preordained.

Work on the scriptural texts, taken as an object of study in itself, demonstrated a diversity of methodologies and gave rise to a multitude of "Islamic sciences," each having its methodology, its field of investigation, and its limitations. Exactly the same logic should guide us in all areas of knowledge.

Faith connects the believer with the Creator in all areas of life, and life should stay committed as much as possible to the centrality of *tawhid*. Intellect, committed to *tawhid* and the scriptural sources, will produce, as we have seen, a system of ethics built upon the meaning and the finality of life, which lie at the heart of the universal message of Islam. That same intellect will also, nevertheless, work out, completely autonomously and on the basis of its object of study, appropriate rules and methods that will set the boundaries for the science in question. In other words, and completely consistently, reason connected with the Source (God and the Texts) formulates ethical teaching on the one hand and on the other sees itself as obliged by its object of study to set completely autonomous scientific rules and methods. There is no need to Islamize the sciences or to combine and confuse ethics and scientific methods: the universality of Islam offers a coherence that implies no confusion. So we must propose a new representation of the scientific universe if we want to avoid the dualistic impasse into which we were carried by the representation referred to earlier and produced by the medieval Muslim mind. We might present the picture as shown in figure 2.2.

In figure 2.2, from the centrality of *tawhid*, the arrows pointing from the center represent ethical teaching drawn from the scriptural sources. Along the concentric circles are the various sciences, each of which has its own methodology established by the autonomous efforts of reason on the basis of the object of study (e.g., the Texts for the religious sciences, the human body for medicine, social dynamics for sociology). The various circles represent the various degrees of proximity (without any kind of

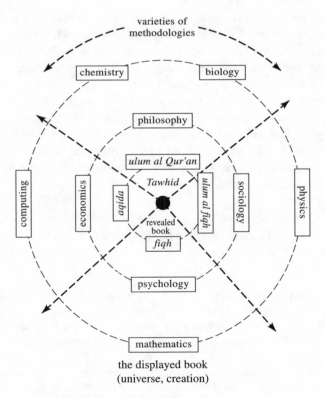

Figure 2.2.   Tawhid, Ethics, and the Sciences

hierarchy) that the different sciences may have with the scriptural sources. Thus, the sciences traditionally called "Islamic" are naturally in the first circle; the humanities, where the scope for interpretation, subjectivity, and ideological orientation is considerable, are in the second circle (a particular view of the world may influence work in these sciences): the hard or pure sciences are in the last circle because their methodologies are virtually autonomous and are connected to the structure imposed by the object of study.[59] The universal and comprehensive message of Islamic ethics penetrates all the sciences without exception, calling for moral consistency, but it does not confuse the latter with the autonomy of scientific methods (in themselves morally neutral).

Thus, human reason finds itself between two books, each of which, as an object of study, determines and imposes specific methodologies. From the revealed Book we must extrapolate and organize a grammar, a typology of rules, or the content of the credo. From the book of nature, we must discover the laws, functions, and logical patterns of organization, which give birth to medicine, chemistry, and physics. Ethics is the light that allows a "faithful" reading of the two books: it requires understanding of the laws, as well as respect for their balance.

This new representation makes it possible for us to change the old paradigms and rediscover ways that make a union possible. With reference to the elements that constitute the human being, we have shown that none of them is positive or negative "in itself" and that a moral quality can be acquired only through exactingness, discipline, self-control, and humility. It is exactly the same in the sciences, and it is the union of controlled scientific method and applied ethics that makes people faithful to the source at the heart of the various fields of knowledge. So, like all the elements that make up the human being, all the scientific methods (imposed by creation itself, the open book) are "Islamic" *by nature;* mastered by mankind in the name of the ultimate values of life, they must, ethically, become so *by conscience.*

In order to achieve this, the consciousness of the believer will have to respond, in the very midst of scientific research and its application, to the three fundamental moral questions of the Islamic universe of reference:

1. What are my intentions (*al-niyya*) in engaging in the study of this science? There must be an active connection with *tawhid.*
2. What ethical boundaries must I respect? The concrete application of the ethical teaching must be rationally connected with the scriptural sources.
3. What are the ultimate objectives of my research? Scientific activity must be integrated into the "way of faithfulness," the "path to the Source."

At the end of this analysis we have come to understand that the principle of *shumuliyya*, the comprehensive character of the Islamic message, constitutes anything but a confusion of categories or, at the other extreme, a split between them such that one might legitimately be anxious about the emergence of a "science without conscience," to use Rabelais's phrase. The same logic we have already encountered, when considering relations with the Texts, the human being, or the principle of integration, is at work here. Drawing on *tawhid*, faith demands of reason that it should unite, marry, pacify in full faithfulness: as a testimony to consciousness of the covenant. It is also an expression of how demanding is this concept of "universality": in practice, it means that Muslims must engage, within their own areas of competence, in groundbreaking specialization in all the areas of contemporary knowledge and that, far from becoming intoxicated by that knowledge and changing it into a new idol of modern times, they must make their contribution to the ethical questions that it raises. The scientific challenges facing the new Muslim presence that seeks to act from within, not from the margins of society and science, are to master the rules and methods of the various humanities and pure sciences, to discuss hypotheses and applications, and to put forward new perspectives. The greatest challenge is to preserve the centrality of what is essential—the connection with the Source, a sense of responsibility, and retention of an awareness of "the need of Him," which gives birth to humility—even, and especially, in scientific activity.

3

IN THE WEST

First Attempts at Reform

The two preceding chapters have sketched at various levels the outline of an Islamic structure of reference. *Tawhid* (the oneness of God), the *Sharia* (the path to faithfulness), and the three notions of *maslaha* (the common good), *ijtihad* (intellectual effort and critique of legal formulations), and *fatwa* (circumstantial legal opinion) represent respectively the Source in the absolute, the way that leads to it in the relative circumstances of time, and the instruments that allow the human intelligence to make the connection between the absolute and the relative, the essential and the accidental, or, in other words, universal principles and the contingent realities of human societies. We should be even more precise in affirming that the "path to faithfulness" *requires* the definition of the "common good" in a given society, the continuous exercise of "critical work on legal formulations," and the exposition of "legal opinions" in step with the new realities of the world. Faithfulness in time is possible only if human reason, using the instruments put at its disposal, is active and creative in putting forward original proposals in tune with the time and place. In this sense, new answers connected with the Source are *faithful* answers, just as there is no faithfulness without renewal.

Western Muslims cannot take short cuts in this work: if they want to live in the "way of faithfulness," if they want to determine the direction of their "path toward the Source," they have to engage in a deep and constant labor of reform inspired by the "comprehensive nature of the message of Islam." In the last analysis, it is a matter of avoiding an integration that depends on a collection of legal opinions aimed at protection and instead suggesting a route that will allow Muslims to establish themselves freely and confidently and that will open the way for them to make a contribution. With regard to the classical Islamic works to which contemporary ulama have been referring for a long time, and taking into account the social, cultural, and political realities Muslims are facing, three questions are fundamental and urgently demand precise answers if we are to build a future for ourselves in the West: *Where are we? Who are we?* and finally, *In what way do we want to belong?*

If the old answers seem to us today to be obsolete, we are nevertheless bound to propose something other than a hodgepodge of ideas that drag Muslims either into "living in the West out of the West" or into "becoming Muslims without Islam." Between the ghetto and dissolution, Western paths toward faithfulness must be constructed on solid, consistent, and coherent foundations, based on a double dialectical approach, encompassing both the contextualized study of the texts and the study of the context in the light of the texts. The foregoing analyses provide us with some keys to this.

The West: The Abode of Testimony

We know the two old widespread concepts of *dar al-islam* and *dar al-harb.* If we do some research into them, we find that they do not occur either in the Qur'an or in the Sunna.[1] In fact, they do not belong to the fundamental sources of Islam, in which principles are essentially given for the universe (*lil-alamin*), for all times and across all frontiers.

It was the ulama who, during the early centuries, when considering the state of the world—its geographical divisions, the powers that were in place across religious affiliations, and their influence and the forces at work in changing allegiances—began to classify and define the various areas in and around the places in which they lived. This process was important and necessary for at least two reasons. On the one hand, by identifying which were the Islamic territories, the ulama were able to indicate both what the essential conditions were for an area or a nation to be considered Islamic and also what regulations should govern political and strategic relations established with other nations and empires. On the other, it allowed them to make a clear distinction in legal matters between the situation of Muslims living within the Muslim world and that of Muslims living abroad, or of those who traveled a lot, such as merchants (who, consequently, needed specific regulations).

After studying the attitude of the Prophet after the peace of Hudaybiyya (*sulh al-Hudaybiyya*), his sending of numerous messengers to various rulers during the five years that followed,[2] and his behavior toward neighboring countries, the classical scholars arrived at the conclusion that four elements had to be identified and taken into account: (1) the population living in the country; (2) the ownership of the land; (3) the nature of the government; (4) the laws applied in the country. The Prophet—considering himself in the light of Revelation as a Messenger to the whole world—according to Ibn Hisham, sent at least nine delegations in five years to the peoples of the neighboring countries who knew nothing about Islam, or whose leaders had no real knowledge of the new religion and who founded their judgments on vague conjectures. In two famous cases, the attitude of the rulers toward the Prophet's messengers led to wars (which was certainly not the purpose of these delegations nor the rule that was meant to be applied to relations with neighboring countries). A war took place first against the Byzantines because the Prophet's messenger, Harith ibn Umayr, was killed by Amr al-Ghassani, one of the ministers of the Empire. A second conflict took place with the Persians when their leader tore up the Qur'an in front of the messenger and told his soldiers to go and bring him back "this Muhammad alive." These two reactions were understood by the Muslims as declarations of war, but in most other cases the message was spread without war or hindrance. The priority was clearly to spread the message of Islam among the population. The local rulers at that time were the immediate means of achieving this objective, for Islam was primarily a message for the people (*lil-nas*), according to the Qur'anic formula, rather than a guidance addressed to the authorities.

Basing their thinking on these facts, the ulama strove to deduce clear principles and to distinguish and categorize the characteristics of so-called Islamic areas and countries and those of non-Islamic territory. In the first centuries of Islam, taking into consideration the reality with which they were confronted, the ulama could formulate a general conception of the world only in terms of this binary vision. Thus, before there was any contextualized definition, the first fundamental rule dealing with relations between Muslims and non-Muslims on the basis of the actions of the Prophet was that there was considered to be a "state of peace" and not "a state of war." The second was that the Prophet wanted above all to address the people and not to seize power. The tradition shows that he always decided to fight the rulers because of their murders, treachery, and injustices and that he never fought against populations because they refused to convert to Islam. He wanted them to choose Islam in full knowledge of what it was; when they knew, he accepted their choice and recognized their right to stay where they were living and practice their religion. Non-Muslim populations paid a tax (*al-jizya*) in exchange for the protection of the State.

Having drawn out these essential points, the ulama still had to define the two entities, *dar al-islam* and *dar al-harb*, so as to have a clear vision of the geopolitical reality of their time. Numerous definitions were proposed, specifically within the four principal Sunni schools of law. We cannot here give a detailed study of their respective studies, but it is useful to make the following points.

Dar Al-Islam *(The Abode of Islam)*

Taking into account two of the four elements mentioned in the preceding section, al-Dusuqi, of the Maliki school, declared that the abode of Islam[3] must be the property of Muslims where the Islamic legal system is applied (even if non-Muslims are in power).[4] This is the current legal opinion, also held by Ibn Taymiyya, while the ulama of the Hanifi school focused on the very specific issue of whether practicing Muslims were in a position of safety. So, in their opinion, as expressed by the Hanafi al-Sarakhsi, one could know that one was in the "abode of Islam" by the fact that Muslims there were secure and had nothing to fear by practicing their religion. For this school of law, it was the question of security and protection, and not the strict question of Islam and *kufr* (here in the sense of nonacceptance of Islam), that had to be taken into consideration in making the judgment.

Dar Al-Harb *(The Abode of War)*

Numerous definitions for the concept of *dar al-harb*[5] have been proposed, and there are important differences between the ulama with regard to the best of them. Nevertheless, the ulama are unanimous in holding that a country is called *dar al-harb* when the legal system as well as the government are non-Islamic. The consensus is that this description is dependent not on the population, which may be majority-Muslim, but rather on the law and the political system. For the Hanafi school, in contrast to *dar al-islam*, *dar al-harb* is a territory where Muslims are neither protected nor able to live in peace. But, as the various definitions show, the existence of an "abode of war" does not necessarily mean that a state of war exists between the opposing "abodes."

An intensive study of these definitions (though they cannot be presented here very exhaustively or in great detail) shows that the criteria on which the specific and reliable recognition of an "abode" depends are not strictly antithetical. Most of the ulama insist on ownership of the land and the application of the Islamic legal system in order to declare the existence of a *dar al-islam*, while it is the nature of the legal system and that of the government that are the relevant factors for a *dar al-harb*. In the first case, the stress is on the population and in the second on the government. This asymmetry is actually the cause of a deep divergence between contemporary ulama, for they all admit that the Islamic system (which is the second condition that must apply to allow an area to be defined as Islamic) is not truly or fully implemented anywhere today.

Thus, some ulama take the population into account and are of the opinion that Muslim countries should continue to be considered as *dar al-islam*, while others, focusing on governments that according to all the evidence do not apply the teachings of Islam, maintain that these countries cannot be called *dar al-islam*. If, however, we take into account the criteria based on notions of safety and security that are considered by some ulama of the Hanafi school, the conclusion might be very different, even diametrically opposed: Muslims may feel safer in the West, as far as the free exercise of their religion is concerned, than in some so-called Muslim countries. This analysis could lead us to conclude, on the basis of the criteria of safety and security, that the description *dar al-islam* is applicable to almost all Western countries, while it can hardly be given to the great majority of actual Muslim countries, whose population is 60, 70, 80, or even 95 percent Muslim. This reversal in the respective descriptions of the West and Muslim countries is "certainly impossible," states Shaykh al-Mawlawi:[6] apart from the measure of security, all the evidence points to the fact that we really are not in a "Muslim country."

This debate, apart from the problems of definition that it raises, is based on old concepts that seem to be neither operational nor relevant in our time. To apply them to our contemporary reality, just as they were thought out by the great ulama more than ten centuries ago, would be a serious methodological error. In today's world, where populations are in constant movement and in which we are witnessing an increasing complexity in the distribution of economic, financial, and political power, as well as a diversification of strategic alliances and spheres of influence, it is impossible to hold to an old, simple, binary vision of reality. That being so, this set of readings is totally inappropriate: it could lead to a simplistic and clearly erroneous perception of our times.

Even the addition of the third concept, introduced by al-Shafii, which refers to the "abode of treaty" (*dar al-ahd*), is not enough to extract us from this binary view of the world. This description assumes that there are countries that, although not Muslim from a political point of view, have nevertheless signed a treaty of peace and collaboration with one or several Muslim nations. The treaty may be temporary or permanent, and this concept of *dar al-ahd* presents an interesting opening if it can be adapted to the current political situation on an international scale. The existence of organizations such as the United Nations or the Organization of African Unity and the numerous treaties signed by states represent a clear implementation of this notion of *dar al-ahd*. This is the opinion of Shaykh Manna al-Qattan, according to whom "this is the appropriate description to be applied to the majority of countries as far as relations with

Muslims are concerned."[7] Perhaps this concept can shed new light on our way of looking at the world that surrounds us. However, a careful analysis shows that this category cannot give an adequate vision of our present situation. The concept of *dar al-ahd* has specific meaning only in the light of the other two notions discussed earlier. To define the nature of a treaty, we would have first to know the nature of the countries that agreed to its clauses—that is, to have a clear idea of what is and what is not *dar al-islam*. We have already come up against the difficulty of defining this concept, and it seems that, if used to explain our contemporary world, the concept of *dar al-ahd* is more a description of a "war-free situation" than an adequate definition of an "area where Muslims live." This makes it an interesting and useful idea, but it is not completely appropriate, for three reasons:

1. It no longer seems possible to use this concept founded as it was on a vision of two independent entities (*dar al-islam* and *dar al-harb*) reaching an agreement. For in today's complex geopolitical climate, where economic and political influence and asymmetrical struggle for power prevail, such expressions of agreement can hardly be described as independent.

2. To use the same word (*ahd*) to refer both to treaties between countries and relations between Muslims and a State (and its constitution) would lead to a deep blurring of its meaning, because the content to which it refers is not in the least of the same nature in both cases. It appears that the use of these three old concepts has drawn some ulama to neglect some important geopolitical facts that should, on the contrary, be taken into consideration, since they influence profoundly the new vision of the world that we must develop.

3. At a deeper level, to consider that we are, as citizens, in a kind of contract with a "non-Islamic" society perpetuates the idea that we are not in *our own* society but that we are coming to terms with an entity with which we do not identify. The notion of *ahd* used in this way is quite different from the idea of a "social contract" between a citizen and an entity of which he is part and in which he feels himself to have full membership. To speak of *dar al-ahd* does nothing to make this an effective reality in the minds of Muslims.

Thus, a study of the debates taking place between the ulama shows that there is quite a gap between the classical concepts and the current state of affairs (*al-waqi*). A few ulama give the latter priority and try to adapt and modify the content of these concepts, while others, held by the *fiqh* tradition, end up simplifying the reality and perpetuating a binary view of the world that is no longer at all appropriate.[8] These developments reveal the gaps in the approach of many ulama: it is clear that, as well as having an inadequate conceptual framework at their disposal, they lack a deep understanding of the new political and economic landscape that confronts them.

The four elements referred to—the nature of the population living in the country, the ownership of the land, the nature of the government, and the laws in force in the country—are no longer relevant if we wish to set out a correct perception of the real situation of Muslims in the world. Three points must be made on this subject: for something between 150 and 175 years, colonialism and then political actions defined as various kinds of "protection" have caused major changes in Muslim countries. Alliances between a significant number of Muslim rulers and Western governments and the progressive introduction of a foreign and Westernized legal system have led to major modifications in the markers of Muslim societies themselves. They do not constitute—and never will—a unique and closed world, "unsullied" by any "foreign" influence.

Political and economic factors have pushed millions of people to leave their own countries to look for work and security in the West. This process has led them to settle abroad, and they now form part of societies whose main characteristics seem to be diversity and religious and cultural pluralism. These Muslims represent minorities in the West, though the children of the second and following generations are at home there, as are all those who have converted to Islam. The West is therefore permeated by a new religiously based citizenship dynamic based on the fact that there are individuals who consider themselves both Muslims and completely European or American.

So we are living in an age of diversity, blending, and extremely deep complexity that cannot be understood or evaluated through a binary prism, which is as much simplistic as reductionist. It is apparent that today it is neither sufficient nor relevant to concentrate on questions of the nature of government, the laws that are in force, or ownership of the land, given that the state of the world makes these questions as difficult to deal with comprehensively in Muslim countries as in the West.

The process of internationalization and globalization brings us back to an analysis that should take into account the realities in which people live. Such a study would show that a radical change in our state of mind is needed. It is difficult today to be a consistent and balanced Muslim in every aspect of life because the world that surrounds us and the criteria on which evaluations are based, whether in Islamic areas or in the West, are not themselves very consistent. This is the least one can say. This means that we must go back to the sources of Islamic teaching in order to find out whether we can discover a framework, a guide, or a direction that will enable us to fully take on the challenge represented by our contemporary situation.

Two things must be constantly kept in mind. First, for a Muslim, the teaching of Islam—when it is well understood and well applied—is valid in every time and place, and this is the meaning of the idea of the *ala-miyyat al-islam* (the universal dimension of the teaching of Islam). Second, the concepts of *dar al-islam*, *dar al-harb*, and *dar al-ahd* were not first described in the Qur'an or in the Sunna. In fact, they constituted a human attempt, at a moment in history, to describe the world and to provide the Muslim community with a geopolitical scheme that seemed appropriate to the reality of the time. This reality has completely changed: it is becoming necessary today to go back to the Qur'an and the Sunna and, in the light of our environment, to deepen our analysis in order to develop a new vision appropriate to our new context in order to formulate suitable legal opinions. To reread, reconsider, and "revisit" our understanding of the teachings of Islam therefore appears to be a necessity.

At a time when all the old criteria have been overthrown because of the great changes that have come about in society, and when it is becoming difficult to find guidance or solutions in the old works of the ulama, it seems imperative to go back to the sources and to set out clearly, from an Islamic point of view, the priorities in the life of a believer, both as an individual and as a community. It is a question of defining *who we are* and *what our religion expects of us as Muslims*. At first sight, these two questions may appear simple, but they are crucial: by setting a general framework for the Islamic identity, beyond the contingencies of a particular setting such as Europe or North America, they permit us to decide what is already acceptable and what is needed by way of reforms and improvements in order to create both a balanced existence and a positive coexistence.

The Islamic sciences are only the means by which Muslims can protect their faith and live and practice their religion as it is required of them. They are instruments that the ulama use to provide the Muslim community with a general understanding and a legal framework that allows them to be and remain Muslims, whatever their circumstances. In the same way, we could say that the environment, whatever it may be, is a space within which Muslims should find the resources necessary for them to be in harmony with their faith: understood in this way, the environment must be thought of as a means through which an identity may come into being and flourish.

The philosopher Bergson stated that there are two ways of knowing an object: from the outside, by adding up the points of view, and from the inside, through a sort of "intuitive experience" of the object. Without pursuing this "experience" to its extreme, we may take inspiration from this distinction at the point when we want to define the "space" in which we live, in interaction with the identity by which we define ourselves, and to do this in the light of our sources. Before studying the foundations of Muslim identity,[9] it seems necessary to set out the fundamental principles that are the prerequisites of *living space* and that allow that identity to flourish. We shall also avoid the methodological error of reading reality through pre-established concepts formulated in another age for another context. Our reflection will thus put forward a classification of the preliminary basics for developing a "positive space" that may serve as a measure by which we can evaluate the Western sociopolitical environment. This new method is, as we shall see, in some sense close to the approach of some Hanafi ulama who, as we have seen, preferred to define areas (as *dar al-islam* or *dar al-harb*) on the basis of the security (*al-amn*) of the believers before they turned their attention to the form of the legal system or government. In doing this, they not only considerably modified the criteria and conditions according to which the various "abodes" had been defined but also acted as the precursors of the global vision we need today as a result of the massive upheavals we have witnessed in the past century.

An environment that guarantees freedom of conscience and worship to Muslims (that is, of their faith and their practice), that protects their physical integrity and their freedom to act in accordance with their convictions, is not in fact a hostile space. In North America, as in Europe, five fundamental rights are guaranteed that allow them to feel at home in their countries of residence:[10] the right to practice Islam, the right to knowledge, the right to establish organizations, the right to autonomous representation, and the right to appeal to law.[11]

An evaluation of the "Western abode" could be made on the basis of the comparative analysis of the two sets of considerations referred to earlier: on the one hand, the conditions essential for the expansion of the Muslim personality, and on the other, the five general and fundamental rights already acquired in the West. It is immediately clear that many of the legal conditions we have set down are already met and that Muslims enjoy, to a large extent, the right to live as Muslims in Europe and North America, though we must not forget that there exist important questions on which we must reflect, insofar as they appear to be obstacles to the positive and full existence of Muslims in the West. For example, we must not minimize the difficulty we have in protecting a *living faith* in industrialized countries subject to the logic of production and consumption. Spirituality is of great significance in Islam, and the neutrality of the public space in secularized societies has often been taken to mean a total absence of religiosity (even a categorical rejection of it), or the primacy of an atheistic ideology that does not call itself by its name. This is not an area where Muslims are in conflict with the legislation, laws or regulations: it is a fundamental problem rooted elsewhere. It is connected with an issue that is vital for Muslim communities in the West: the issue of how to preserve the vitality of a spiritual life in a society that has become so modern—modern in the popular sense of the word, which is to say secularized and industrialized—and then how to pass on the necessary knowledge, which alone is able to provide authentic freedom, the necessary condition for making any choice? This point uncovers another series of fundamental "problem areas" concerning issues of education in general and Islamic education in particular in a secular environment, issues of social and political participation and of culture, questions to which we shall return in part II. Nevertheless, we must add here a problem that grows daily more acute—the image of Islam that is conveyed by events taking place on the international stage. The fallout from political situations in Muslim countries and the active interests, and sometimes manipulations, of governments cast a very negative light on Muslims living in the West and give rise to a whole range of prejudices and preconceived ideas about Islam and Muslims. The consequence is that laws, whose letter protects the rights of Muslims, are read, interpreted, and used tendentiously because of this atmosphere of suspicion and so become the "official" and legitimate justification for obvious acts of discrimination. It would be stupid today to avoid this reality simply because it is not immediately quantifiable or "legally identifiable": the fact is that it constitutes the daily experience of thousands of Muslims in the West who are confronted by the imagined vision of their interlocutors more often than they find themselves clashing with constitutions or laws. This representation of Islam and Muslims is at the bottom of the difficulties lived by Muslim communities at the present time. Perhaps it is even the main factor. This phenomenon is sometimes hidden behind the veil of a supposed "total legal incompatibility" that does not stand up to serious analysis. The security-based treatment of the question of Islam perceived as a threat raises the same kind of problems. Well before 11 September 2001 and the outrages in the United States, Muslims were already experiencing every day the reality of suspicion and discrimination. Since 11 September, things have worsened, and now the problem of "living together" in the pluralist societies of the West is dealt with more on the level of "representation" than on the level of seeking equal treatment for the practice of religion and its laws. Responsibility in this is mutual, and we shall return to this in our next chapter.

Apart from all these pitfalls (though they should not be minimized), the West still appears to be a place where Muslims can live securely with certain fundamental rights granted and protected. What name should we then give to this space? What appellation can we find that suits both the Islamic references and our current situation? There is no consensus (*ijma*) on the question of identification, definition, or appellation of the "Western abode" generally. We can broadly distinguish here three different—though not completely contradictory—positions that are the expression of three specific legal opinions on this question.[12] Some ulama consider that the old concepts of *dar al-islam* and *dar al-harb* are still valid, even if all the relevant conditions are not completely met. Other ulama are of the opinion that the considerable changes that have taken place must be taken into account and that the conditions (*shurut*) referred to earlier that would allow an area to be defined as *dar al-islam* or *dar al-harb* today do not occur in the same way in one place as in another. In their view, these elements should be underlined when the situation of Muslims in the West is discussed. In order to define Western countries, they use the Shafii concept of *dar al-ahd* ("abode of treaty") or *dar al-amn* ("abode of safety"). The third group believe these concepts are no longer valid: to continue to use them forces us to avoid questions about both the concepts and the reality we are facing. They think that the ulama should think of new appellations that are faithful to the Islamic sources and also appropriate for our current situation. Faysal al-Mawlawi, for example, states: "We are not, in the West, in the 'abode of war'; we are either in an 'abode of treaty' or in an 'abode of invitation to God' [*dawa*]. If we wish to maintain the [traditional] classification of the world as set out in *fiqh* with the 'abode of Islam,' the 'abode of war' and the 'abode of treaty,' we are in that case, in the West, in an 'abode of treaty.' If, on the other hand, we consider that the old *fiqh* classification is no longer applicable in our current situation—and this is the view we prefer—then on that basis, we say that we are in an 'abode of *dawa*,' as were the Prophet and the Muslims in Mecca before the Hijra. Mecca was neither *dar al-islam* nor *dar al-harb*, but *dar al-dawa*[13] and in the eyes of the Muslims, the whole of the Arabian Peninsula, was *dar al-dawa*."[14]

It is important to note here a double phenomenon: first, the traditional appellations are discussed—and almost set aside—and a new name is suggested in the light of the source (the Meccan period) that corresponds more with our own reality in numerous points. This last approach (formulating a new appellation) is, in our opinion, following our analysis, the most correct and relevant. If the "abode" where Muslims live provides them with security—as we must honestly recognize is the case in the West—this must be taken into account. And, beyond all sectarian and inadequate classifications, Muslims should also remember, in this age of globalization and the "new world order," that they must face up to their responsibilities in order on the one hand to bear authentic witness to their faith in the oneness of God and their respect for the values of justice and solidarity and on the other hand to take appropriate action, whether individually or as a society. Indeed, wherever a Muslim who declares, "I bear witness that there is no god but God and Muhammad is His messenger" lives in security and can fulfill his fundamental religious obligations, he is at home, for the Prophet taught us that the whole world is a mosque. This means that Muslims living in the West, individuals as well as communities from various countries, not only *may* live there but are also the bearers of an enormous responsibility: they must give their society a testimony based on faith, spirituality, values, a sense of where boundaries lie, and a permanent human and social engagement.

This vision reverses the perception based on the old concepts, which inevitably encouraged Muslims to adopt a reactionary stance as a minority and consequently led them to decide on, and work only to protect, their minimal rights. Even if this attitude was understandable during the first decades of the Muslim presence in the West and among the first generations of migrants, it should now have been superseded. It is high time to define the responsibilities of Muslims in the West, and first, with the insight provided by these considerations, we should be able to call the place where we live the "Western abode."

Al-Mawlawi proposed the concept of *dar al-dawa* with reference to the Meccan period during which the Muslims, although a minority in a society that rejected the new Revelation (which he called *dar al-kufr*), considered themselves responsible for bearing witness to their faith before their people and their tribe. In the same way, we could say that, in the present new world order, which seems to have forgotten the Creator and to depend on a logic that is almost exclusively economic, Muslims face the same responsibilities, particularly in industrialized societies. Positive and sure of themselves, they must remind the people around them of God and spirituality, and when it comes to social issues, they must be actively involved in supporting values and morality, justice and solidarity. They should not submit to their environment, but, on the contrary, once their position is secure, they should be a positive influence within it.

From within the West, it seems essential to clarify this perspective, for the concept of *dawa*, although vital, has many shades of meaning and so is difficult to translate.[15] Beginning with the same approach of rereading the sources in a manner faithful to their intention, but also in light of the universal message and teachings of Islam (*alamiyyat al-islam*), we might fairly, I believe, consider the notion of *shahada* (testimony), insofar as it takes two important forms. The first goes back to the *shahada* that every Muslim, in order to be recognized as such, must pronounce before God and the whole of humankind, and by which he establishes his identity: "there is no god but God and Muhammad is His messenger." The second is connected with the responsibility of Muslims, according to the Qur'anic injunction, to "bear witness [to their faith] before humankind."[16] In the idea of *shahada*, testimony, we bring together essential elements of the Muslim faith: a clear remembrance of the fundamental core of our identity via faith in the oneness of God (*tawhid*) and His last revelation to the Prophet Muhammad and an elevated consciousness that gives us the responsibility to remind others of the presence of God and to act in such a way that our presence among them and with them is, in itself, a reminder of the Creator, spirituality, and ethics.

This double function of *shahada* should be more explicitly expressed in the six points enumerated here, of which the first three refer to the very identity of Muslims and the last three to their role in society:

1. In pronouncing the *shahada*, Muslims testify to their faith and state a clear foundation for their identity: they are Muslim, believe in God, in His messengers, in the angels, in the revealed Books, in fate, and in the day of judgment. They believe that the teachings of Islam come from a Revelation and that they are members of the Islamic community (*umma*).

2. Not only is the *shahada* closely linked with religious rites and practice, being the first of the five pillars of Islam, but there could actually be no true rites or practice without it. An equal part of the Muslim identity is the fact of being able (and having the right) to pray, to pay the *zakat*, to fast, and to perform the pilgrimage. This is clearly referred to in the Qur'an in connection with "pious people who believe in what is beyond human perception and perform the prayer."[17]

3. More broadly, this means that Muslims should, or at least should be allowed, to respect the commandments and regulations of their religion and to act in observance of what is legitimate and illegitimate in Islam. They should not be compelled to act against their consciences, for this would be a "denial of identity."

4. To pronounce the *shahada* is to act before God in respect of His creation, for *al-iman* (faith) is in fact a pledge (*amana*). Relations between human beings are based on respect, trust, and, above all, absolute faithfulness to agreements, contracts, and treaties that have been explicitly or silently entered into. The Qur'an is clear: "And be true to every promise—for, verily, [on Judgment Day] you will be called to account for every promise which you have made,"[18] and believers are those "who are faithful to their trusts and to their pledges."[19]

5. As believers among other human beings, Muslims must bear witness to the meaning of the *shahada* before them. They must present Islam, explain the content of their faith and the teaching of Islam in general. In each type of society, and of course in a non-Muslim environment, they are witnesses, *shuhada*, and this encompasses the idea of *dawa*.

6. This *shahada* is not only verbal. Muslims are individuals who believe and, as a result, act, constantly. "Those who believe and do good," says the Qur'an over and over again, insisting on the fact that the *shahada* has inevitable consequences for the behavior of Muslims, no matter what the society in which they find themselves. To bear the *shahada* means to be engaged in society in every area where a need

makes itself felt: unemployment, marginalization, delinquency, and so on. It also means being engaged in the process that might lead to positive reform, whether of institutions or of legal, economic, social, or political systems, with the aim of introducing more justice and real popular participation. "God commands justice,"[20] says the Qur'an, insofar as it is the concrete manifestation of the "testimony."

Thus, in our opinion, this concept of *shahada* seems to be the most appropriate way of expressing a conception that unites the identity and function of Muslims in light of the teaching of Islam. It also suits our present situation, since *it allows the identity and social responsibility of Muslims to be both expressed and linked.*

It is also appropriate to study its relevance in relation to the present state of the world and to the geopolitical configuration of the planet. It seems difficult, when we are experiencing a worldwide process of globalization,[21] to continue to refer to the notion of *dar*, translating it in the sense of "house," dwelling, rather than considering the whole world as our dwelling. Our world is now, whether we like it or not, *an open world.* Indeed, this is the intuition upon which is based the original appellation proposed by Faysal al-Mawlawi when he concludes: "In our opinion, the whole world is a *dar al-dawa.*"[22]

Consequently, it seems appropriate not to translate the notion of *dar* in its limited sense of dwelling but to choose to give it the sense of *space*, which, while referring to the environment, expresses more clearly the idea of being open to the world, for Muslim populations are now dispersed across the continents. These migrations have been significant, and, despite very restrictive regulations, it appears that population movements are destined to continue: these days, millions of Muslims are settled in the West. Their fate is connected with that of the societies in which they live, and it is unthinkable to draw a line of demarcation between them and non-Muslims only on the basis of considerations of space. In our world, we hardly have to deal with the issue of relations between two distinct "houses." It is rather a case of relations between human beings belonging to and identifying themselves with various civilizations, religions, cultures, and moralities. It is also a question of relations between citizens in constant interaction with the social, legal, economic, and political framework that forms and directs the space in which they live. This process of compounding complexity, which is a specific characteristic of globalization, mingles the factors that previously permitted us to define the various "houses."

And we must go even further: the old binary geographical representation, with two juxtaposed universes that could stand face to face in relative stability, no longer bears any resemblance to the reality of hegemony and spheres of influence in civilization, culture, economics, and subsequently, of course, politics. Westernization, the legitimate daughter of multidimensional globalization, is much better expressed by the use of the notions of *center* (the West and its outposts in the South) and *periphery* (the rest of the planet) than by a schema of two "houses" living the reality of a "confrontation" (see figures 3.1 and 3.2). The Muslims settled in the West are at the *center*, at the *heart*, in the *head* of the system that produces the symbolic apparatus of Westernization. In this very specific space, in the *center*, and in a more demanding way than at the *periphery*, Muslims must bear *witness*, must be *witnesses*, to what they are and to the values they hold. The whole world is indeed a *land of witness*, but there is a space, the fortress charged with an incomparable symbolic responsibility, which is the heart of the whole system and in which millions of Muslims now live. At the center, more than anywhere else, the principle of the *shahada*, which both is pivotal and extends outward, acquires its full meaning. We may schematize the evolution of this representation of the world as shown in figure 3.1. The representation in figure 3.2 brings us out of the logic of confrontation.

For Muslims at the heart of the West, there can be no question of falling back into the old binary vision (figure 3.1) and looking for enemies; it is rather a matter of finding committed partners like themselves who will make a selection from what Western culture produces in order to promote its positive contributions and resist its destructive by-products at both the human and the ecological level. More generally, it is also a matter of working for the promotion of a true religious and cultural pluralism on an international scale. Many European and American intellectuals are fighting to ensure that the right of civilizations and cultures to exist is in fact respected. Before God, and with all men, in the West Muslims must be, with them, *witnesses* engaged in this resistance, for justice, for all human beings of whatever race, origin, or religion.

The notion of *shahada* protects and safeguards the essential features of Muslim identity, in itself and in society: it recalls the permanent relation to God (*al-rabbaniyya*) and expresses the *duty of the Muslim to live among people and to bear witness*, in both action and word, to the content of the message of Islam before all humankind. And this is to happen in any society, for it is the basis of our relations with others. Western countries,

Figure 3.1.   Old Binary Representation, Face to Face

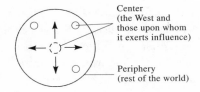

Figure 3.2. New Representation of the
World: Center and Periphery

Center
(the West and
those upon whom
it exerts influence)

Periphery
(rest of the world)

called *dar al-shahada* or *alam al-shahada* (area, or world, of testimony), represent an environment in which Muslims are brought back to the fundamental teaching of Islam and invited to meditate on their role: considering
themselves as *shuhada ala al-nas* (witnesses before humankind), according
to the Qur'anic expression, should lead them to avoid all reactionary and
oversensitive attitudes and to develop a self-confidence based on a deep
sense of responsibility, which in Western societies should be accompanied
by real and constant action for justice. This approach "from the inside"
makes it possible to define the European environment as an *area of responsibility* for Muslims. This is the precise meaning of the *area of testimony*
that we are proposing here and that completely upends the existing perspective. If, for years, Muslims have asked themselves the question of
whether and how they were going to be accepted, a serious study and
evaluation of the Western legal environment entrusts them, in the light
of their Islamic terms of reference, with a mission of supreme importance.
If they are truly with God, their life must bear witness to a permanent
engagement and infinite self-giving in the cause of social justice, the well-
being of humankind, ecology, and solidarity in all its manifestations. Once
legitimately oversensitive and even hidden in the realms of the "abode of
war" and the "abode of unbelief," Muslims can now enter into the *world
of testimony*, in the sense of undertaking an essential duty and a demanding responsibility—to contribute wherever they can to promoting goodness
and justice in and through the human fraternity. Muslim thinking must,
as we have said before, move on from "protection" alone to making an
authentic "contribution," and this model, based on the scriptural sources,
should help. Muslims are, along with so many other human beings, rich
in this ethic of giving. And this giving, all together, will consecrate the
richness of their societies.

Identity and Culture

Who are we? We touch here on the central question of identity that has
occupied people's minds and continues today to be the nub of much reflection and debate. The question is a vital one for Muslims living in the

West. If the message in which they believe is universal, if they must try, wherever they live, to remain faithful, and if the West is a "place of witness" that allows them to be themselves and feel at home, it is imperative that they define what they are and what they want to be in order better to treat the malaise that can result from not knowing very well how the outlines of that identity are drawn. This malaise is, to tell the truth, an almost permanent feature of the Muslim psyche in the West: the old immigrants were not very clear about whether they wanted to be "Muslims" in the West or rather "Pakistani, Turkish and Arab Muslims" in the West, and, as for native European and American converts, they were divided between exiling themselves from their own culture by Arabizing or Pakistanizing themselves and simply staying what they were at a distance from Muslim communities that had come from elsewhere and were culturally distinct.

The encompassing character of the message of Islam, its universality, and the instruments we have been given to help us live in time should help us to cure these troubling disorders and finally to overcome them. Once again, a return to the scriptural sources allows us to establish a distinction between the religious principles that define the identity of Muslims and the cultural trappings that these principles necessarily take on according to the societies in which individuals live. This is a fundamental distinction: just as the universality of the principles allows Muslims to cloak this universality with the specificity of their national cultures through the process of integration we have spoken of, so it must not happen that any one culture becomes so identified with Muslim principles that it interferes with adaptation to another context, or more pernicious, that it accords itself a false right to represent the only way of being authentically Muslim (as is sometimes the case with Arab culture).

So we must distinguish between on the one hand the elements of Muslim identity that are based on religious principles and that give it a necessarily open quality that allows the believer to live in any environment, and on the other hand cultures that are a specific way of living out these principles, adapted for a variety of societies, none having more legitimacy than any other provided that it respects the religious injunctions. If we embark on the first stage of this stripping down, it is possible to define the import and the meaning of "Muslim identity" by exposing four foundational pillars with specific dimensions. Let us remember that our task is to extrapolate the essence of the identity from the accident of its actualization in a particular time and place. In other words, our purpose and aim consist in discerning and abstracting Islam from the incidentals of Arab and/or Asian culture, tradition, and dress in order to arrive at a conception of the universal principles to which Muslims in the West must hold if they are to remain faithful and then to dress them in that culture. At the end of this process, the means of becoming a European or American Muslim will emerge.

One Faith, One Practice, and One Spirituality

The first and most important element of Muslim identity is *faith*, which is the intimate sign that one believes in the Creator without associating anything with Him. This is the meaning of the central concept of *tawhid*, faith in the oneness of God, to which the *shahada* affirms and testifies. In this sense, the *shahada* is the purest expression of the essence of Muslim identity beyond time and space. It is naturally embodied in religious *practice* (prayer, *zakat*, fasting). Closely connected with these two realities, and the immediate consequence of them in the life of the believer, is the fundamental dimension of *spirituality*. Spirituality, from an Islamic point of view, is the way in which the believer keeps his faith alive and intensifies and reinforces it. Spirituality is remembrance—recollection and the intimate energy involved in the struggle against the natural human tendency to forget God, the meaning of life, and the other world. All the practices prescribed by Islam, especially prayer, are in fact a means of recollection (*dhikr*): "Truly I am God; there is no god but I. So worship Me and perform the prayer in order to remember Me."[23]

Excellence, defined as the ideal behavior of the Muslim, would be to attain a state where there was no forgetfulness. Excellence (*al-ihsan*), the Prophet said, is "to worship God as if you could see Him, for even if you cannot see Him, He sees you,"[24] that is, to try to be with God in every situation.

In the many debates involving sociologists and political scientists, this dimension is often forgotten, as if faith and spirituality cannot be considered as scientific data with an objective "identity." But the word *islam* itself means "submission" to God, expressing, strictly speaking, an act of worship, with its spiritual horizon. Consequently, recognition of the Muslim identity entails recognition of this first and fundamental dimension of faith, and, by extension, allowing Muslims to carry out all the religious practices that give shape to their spiritual life. Faith and spirituality underpin these practices, which express the presence of an essential conviction that gives meaning to life: to cut Muslims off from them is to cut them off from their very being. Muslim identity, at its central pivot, is therefore a faith, a practice, and a spirituality. It is essentially the dimension of intimacy and the heart.

An Understanding of the Texts
and the Context

There is no true faith without understanding; for Muslims, this means understanding both the sources (the Qur'an and the Sunna) and the context in which they live. This has already been much emphasized in the first two chapters. Muslims' responsibility rests on this twofold understanding: they must develop both an understanding of the texts and an understanding of the context in order to discover how to stay faithful to the injunctions of Islam. This is the fundamental teaching of Islamic legal practice, which has continued since the time of the Prophet and has never ceased to occupy the ulama through the centuries. It follows that Muslim identity is not closed and confined within rigid, inflexible principles. On the contrary, it is based on a constant dialectical and dynamic movement between the sources and the environment, whose aim is to find a way of living harmoniously. This is why the development of intellectual abilities is so important in Islam and actually elevates the very foundations of Islamic teachings. A Muslim must not be satisfied with a hypothetical natural state of affairs: to be Muslim entails struggling to increase one's abilities, seeking tirelessly to know more, to the extent that one might say in the light of the Islamic sources that, when it comes to the cultural dimension, "to be Muslim is to learn." The Prophet said, "Seeking knowledge is an obligation for every Muslim man and woman."[25]

More generally speaking, this knowledge is a precondition for understanding not only the Islamic sources themselves, but also the Creator, the Creation, and created beings. According to the Qur'an, which never stops sending human beings back to use their intelligence, knowledge and understanding are the means of deepening one's awareness of God. This is one aspect of understanding. The second is that Muslims, faced with the calling to act in conformity with the teachings of Islam, should use this ability when making choices between what is good and what is bad in order to find the best way to please God, no matter what the environment in which they are living. If it is clear that there can be no choice without freedom, as we have said, we have to add that neither is there choice without knowledge and, even more important, understanding. Choice and ignorance are antithetical. So the elements of Muslim identity that follow on immediately after faith and spirituality are *understanding based on knowledge* and *choice based on freedom*. These together make up the dimension of *responsibility*.

So, Muslim identity, in its second pivotal point, is seen to be open because it rests on an attitude of intellect that marries an understanding of the Texts and an understanding of the context. It is therefore distinguished by *an active and dynamic intelligence* that needs knowledge, freedom, and a sense of responsibility.

Education and Transmission

Faith (*iman*) is a pledge (*amaana*), and Muslims are required to pass this *amana* on to their children and those close to them and, as we have already explained, to bear witness to it before humankind. To be Muslim entails educating and passing on; this was commanded by the Prophet himself in the first months of the Revelation: "Warn those who are closest to you."[26]

Again, Muslim identity is not closed and confined within the individual and personal domain as if it affected only the Muslim and the individual's relationship with God. On the contrary, to be Muslim entails adopting and articulating a perception of life based on faith, spirituality, and a basic understanding of moral injunctions. Educating one's children in order to make it possible for them to receive the *pledge*, and then to make free choices, is part of the Muslim identity, for a woman, for a mother, for a man, for a father. One of the most important functions of parents, part of their *being*, is to offer to their children the idea and substance of *what they are* so that the children can then choose, as responsible beings before God, *what they want to be*, for, as the Qur'an says, "no one can bear the burden of another."[27]

On a larger scale, and we have referred to this when dealing with the idea of *shahada*, Muslims are persuaded that the Qur'an is the final divine Revelation and that, as such, it has a universal dimension. Their responsibility before God is to make the message of the *pledge* known and to explain its content as well as possible. The responsibility ends there, for the idea of converting people is alien to Islam: to pass on the message is to call and invite people to a real knowledge of the presence of God and to a true understanding of His teachings. Conversion is something that only God can accomplish, through His revelation, with each individual, and no other human being has the right to get involved in it. It is an affair of the heart and so does not lie within anyone else's role or prerogative. This is the real meaning of the expression "bear witness to the message before humankind," which expresses the idea that the Muslim should bear the weight of this enormous responsibility before those close to him as well as before the whole of humanity—through his words, but much more through his behavior.

The third pivot of Muslim identity is an open and constantly active expression of this last element because it is based on "being Muslim," defined by the action of *educating* and *transmitting*.

Action and Participation

The outward expression of Muslim identity is the articulation and demonstration of the faith through consistent behavior. Faith, understanding, education, and transmission together constitute the substrata of Islamic ethics and should therefore guide the actions of the believer. To be Muslim is to act according to the teachings of Islam, no matter what the surrounding environment, and there is nothing in Islam that commands a Muslim to withdraw from society in order to be closer to God. It is actually quite the opposite, and, in the Qur'an, believing is often, and almost essentially, linked with behaving well and doing good. The Prophet never stopped drawing attention to this dimension of Muslim identity, and its authentic flowering entails the possibilities one has of acting according to what one *is* and according to what one *believes*.

This "acting," in whatever country or environment, is based on four important aspects of human life: developing and protecting spiritual life in society, disseminating religious as well as secular education, acting for justice in every sphere of social, economic, and political life, and, finally, promoting solidarity with all groups of needy people who are forgotten or culpably neglected or marginalized. In the North as well as in the South, in the West as well as in the East, a Muslim is a Muslim when he or she understands this fundamental dimension of his or her presence on earth: to be with God is to be with human beings, not only with Muslims but, as the Prophet said, "with people," that is, the whole of humankind: "The best among you is the one who behaves best toward people."[28]

For the individual, to bear the faith has to be translated into action that is consistent with it. One may act as oneself for oneself before God. But this is clearly not enough, and one is bound to move in the direction of participation, which clearly expresses the idea of action with an other, in a given society, with the fellow-citizens of whom it is composed. The fourth pivot of Muslim identity brings together these two dimensions of *acting* and *participating*, or, in other words, the individual and the social being, which define being Muslim in relation to society and the world.

These four elements give an adequate picture of the fundamentals of Muslim identity, individual and social, separate from its cultural reading in a specific region of the world. The kernel of *faith*, with *practice* and *spirituality*, is the light by which life and the world are perceived. *Understanding the Texts and the context* allows one to order one's mind both in relation to oneself and in relation to the environment. In a broader circle, *education* and *transmission* make it possible both to hand on the pledge as a gift and to pass on the message. And, finally, in an even broader context, *action* and *participation* are the full demonstration of this identity through the way one behaves *for oneself*, toward the other, and toward

Creation (action) and *with* one's fellow-citizens and the whole of human-kind (participation). It becomes apparent, then, that the definition of Muslim identity can be only of something open and dynamic, founded, of course, on basic principles but in constant interaction with the environment. The diagram in figure 3.3, beginning with faith at the core and moving on to expression through engagement with people, participation, demonstrates fairly clearly the way we have articulated the definition of Muslim identity.

The great responsibility of Muslims in the West is to dress these four dimensions of their identity in a Western culture while staying faithful to the Islamic sources, which, with their conception of life, death, and Creation, remain the fundamental frame of reference. Keeping in mind both the distinction between the *usul* (the fundamental elements of the religion) and the *furu* (the secondary elements), the three levels of *maslaha*—that is, *al-daruriyyat* (the indispensable), *al-hajiyyat* (the necessary, the complementary), and *al-tahsiniyyat* (the additional enhancing, the perfecting)—as well as the areas in which *ijtihad* may be applied, Muslims, both ulama and group leaders, should provide Western Muslims with appropriate teachings and regulations that will make it possible for them to protect and to actualize their Muslim identity, not as Arabs, Pakistanis, or Indians but as Westerners. This slow process has actually been taking place for only about twenty years, and it is proceeding, making possible the birth of a new and authentic Muslim identity, neither completely dissolved in the Western environment nor reacting against it but rather resting on its own foundations according to its own Islamic sources. In the second part of this book I shall try to give concrete illustrations of these dynamics and the direction in which I believe they should move together.

At a middle point between being *Muslims without Islam* and being *Muslims in the West but outside the West*, there is the reality of Muslims aware

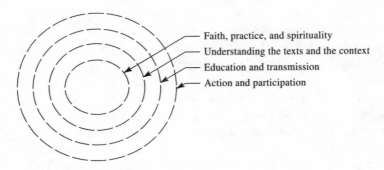

Faith, practice, and spirituality
Understanding the texts and the context
Education and transmission
Action and participation

Figure 3.3.   Muslim Identity

of the four dimensions of their identity and ready, while acknowledging the demands it will make, to be involved in their society and to play their part as Muslims and as citizens. There is no contradiction between these two allegiances as long as Muslims carry out their commitment to be active in conformity with the law and that they are not required to shed any part of their identity. This means that their faith, their perception of life, and their spirituality, which they need in order to learn and understand, to speak and educate, to act for justice and solidarity, should be respected by the country in which they are either residents or citizens.

Neither should there be any legal or administrative discrimination against the freedom of Muslims to organize themselves and to respond adequately and effectively to the demands of their faith and their conscience. These obstacles are met with daily in Western countries both because of the image of Islam that is disseminated by some of the mass media and as a result of the widespread feeling that there is an "Islamic threat," which is reinforced by news of dramatic events in Algeria, Afghanistan, and in the United States in September 2001. Many Westerners—politicians and intellectuals, as well as ordinary people—who are used to living in a secularized society tend to believe that the only Muslims they can trust are those who do not practice their religion and reveal nothing of their Muslim identity. Out of fear, or sometimes out of ill intent, they interpret the law of their country tendentiously and discriminatorily and sometimes have no hesitation in justifying their behavior by recourse to the argument that they must resist the "fundamentalists" and "Muslim fanatics."

Such attitudes are in evidence if we look at numerous rights denied to Muslims (e.g., construction of mosques, general organization of activities, allocation of grants, or simply freedom at a social level), while other religions and institutions, under the same law justly applied, have enjoyed these rights for decades.

It is nonetheless the law that should be the criterion and reference point, and a careful study shows that in most Western countries the constitution allows Muslims to live largely in accordance with their identity in the sense by which we have defined it. Muslim leaders and intellectuals should on the one hand demand and require the just and equitable application of the law with respect to all citizens and all religions. And on the other, they should face up to their responsibilities by using the broad freedom they enjoy in the West and trying to provide Muslim communities, through courses, study circles, and all kinds of institutions and organizations whose essential aims are to keep Islamic faith and spirituality alive, to spread a better understanding both of Islam and of the environment, to educate and pass on the message of Islam, and, finally, to see to it that Muslims get really involved in the society in which they live. There is nothing to stop them from doing so and although many initiatives have been taken in this direction over the past several years, the teaching given has often remained traditional. We shall return later to these forms of Islamic education, which have been provided without much thought to the context in which Muslims live.

This proposal means, above all, that we must develop, as we have said, a new and more confident attitude, based on a clear awareness of the essential features of our "being Western." This understanding should lead Muslims to evaluate their environment objectively and fairly. While respecting the requirements of their religion, they must not neglect the important potential for adaptation that is the distinctive characteristic of Islam. This is what has allowed Muslims to establish themselves in the Middle East and in Africa and Asia and, in the name of one and the same Islam, to give their identity concrete reality in specific and diverse shapes and forms. Again, Islam as a point of reference, is one, but its realization assumes recognition of the history and the social and cultural context in which it exists. In this sense, as we have said, there should be an Islam that is rooted in the Western cultural universe, just as there is an Islam rooted in the African or Asian tradition. Islam, with its Islamic sources, is *one and unique*; the methodologies for its legal application are *several*, and its concretization in a given time and place is by nature *plural*. From the Islamic point of view, adapting, for the new generations, does not mean making concessions on the essentials but, rather, building, working out, seeking to remain faithful while allowing for evolution. With this aim, Muslims should take advantage of the most effective methods (e.g., of teaching, management) and scientific and technological discoveries (which are not in themselves in conflict with Islam, as we have seen) in order to face their environment appropriately equipped. These developments belong to the human heritage and are part of Western society, and Muslims, especially those who live in the West, cannot ignore them or simply reject them because they are not "Islamic."

On the contrary, the teaching of Islam is very explicit and comes into its own here: in the area of social affairs (*al-muamalat*) all the ways and means—the traditions, arts, clothes—that do not, either in themselves or in the use to which they are put, conflict with Islamic precepts become not only acceptable but *Islamic* by definition. Consequently, Muslims should move toward exercising a choice from within the Western context in order to make their own what is in harmony with their identity and at the same time to develop and fashion the image of their Western identity for the present and the future.[29]

Belonging and Loyalty

To define the space in which we live as well as the open aspects of our identity is essential but still not enough. Muslims today experience, sometimes with a great deal of tension, conflicts of belonging, and if they themselves do not feel it as such, their fellow-citizens sometimes manage to connect them with another belonging—to "their community," "their brothers" from some other place, as if this attribution were one more sign that they do not really belong to the Western nations. For decades the same intentional process has been directed in Europe against Jews, whose genuine loyalty has always been suspect. Muslims face the same judgment, and international events push them even more onto the defensive. So this issue must be dealt with particularly explicitly.

Let us ask the questions clearly and simply: should Muslims be defined in the light of the notion of community (*umma*), or are they simply Muslim citizens of one or another Western country? To which group or collectivity do they belong first, to the *umma* or to the country in which they live as residents or citizens? These are sensitive questions, for behind their outward meaning we find *the* fundamental question—is it possible for a Muslim to be an authentic European or American, a real citizen, a *loyal* citizen?

Belonging to the Islamic Umma

We have explained that the essence of the Muslim personality is the affirmation of the *shahada*.[30] If we had to look for the minimal element on which Muslims agree for the definition of their common identity, we would certainly find that it was this fundamental profession of faith, which, when declared sincerely, makes the individual a Muslim.

This *shahada* is not a simple statement, for it contains a profound perception of the Creation that itself gives rise to a specific way of life for the individual, as for the society. The permanent link with God, the recollection that we belong to Him and will return to Him sheds an intense light on our person because we understand that life has meaning and that all people will have to account for their actions. This "intimate thought of every action" is one of the major dimensions of Islamic spirituality that, without any form of institutionalized influence, prompts every believer to decide on the markers for his social life.

To believe, along with the recollection of the presence of the Creator, is a way of understanding one's life within Creation and among people, for, from the Islamic point of view, to be with God is to be with human beings. This is the meaning of *tawhid* that we have referred to earlier. In Islam, there are four circles or areas that, at various levels and with specific prerogatives, should be highlighted in order to explain the social significance of the teaching of Islam, from the family to the *umma* and finally to the whole of humankind.

Immediately after the recognition of the presence of a Creator, which is the fundamental vertical dimension, a first horizontal area is opened up in matters to do with human relations. The strong affirmation of the one-ness of God and the worship of Him is linked as an essential condition with respect for parents and good behavior toward them. The first area in social relations, which is based on family ties, is basic for Muslims. The Qur'an connects the reality of *tawhid* with respect for parents in numerous verses: "Do not set up any other deity side by side with God, lest you find yourself disgraced and forsaken: For your Lord has ordained that you shall worship none but Him. And do good unto your parents. Should one of them, or both, attain old age, in your care, never say 'Ugh' to them or scold them, but [always] speak unto them with reverent speech, and spread over them humbly the wings of your tenderness, and say: 'O my Sustainer! Bestow Thy grace upon them, as they cherished and reared me when I was a child.' "[31]

To serve one's parents and be good to them is the best way of being good before God. It is one of the most important teachings of Islam, and the Prophet constantly emphasized it with supporting injunctions, such as the famous *hadith*: "Paradise lies at the feet of mothers." Nevertheless, there may be a situation when parents ask something that is against the faith and God's commands, in which case a son or a daughter should not obey, although they should remain respectful and polite. The most impor-tant of these commands is, of course, not to associate any other god with God, and if parents order their children to do this, they should refuse: "But if both try to force you to associate with Me that of which you have no knowledge, do not obey them; keep company with them in this world in an appropriate way, but follow the way of those who turn to Me."[32]

This refusal to obey certain pressures exercised by one's parents clearly shows where the priorities lie with regard to authority from the Islamic point of view: one should please both God and one's parents, but one should not disobey God in order to please one's parents. This was confirmed in general terms by the Prophet: "There should be no obedience to a crea-ture in disobedience to the Creator."[33] This means that despite the impor-tance of parental ties, which are where identity and fundamental belong-ing lie for a Muslim, they are not the first or the most important criterion in determining and guiding human relations. If a Muslim has to choose between fairness, which God has commanded should be practiced and re-spected, and himself, his parents, or his loved ones, he should prefer justice, for such an act bears true witness to his faith: "O You who have attained to faith! Be ever steadfast in upholding equity, bearing witness to the truth for the sake of God, even though it be against your own interests or those of your parents and kinsfolk. Whether the person concerned be rich or poor, God's claim takes precedence over [the claims of] either. Do not, then, follow your own desires, lest you swerve from justice: for if you distort [the truth], behold, God is indeed aware of all that you do!"[34]

A Muslim belongs above all to God, and this belonging influences and illumines with a particular light each social sphere in which he or she is involved. To believe in God and to bear witness to His message before the whole of humankind means that the fundamental values He has revealed, such as honesty, faithfulness, fairness, and justice, all have priority over parental ties. Consequently, Muslims must respect family ties (and by extension ties with community, people, and nation), as long as no one forces or compels them to act against their faith or conscience.[35] The first area of social relations in Islam associates father and mother very closely with the concept of the family, which refers, in the broad Islamic sense, to close relations and to everyone with whom one has a family relationship (al-aqrabun).

The individual affirmation of Islamic faith by means of the *shahada* and the recognition of the family as the first area of social life are the prerequisites for entering into the second circle of social relations in Islam. Each of the four practical pillars of Islamic religious practice has a double dimension—individual and collective. By trying to excel in the practice of their religion, Muslims are immediately called to face the communal dimension of the Islamic way of life. Most Qur'anic injunctions are addressed to the believers in the plural: "O bearers of the faith. . . ." and when Muslims recite the "opening chapter" of the Qur'an (*al-Fatiha*) in each prayer cycle, they present themselves as members of a community by saying: "You alone we worship, to You alone we turn for help. Guide us in the right Way."[36]

Alone before God, Muslims should direct all their efforts toward developing a personal and intimate consciousness of God, but they should also not forget that they belong to the community of faith. The Prophet said: "Communal prayer is twenty-seven times better than the prayer of a man alone in his house."[37] Prayer is the most important pillar of Islam. It is its very essence and explains the link with God but also the fundamental equality that exists between believers, brother beside brother, sister beside sister, all asking for divine guidance based on faith and brotherhood, as they have been taught. This sense of community is confirmed and reinforced by all the other religious practices, particularly *zakat*, which is essentially a tax raised for the poor and needy. The stronger our relationship with God, the stronger our desire to serve others will become, too. A right understanding of *zakat* takes us to the heart of the social message of Islam: to pray to God is to give to one's brother or sister. These are the very foundations of Islam as Abu Bakr understood it, when he warned after the death of the Prophet that he would fight anyone who wanted to make a distinction between prayer and paying *zakat* (what is effectively what happened later with the southern tribes). The same call is found in the requirement to fast during the month of Ramadan. An act of worship in itself, fasting also leads Muslims to perceive, and to feel inwardly, the need to eat and drink and, by extension, to ensure that every human being has the means to subsist. The month of Ramadan should be a time during which believers strengthen their faith and spirituality while developing their sense of social justice.

Pilgrimage clearly has this same double significance: the gathering at Mecca is the great witness to this *community of faith* that exists among Muslims. Men and women together, at the Center, praying to one God, members of a community that share the same hope—of pleasing the Creator and of being forgiven and rewarded in the next life. For Muslims, the daily practice of their religion gives birth naturally to a deep sense of being members of one community. This is a dimension that is inherent in the Islamic faith and way of life, which in turn are strengthened, guided, and shaped by this communal feeling: "Certainly the believers are brothers,"[38] the Qur'an tells us. Wherever Muslims live, we are present at the birth of a community that is created and confirmed by prayer and the prescribed religious practices and that then develops progressively as the Muslims begin to use their imaginations and to put in place social activities centered around the mosque (or to create an Islamic association). This process is evident everywhere in the world, in Muslim countries as well as in the West. To pronounce the *shahada*, which is, as we have said, the essence of Muslim identity, is to share in this community spirit with its immediate implication, which is the promotion of social activities. In philosophical terms, one might say that this feeling has a part in Muslim identity at the heart of the practice and that it constitutes one of the distinctive characteristics of such an identity. As the Prophet said: "Gather together, for the wolf picks off only the sheep that stand alone."[39]

A rereading of this analysis concerning the communitarian aspect of the four practical pillars of Islam shows a development in the sense of belonging. Prayer establishes connections with our Muslim neighbor in a specific place, while *zakat* enlarges the circle of our social relations, for the whole of the sum must be spent on the needy people in the area where it is raised.[40] Fasting develops an even broader feeling, for by fasting and by thinking about it, we are in spiritual communion with the poor of the whole world. And this communion finds a final, tangible, and physical realization in the pilgrimage to Mecca, the sacred place of gathering for millions of Muslims, symbolic of the *umma*.

This is in fact the third circle that delineates the belonging of a Muslim: the *umma* is a community of faith, feeling, brotherhood, and destiny. All

Muslims who say the *shahada* should know and understand that their individual actions are part, an essential part, of the *shahada* borne by the whole community of believers: all Muslims are individually invested with the common responsibility of bearing witness to the message before the whole of humankind. This is the exact meaning of the verse already quoted that links the notion of *umma* (the body, in the singular) with the duty of the believers (the members, in the plural): "So we have made you one community justly balanced, so that you might be witnesses before humankind."[41]

Consequently, every Muslim is not only personally attached to this dimension but also understands that it is his or her duty to spread it and pass it on to his or her children. It is an active belonging coming from a deep understanding of the principle of *tawhid*, the oneness of God, which sheds a particular light on the *umma* and its responsibility toward Him. It follows that what takes place within the *umma* should interest all Muslims, because this connection is part of their identity. The Prophet's statement is clear: "Whoever is not interested in the affairs of Muslims is not one of us."[42] To be Muslim, anywhere in the world, means feeling and developing this sense of belonging to the *umma* as if one were an organ in an enormous body. The Prophet said: "The *umma* is one body; if one of its members is sick, the whole body experiences the fever and the affliction."[43]

Does this mean that this belonging, resting on faith, brotherhood, and love, knows no limit and is the only criterion by which we should judge, so that we might say, for example, that everything done in the name of the *umma* is good and that what is not should be rejected? This statement, which is sometimes made by Muslims themselves, absolutely does not express the teaching of Islam, for just as there were limits to obedience to parents, there are principles on which Muslims base their belonging, their allegiance, and therefore their support. The greatness of the Islamic *umma* must be understood in the fact that it is "a community justly balanced" that must bear witness to the faith before all humankind by defending and spreading justice, solidarity, and the values connected with honesty, generosity, brotherhood, and love. This feeling of belonging does not mean that Muslims are required to accept or support an injustice simply because it is committed by another member of the faith. On the contrary, in the name of their religion and as members of the *umma* they should stop it and even oppose it. The Prophet clearly said: "Help your brother whether he is unjust or the victim of injustice." One of the Companions asked: "Messenger of God, I understand helping someone who is the victim of injustice, but how should I help one who is unjust?" The Prophet replied: "Prevent him from being unjust. That is how you will help him."[44]

This sense of belonging must be founded on the principles revealed by God, without which it becomes a kind of blood-bond or tribal attachment in total opposition to the universal message of Islam. We have shown that even the closest relationships, like those between parents and children, are subject to the principle of justice, and this is also without question the case with regard to relations within the *umma* as well as with other peoples and nations. Justice takes precedence over sentiment, whether the sentiment is affection or aversion: "O you bearers of the faith! Stand firm as witnesses before God, practicing justice. Let not hatred toward a people incite you to commit injustices. Be just: this is closest to piety [awareness of God]. Fear God; God well knows what you do."[45]

If the sense of belonging to the *umma* is inherent in the Islamic faith and part of the essence of *tawhid*, we should underline the fact that this attachment is based on a true understanding of the mission of the Muslim community as a whole, which is, for all Muslims, to bear witness to their faith in the presence of God before the whole of humankind by standing on the side of justice and human dignity in all circumstances, in relation to Muslims and non-Muslims alike.[46]

The principle of justice is the criterion. In the body of literature that illustrates its correct application, the Qur'an and the Sunna refer to a very specific situation which serves to guide—and maybe restrain—involvement in and for the *umma*, by showing when Muslims, whether members of a group or nation, are bound by a contract or agreement. We have noted earlier, in dealing with the notion of *shahada*, the importance of contract in Islam, and the Revelation is clear on this point: "An account will be required of every contract,"[47] and the believers are those "who respect the pledges entrusted to them and their commitments."[48]

This principle is true to the point that if Muslims are treated unjustly or persecuted in a country with which another Muslim community has signed an agreement, it is impossible for the latter to intervene because respect for the contract overrides everything. This is explicitly stated in the Qur'an: "Those who believed, who emigrated and struggled with their goods and themselves in the way of God, and those who gave them refuge and succor, they are allied with each other. And as for those who believed but who did not emigrate with you, you will not be bound to them as they did not emigrate. If they ask for your help in the name of religion, you must help them, except against people with whom you have concluded a treaty. God sees perfectly what you do."[49]

Although this verse refers to a situation in which two entities exist—for example, a Muslim state such as Medina and a non-Muslim neighbor—it is still possible to deduce at least three essential teachings:

1. Muslims are not responsible for those of the coreligionists who choose to live elsewhere and are bound to another state (by an explicit or tacit agreement).

2. It is the duty of Muslims to react when their brothers or sisters are exposed to persecution by reason of their religious beliefs.[50]
3. However, the duty to help persecuted believers cannot be carried out if there is a treaty (of alliance or nonintervention), for such an intervention would mean a unilateral breach of the obligations of the agreement.

These three observations are of prime importance in discussions of the notion of *umma* and what is implied by being connected to it. One part of Muslim identity is guided by the principle of justice, but this may be restricted in certain circumstances when there are pacts which may be signed by Muslims—in their capacity as individuals or a community.

The *sira* of the Prophet teaches us that he submitted to the clauses of the pact he had signed with the tribes of Quraysh at al-Hudaybiyya. The agreement, as we have said, meant that if someone left Medina for Mecca, he would be allowed to stay there, but if someone had escaped from Mecca, the Prophet should not accept him but should send him back to Mecca. Later, when a Muslim escaped from Mecca and arrived in Medina, the Prophet refused to keep him because this would have been a betrayal of the pact: to the great amazement of the Companions, the Prophet sent him back, showing them by his attitude that an agreement applied without exception. It was only later, when the tribes of Quraysh had first broken the terms of the pact of al-Hudaybiyya, that the Prophet decided to send his army to Mecca.

Thus, by way of synthesis of our study of the notion of *umma*, three observations should be made. First, the notion of belonging based on faith, religion, and brotherhood brings out the very essence of the teaching of Islam and constitutes one of its distinctive characteristics, for it explains that the link with God (*al-rabbaniyya*) is fully realized through an active and positive involvement in society, from the small family unit up to the wide reality of the *umma*. Next, in the light of their faith, Muslims are bound to "the prime aim of justice," which must be their criterion in every circumstance, rather than to an abstract feeling of belonging founded only on the fact that "we are all Muslims." In other words, Muslims should feel that they belong above all to God and that the Creator will never accept a lie, a betrayal, or an injustice, especially on the part of a Muslim individual or community, for they should be models of rectitude, honesty, justice, and loyalty. Finally, contracts determine our status, define our duties and rights, and guide the direction as well as the content of our actions. Once settled, the terms of an agreement must be respected, and if one of its points seems to go against the rights of Muslims—or even against their conscience as believers—it must be discussed and negotiated, for Muslims do not have the right to break a treaty unilaterally. On this point, their loyalty must have no exceptions.

Civil Allegiance in the West

The preceding analysis should help us to deal with the problem of Muslim residents and citizens in Europe and in North America and to respond to questions related to the nature and integrity of loyalty. We have explained the kind of attachment that is linked to the notion of *umma* and how it should be realized in the light of the principle of justice and respect for treaties. This explanation is of great interest when it comes to the question of citizenship, insofar as it structures the various levels of belonging.

Before starting this study, it is perhaps important to pay attention to an essential point that recurs constantly in discussions about the status of Muslims in the West: do they consider themselves first Muslims or Westerners? Behind this apparently simple question we see a series of concerns in which are mixed doubts and suspicions about these residents or new citizens. And, even if at first sight it seems to be a legitimate question, deeper consideration shows that it really centers on a false problem, for faith and nationality, as they are embodied in actual national constitutions, are not of the same order. To be Muslim means to be entrusted with a pledge (*amana*) that gives a meaning to life: it is to be indwelt and pregnant with a comprehensive perception of life, death, and destiny, guided by faith in one Creator. Philosophically speaking, "Muslim identity" responds to the question of being and as such is essential, fundamental, primal, and primordial, because it contains the justification for life itself. The concept of nationality, as it is understood in the industrialized countries, is of a completely different order: as an element of identity, it organizes, from within both a given constitution and a given space, the way in which a man or woman is related to his or her fellow-citizens and to other human beings. Muslim identity is a response to the question: "Why?," while national identity is a response to the question: "How?," and it would be absurd and stupid to expect geographical attachment to resolve the question of being. In short, it all depends on what one is talking about: if it is a question of a philosophical debate, the individual is a *Muslim of American, British, French,* or *Belgian nationality,* as is the case with any humanist or Christian involved in explaining his or her ideas about life. If the discussion is of legal, social, and/or political questions, the individual is an *American, English, French,* or *Belgian person of the Muslim faith,* as others are of the Jewish or Christian faith. In fact, the terminological dispute about whether to say, for example, "Muslim American" or "American Muslim" is, properly speaking, void of meaning.

The real question is not, from the Muslim point of view, about justifying the primary attachment of believers—which is naturally that which they have to God and their faith—but rather, more specifically, to clarify the nature of the connection that exists between Islamic requirements and the concrete reality of citizenship in Western countries. Do the Islamic sources allow a Muslim to be a true American or European citizen, or does a contradiction exist such that the notion of "Western Muslim" cannot be realized? A few points in response to this have already been made in our discussion of the *umma*, but we must push our thinking further, particularly on the question of the "social contract."

To begin with, the first principle is that one expects Muslims, in whatever context, to struggle to promote justice and try to reform and improve the situation, according to the saying of the Prophet: "If one of you sees an abhorrent action, let him correct it with his hand; if he cannot, let him do it in words; if he cannot, let him do it in his heart—which is the weakest degree of faith."[51] However, in the social, political, and even financial domains, human affairs are based on agreements and contracts, which, as we have said, Muslims are bound to respect and which must take priority in their eyes. Faysal al-Mawlawi rightly underlines the fact that, according to the majority of the ulama, Muslims are bound by the decisions and actions of an unjust ruler or dictator "as long as he does not commit a sin or an action that goes against the teachings of Islam."[52] In such a situation, they are not bound to his actions, because by so acting he has broken the tacit agreement between him and his people with respect to the authority of the Islamic sources. Consequently, they have the right, and the duty, to abandon him and to take power from him within the framework of the legislation in force, that is to say "by all legal means."

Following on from this first observation, which has already emphasized the importance of contracts, we must note that Muslims today, even if they do not recognize the corrupt leaders or totalitarian political systems in their country of origin, are bound by agreements that these governments may have signed with other countries as long as the agreements do not force them to accept anything contrary to their religion. Consequently, these international agreements, as well as the visas Muslims obtain in order to travel to a country, are legally binding on Muslim residents, as they are on citizens under the authority of the national constitution. The general rule here is that *Muslims are bound by the terms of their contract*,[53] except in a specific case where they would be *forced* to act against their conscience. This precise use of terms is necessary because some radical Islamic groups state that a Muslim cannot be bound by a constitution that authorizes bank interest (*riba*), consumption of alcohol (*khamr*), and other types of behavior that contradict the teachings of Islam.

Now, even if in practice European constitutions do authorize such transactions and behaviors, they do not *compel* Muslims to use them or do them. Consequently, they are able both on the one hand to respect the law in force—because their presence in the country is based on a tacit or explicit agreement—and on the other hand to abstain from all activity and all involvement that would contradict their faith. Thus, we see that it is clearly in the name of respect for the Islamic teachings of the *Sharia* that Muslims are able to live in the West and that they should respect the law of the country. So, in other words, Islamic law and jurisprudence *command* Muslim individuals to submit to the body of positive law enforced in their country of residence in the name of the tacit moral agreement that already supports their very presence. Put in yet another way, *to apply the Sharia* for Muslim citizens or residents in the West means explicitly to respect the legal and constitutional framework of the country of which they are citizens.

When this is understood, it is the responsibility of Muslims to study with legal scholars every situation in which difficulties could arise, for example, in matters concerning obligatory insurance, inheritance, and marriage. Rules would have to be formulated—as they already have been on numerous points—taking into account the legislation of the country, the teachings of Islam (in the light of its five essential rules, already noted), and needs arising from the environment Muslims are faced with. This requires meticulous legal work: the legislation in the various Western countries is not the same and is not closed; it provides scope for interpretation and application. Moreover, there are legally recognized procedures to which Muslims may revert to deal with their situation in a way that accords closely with their conscience. This requires that they work within the limits of what the law allows in order to find an adaptation as close as possible to the teachings of Islam.

One often finds that only an apparent contradiction exists and that working toward adaptation within the margins allowed by the law provides some interesting solutions (in the areas of legal interpretation and strict jurisprudence). It is for Muslim jurists to consider how these arrangements can be managed by working in phases and in various areas of law—from marriage contracts and inheritance to the area of finance and commerce. At the end of this stage in our reflection, three principles can be explicitly formulated: first, the Islamic sources allow Muslims to live in the West. Second, they are under the authority of an agreement whose terms must be respected as long as they do not force Muslims to act against their conscience. Third, if a clear conflict of terms of reference occurs, which is very rare, a specific study should be carried out by Muslim jurists to determine, by formulating a legal opinion (*fatwa*), the types of adaptation that may be possible and that might provide the Muslim with a satisfying solution, both as a practicing believer and as a resident and/or citizen. It is clear, from the preceding observations and in the light of the Islamic sources, that it is illegitimate for a Muslim living in the West to act against the law, or to commit acts of abuse, embezzlement, or fraud. Once an agreement is concluded, to act according to the law is in itself a way of worshiping God. Even Abu Hanifa, who went a long way toward allowing Muslims, under certain conditions, to practice interest (*riba*) when they were trading in non-Muslim countries (*dar al-harb*, to use binary terminology), clearly indicated that it was permissible to trade with non-Muslims according to the rules in force in their countries, but not in any way to deceive or defraud them. For Muslim citizens and residents [in non-Muslim-majority countries], to act with honesty, rectitude, and dignity is the best way of protecting and affirming their identity as Muslims and of bearing witness to the Islamic message of justice among their fellow-citizens and neighbors.

The Conscience Clause

We have shown how the idea of belonging to the *umma* is formed and structured at various levels and how, through the notion of contract, the apparent opposition between the *umma* and the state should disappear. Moreover, the foregoing analysis has clearly indicated that it is permissible for Muslims to live in non-Muslim countries as long as they able to protect their identity and practice their religion and the fact of residence is bound to a tacit or explicit agreement which, in the light of the teaching of Islam, must be respected. As residents or citizens, Muslims are required to respect the terms of the constitution of the country in which they live. This is clear when Muslim immigrants have to make a declaration if they want to be naturalized, after residing for several years in a Western country: the oath (*qasam*) they must pronounce[54] means that they will respect both the country and its constitution. They are not required to accept or like each law and regulation in force in the country or to do everything that is permitted by the legislation. Rather, what is expected of them is both to recognize (*yatarif*) the legislation and to act within the framework of the law (*yaltazim bil-qawanin*). These are the conditions of the oath, and once the oath is taken Muslims must respect it, as the well-known Islamic rule stipulates: *al-muslimun inda shurutihim* (Muslims are bound by the conditions they accept).

So Muslims, as citizens, must make choices and find their way in the Western environment. Within the vast range of what is permitted in these societies, they must decide, as Muslims, what they may do in conscience and what they should avoid. With regard to the latter, things are sometimes very clear, as when things forbidden in Islam are permitted in Western legislation—for example, alcohol and sometimes what are called soft drugs, interest derived from financial dealings, and extramarital sexual relations. They have the choice and should develop the will to keep away from everything that is not consistent with their identity and the correct practice of Islam. But on many points the appropriate behavior is not obvious and requires analysis and clarification, for some questions (e.g., education, culture, leisure activities, economics) need specific responses, to which we shall return in part II. These admittedly real problems must nevertheless be distinguished from the primary issue, the legislation within whose framework Muslims have to act.

In other words, what is allowed by the latitude of the national constitution is one thing, but what Muslims should choose within the options permitted by this latitude, in order to live in accordance with their faith, is another. Muslims are brought back to taking responsibility for their involvement in social, educational, and cultural activities in the West, with the aim of working out better ways of behaving and finding answers (even adapted institutions) appropriate to their reality. So the question is not strictly legal, for it is more generally a matter of thinking through how to undertake a specific and participatory engagement that will allow us to live peacefully in the West, with all its demands and choices.

Once this distinction has been formulated and understood, it becomes clear that Muslim citizens in the West bear an immense responsibility. Not only should they be citizens who take their duties seriously, but they should also decide what should be the basis and content of their "Western-Islamic identity," which will make it possible for them to develop an integrated personality from childhood to adulthood in this environment. This is certainly a challenge and a difficult task, but it is unavoidable, for it seems to be the only way by which Muslim communities themselves can take control of and prepare for their future in such a seemingly troubling context. It in fact means that in each Western country Muslims should increase their efforts, in partnership with official organizations, to provide their respective communities with all the institutions, organizations, and places of worship necessary for them to fulfill their task well. There is absolutely no contradiction in this area between their citizenship and the fact that they are Muslims; the law permits them to act in this way, and their faith commands it.

In Western legislation, more is permitted than is imposed. Nevertheless, it may happen that citizenship leads some to come up against, or feel, a serious tension between their faith or conscience and the requirements attached to their national status. In such situations, they should be able to refer to the legal notion of a "conscience clause" that allows them to state that certain actions or behaviors are against their faith.

These cases arise only rarely as far as the law is concerned, but it is still necessary to study them, because they complete the picture we are trying to give of the Muslim European, American, or Canadian citizen. Three things should first be noted: the first two introduce the notion of the "conscience clause," while the last is connected with recognition of "necessity," which sometimes implies the development of Islamic *fiqh* within the Western context.

We have said that, for Muslims, the principle of justice constitutes the fundamental criterion, after their faith in the oneness of God, for their social, economic, and political activities. This principle takes precedence over their own interest, their relatives, the rich, the poor, and so on, as far as the *umma* itself. The same applies to citizenship. If, for example, Muslims are called to participate in a war that is unjust or based solely on the desire for power or control (of territory, interests, or other people), they should not, in conscience, take part. They are not allowed to fight or to kill for money, land, or power, and they should absolutely avoid being implicated in a colonial or oppressive war. In this case, they should, under the "conscience clause," plead "conscientious objection," for their faith and conscience cannot bear to be torn away from the principle of justice before God. This principle should be upheld by individuals in every situation where it is clear that the motive for war has nothing to do with the defense of justice, whatever the identity and religion of the enemy. Many people have pleaded conscientious objection through history, and the cases of the boxer Muhammad Ali (Cassius Clay) and many Christians during the Vietnam War are memorable. They accepted, as objectors, being sentenced to imprisonment for refusing to obey the state and military orders. This is how Muslims should act in similar circumstances. Prison is preferable to committing injustice, as Joseph said when he was urged to act unjustly: "Lord, I prefer prison. . . ."[55]

There is a general Islamic rule that forbids Muslims from fighting or killing another Muslim, and such behavior should be avoided. Some people put this argument forward without any kind of analysis, but it must be remembered that it is the principle that is decisive when it comes to entering into conflict with a Muslim, as with a non-Muslim. It might well happen that the attitude of the Muslim leader of an enemy country is unjust and that he is clearly in the wrong.[56] In this case, a specific decision must be made after a serious study of the whole context, and it would be up to the ulama to formulate an opinion, in the light of both the teaching of Islam and the context, as to whether Muslims were permitted to be involved in such a conflict. The prohibition on killing Muslims remains the general rule, but it is the principle of justice that must first be taken into consideration. (Debates between ulama on this subject have been intense and sometimes passionate throughout history, but it seems to me that the view we are developing here is the one that should be taken and preferred [*tarjih*], particularly in the light of our context.) In a case where two unjust causes confront each other, conscientious objection is also the way of wisdom and is to be preferred. Muslim citizens of Western countries should therefore develop the maturity to analyze and take responsibility for their choices—alone, before God, in conscience, and after consulting competent legal authorities.[57]

It sometimes happens that the residents or citizens of Western countries find themselves obliged to take part in transactions forbidden by their religion. We have already said that the "range of the possible" is very wide and that, when they have the choice, Muslims should avoid anything that does not conform to the requirements of Islam. However, a number of regulations are compulsory (e.g., with regard to some kinds of insurance, banking, slaughter of animals, burial), and these need specific examination. Muslims living in a country whose laws they have decided to accept therefore have to find a way, between the sometimes constraining nature of those laws and their Islamic sources, of living at peace with their conscience. A very pointed evaluation of each of these sample cases should be carried out (by ordinary Muslims as well as by ulama) in order to determine the extent of the relative obligation (and consequently the degree of "necessity"). This should take into account the nature and substance of the constraint, the degree of difficulty, the possible existence and nature of a possible *maslaha* (if there really is one), and the scope and means available for acting *more or less* in accordance with Islamic requirements. It is only after the work of analysis, evaluation, and consideration that an adaptive *fatwa* should be formulated. This is a case of *fiqh*, law and Islamic jurisprudence being explicitly developed on the principle of adaptation to the environment. This mechanism can only be dynamic, ongoing, refined, and constantly elaborative over the years. It is a far-reaching process of *legal integration* in that these legal opinions, put together with each other, will give rise to a corpus of adapted law, a *fiqh* for the West. It can be seen that this has taken place in Western countries over the past twenty years, and numerous *fatawa* have been given, for example, about prayers during working hours, exclusion of Muslim girls from educational institutions, relationships with banks, or insurance.[58] In recent years, Muslims have felt more strongly the need to reflect and adjust, and initiatives of this kind have become more numerous, as we have already seen. It must be noted that these *fatawa* are very specific and sometimes even temporary, because they provide Muslims with responses in a precise context. Western systems of legislation are neither absolute nor eternal, and it is appropriate to think of *fiqh* as being responsive to evolution and change. The laws of Western countries have been thought out and elaborated for a society from which Muslims were absent; basically, it should be emphasized that they do not present a major barrier to the legal and social integration of Muslims (if, as we have said, they are applied according to the intention of the Texts and not through the distorting prism of currently held views of Islam).

However, we should not deny that, in very specific and narrow situations, one may occasionally have to arrive at an arrangement with regard to the law and its application (perhaps only at the level of case law) in order to reach a greater legal equity for a population recognized as being religiously diverse. It is neither realistic nor wise to oppose the very idea of such arrangements: the evolution of individual laws is the very essence of the law, and one would be ill advised to press, in the name of the diffuse fear of a "new presence of Muslim colonizers," for a very dogmatic reading of legislation on the pretext of combating the resurgence of religious dogma. This does not at all mean that, by looking at things from this angle, we are trying to undermine the foundations of the nation or demand "special laws for Muslims," as has been rumored here and there. The contrary is true. Muslim citizens really are *citizens*, and they too have the right, within the framework of the national legislation, to be respected as *Muslims*. The landscape of Western societies has undergone major evolution during the past forty years, and it is simply a matter of being just and consistent and having the wisdom to take these changes into account. As part of Western societies, Muslims now have the responsibility, in accord with the teachings of Islam, to honor their commitment to the laws [of their adopted countries], to protect their identity, and, within the extensive limits of the liberty open to them, to work and act in all the various areas (social, legal, economic, and political) and to think through as far as possible the dimensions of an improved harmony between the Muslim personality and the Western landscape.

In fact, apart from the two considerations referred to, I do not think it is possible to invoke the conscience clause. There are some limited cases that must be closely considered. Many Muslims state that they cannot accept the way marriages are officially conducted in the West or Western educational programs, or other similar practices, because they are not consistent with their faith and therefore are "in conflict with their conscience." We must here be very clear and precise, for these statements are of a quite different significance. There are some questions that arise from the essence of Islamic faith and that therefore have priority and must be taken into account wherever a Muslim lives. Freedom of worship, respect for the principle of justice, and the prohibition on killing for power or money are of this nature: lack of respect for these requirements undermines the foundations of Muslim identity. These constitute, as we have said, a limited number of cases, which is why we have referred to the "conscience clause." As far as the other matters are concerned (school, education, marriage, cemeteries), they do not demand the same level of consideration in the light of Islamic teachings. They are certainly of primary importance, but it is still possible to find solutions within the framework of legislation, that is to say, in accordance with the terms of the agreement tacitly or explicitly entered into with the country. Consequently, these issues do not fall within the reach of a conscience clause but rather require Muslims to make a genuine effort to find appropriate solutions, and this is what we shall try to study in part II.

4

AN INVENTORY

W e are here beginning a transitional chapter between our statement of fundamental principles and the tools that construct Islamic thought and a more concrete consideration of the realities on the ground with the dynamics that run through, or in my opinion should be running through, Western Muslim communities. The first three chapters of this part are essential because they have made it possible for us to present, from within the Islamic framework of reference, the nature of its universal teaching as it affects the awareness of Muslim believers and the ways in which it may be articulated and take root in the future. In the West, as in the East, Muslims are already engaged in the "Way of faithfulness"; they are already trying to journey "toward the source" by seeking to apply the teachings of their religion at their own level, to be consistent with the requirements and to organize themselves to be and do better. They are more or less deeply aware of how demanding the Way is, but they are nevertheless seeking peace and growth by traveling along it.

For decades the context of American and European societies has challenged them, even unsettled them, and has invited them, or rather summoned them, to go back to their Texts and reread them with a new understanding, to understand the substance better, to formulate new responses and propose fresh pathways. Following on from the study of the scriptural sources and classical scholarly works, a very substantial part of the theoretical schema that we have set out naturally comes from our experience of life in the West. Nothing could be more normal, and this is moreover the logical consequence of the connection that the Islamic message itself establishes between the universal principles it defines and active reason, which is invited to consider the principles and actualize them in the midst of historical and social contingencies.

We now need to find out how to use these fundamental sources and their tools in the Western universe to make them effective in practice. How, between the universal message of Islam, the legal instruments available, and the reality of North American and European societies, can we outline a project, a "vision" in the English sense of the word? Where are we going? What do we want? Before considering further, we must take a look at the reality facing us and ask another central question: from where are we setting out? In fact, it is impossible to speak of a vision for the future if we do not take time to establish, even in general terms, an inventory of the assets and deficits of the current situation of Muslims in the West.

Assets and Deficits

In my book *To Be a European Muslim*, I recalled that the "new presence" of Muslims in Europe, as in North America, was a recent phenomenon that went back to the interwar period in the most advanced countries. Some of my critics then drew to my attention the fact that Muslims had been settled on those two continents for centuries and that this was nothing new. Without denying these well-known facts, I had in fact deliberately spoken of a "new presence" in order to mark a clear difference in nature between the past and the present: immigration and conversion in the West during the twentieth century have given rise to strong Muslim communities made up of millions of souls, more and more of them citizens, which makes it an entirely new situation. Today we are talking about substantial sectors of Western societies, and in many countries Islam has become the second religion in terms of numbers. Their numbers and the fact of their permanent settlement are completely new experiences for the Muslims themselves, as well as for the societies that originally welcomed them as temporary migrants, seasonal workers, or political exiles, without ever thinking that these immigrants and their children would one day be full citizens. The same is true of African Americans, with their reclamation of their past and their rights (remembering that they were treated as slaves, that they were ripped from their roots, and that they were denied the Muslim religion of their ancestors); we would say that in their case, and we might add to them the Muslims of Eastern Europe, their effort to reclaim their belonging to Islam and their desire to be faithful to it did not become widespread or attract many adherents until the past few decades.

Assets

One thing that is extraordinarily to the credit of this new presence is the rapidity with which an awareness of the issues and the seeds of new solutions became established. Within the space of a few years, in North America as well as in Europe, communities whose members were mostly of immigrant origin were grouping, organizing themselves, building mosques, setting up various organizations and institutions, and developing an impressively dynamic sense of belonging. It is true that one might have thought it entirely normal that first-generation immigrants would try to preserve their religion and culture but that in time their children would become assimilated by force of events. But the opposite has happened and continues to happen for a significant number of these children: they take up the baton and continue the enterprise begun by their fathers and mothers, and throughout the West, we note with astonishment that the active practice of Islam among Muslim men and women is increasing and that they are becoming more and more "visible." The same phenomenon is also at work among the "native Muslims": the multiple African American Islamic organizations (among them the very organized and dynamic Muslim American Society of WD Muhammad) and the numerous converts (or "reverts") are going through the same positive trend.

In fifty years, the growth in awareness has been phenomenal, and Muslim communities are everywhere witnessing renewed passion and enthusiasm. The passion is first for study: adolescents, students, parents, of all backgrounds and all ages, all together, are following regular courses in religion, Arabic, even history and culture. The demand usually exceeds what the Muslim organizations and institutions can supply. Some even decide to go abroad for a few years' education, usually in an Islamic university or through direct contact with reputable scholars. These realities point to another and consequential asset: the children often know more about Islam than their parents, and knowledge itself is more widespread because of the obvious desire of these younger generations to learn. Translations of classical works and the production of books and audio- and videocassettes with varied content are multiplying exponentially in all languages. Western realities, as we have said, are forcing Muslims to reflect on their Texts in this context, and, more and more, initiatives on the part of ulama,[1] intellectuals, and leaders of organizations are moving in the direction of this contextualized approach. People are searching, asking themselves questions, experimenting on the educational, social, political, and cultural levels: we are living in a time of deep intellectual ferment and transformation. For myself, I have not hesitated to speak of a "silent revolution" in Western Muslim communities because the dynamism, movements in gestation, and innovative perspectives are already tangible and will certainly surprise observers who pay little attention to these grassroots movements . . . too slow to attract the media but extraordinarily rapid for such a short period of history.

A third notable asset is undoubtedly the emergence of an awareness of citizenship in all the countries where Muslims have been present longest—notably in France, Great Britain, and the United States. In practice, it is a matter of a more fine-tuned and internal awareness of relational logics among the individual, the law, and the institutions in a state based on the rule of law. It is not simply a question of promoting the right to vote (which is in itself a notable asset), but one of claiming one's rights of citizenship and at the same time being aware of one's responsibilities and duties. In these three countries, more than elsewhere at present (though there are signs that citizenship movements are growing in other countries, too), Muslim citizens participate at various levels in social and political life and sometimes do not hesitate to demand respect for their religion and/or their origin as participants in a society that is, after all, theirs. This movement is still in its infancy, and we shall come back to it, but the direction it is taking here and now is of special interest.

One of the assets we shall also come back to at greater length is the new and strong participation of women in this process of reappropriation and affirmation of identity. Being more and more educated and experienced, some who are more capable of contributing in the area of religious regulations and cultural adaptations are increasingly taking part in religious, social, and cultural debates and also have an increasingly significant access to leadership. This movement is evident throughout the West, and many women, while affirming and often explicitly demonstrating their attachment to Islam through their style of dress, make themselves heard and enter into discussion as much about the so-called authentic Islamic ideas of their coreligionists (both men and women) as about the hasty and sometimes offensive views of their fellow-citizens.[2] We shall return to this phenomenon, which everything indicates is growing.

Deficits

An observer of Muslim communities cannot fail to notice, even after only a few days' fieldwork, that Muslim communities are very diverse and diversified and that they are shot through with strong currents of identity awareness that are often tied to more than their shared religion. There would be nothing to say about this if it were a matter of confident diversity, and so of richness, in which these various levels of allegiance were not contradictory. But, in practice, this kaleidoscope is often an expression less of diversity than of divisive animosity, or rejection and separation on the basis of origin or social class. Western Muslim communities have not usually succeeded in overcoming a number of barriers essential to the growth of a semblance of unity (not in the sense of uniformity). Some immigrants arrived in the West believing in ideology of a particular school of thought, one that was sometimes in conflict with another school. Often they simply imported their old disputes into Europe and North America. We are witnessing conflicts between ideological trends, the origin and meaning of which are often not very well known, and a multiplication of overlapping organizations, mutual rejections, disputes about Muslim representation, and so on. Intracommunal dialogue between trains of thought, as well as among national and local organizations, is virtually nonexistent. People ignore or exclude one another while at the same time they say, "We are all brothers."

To this sad reality must be added two other kinds of separation that are no less operational and no less serious. Although one might have hoped that, in the new territory of the West, Muslims would succeed in overcoming their differences of origin, it is evident everywhere that the norm is still ethnic segregation. It was, of course, to be expected that the first immigrants would form organizations with other people of the same origin and language; it is less normal to note that, after decades, there are mosques for Moroccans, and others for Algerians, for Pakistanis, for West Africans, for Afro-Americans, for Arabs from the Middle East, and so on— and sometimes in the same street. One even finds, in Switzerland, France, Britain, and the United States, that converts who have not found a place within the communities have established small mosques for themselves, which, although they are in their own country, have ended up making them into strangers in their own land. It is a surprising tendency and a serious dysfunction.

On another level, it must also be noted that there are frequent splits between the social classes. Affluent Muslims[3] have less and less contact with their less wealthy, or frankly poor, coreligionists. So we see the emergence of two kinds of belonging: one is related to a very sophisticated discourse on Islam produced by the universities and leaders of organizations that have "a house of their own"—a sort of middle-class Islam; alongside is another, with which the first often no longer has any contact, that has stronger leanings toward reclamation and draws more on the shared Islamic allegiance to the development of social solidarity movements and a spirit of mobilization that is often in confrontation with the social and political system. This split already exists in practically all the Western countries, more or less sharply according to the social circumstances, but it is clearly in the United States that the rift is most evident between a so-called educated Islam and that of the less affluent, who refuse, usually with reason, to be treated as second-class Muslims who have not understood the "wisdom of the message of Islam." The response of some is that there is a great difference between "wisdom" and the "compromise" and "resignation" actually displayed by some well-off and comfortably settled Muslims. Without denying the relevance of these discussions, it has to be stated here too that there is a real division at the heart of the Muslim communities and that they should find a way to deal with it.

Another patent deficit is the mentality of isolation that burdens Muslims everywhere in the West, whether because this is the way the organization of society in the Anglo-Saxon system treats its citizens or because of a natural inclination to protect oneself from an environment perceived as dangerous. Again, this attitude may have been normal during the first years of the Muslim presence in the West, but it is nevertheless a major handicap when it comes to improving the quality of life of the community. Confusing the "community of faith" we have referred to earlier with a communal withdrawal, even communitarianism, some Muslims live entirely on the margin of society and never interact with it. *In the West but outside the West*, they identify themselves only in terms of difference, otherness, and even confrontation. Although the various discourses may tend to express a deep awareness of the urgent need to stop taking this kind of stance, it is still true in practice, and even more perhaps in the psychology and "feeling" of Muslims, that a significant number of them are feeding this reactionary isolation. The "ghetto" is as much intellectual as social, and the evidences of this thorny problem can already be seen in the kinds of "Islamic education" proposed for Muslims in the West and in the motivations that have prompted the emergence of some private educational bodies that sell their particular advantages more on the basis of their being *different* than on the basis of their being *original*. This frame of mind is significant.

The consequence of this kind of isolationist stance is the emergence of a "minority consciousness" that comes into play at several levels and in sometimes contradictory ways. Muslims are, of course, on the simple basis of numbers of religious adherents in the West, in a minority in the various countries, but this does not mean that they have to hold and refer to this "minority" character and behavior in all the areas where they act as citizens.[4] Nevertheless, what happens is that, on the social level and in the political arena, Muslims continue to consider themselves a minority on the defensive. It is as if the Western Muslim personality has to be formed around a minority consciousness alone, and we see the clear result in everything that follows: social and political discourses and demands that almost never express a sense of true belonging to a shared citizenship, or even to a universality of values, but are reduced simply to a declaration of distinctness, even oddness, and of protectiveness and action *in reaction*.[5] This mentality has perverse and contradictory effects: minority claims that were expressed so powerfully and so forcefully in demanding religious rights seem to have had the exactly opposite result when it comes to sensitive national and civil issues. For the very reason that they feel they are a stigmatized minority, people cannot now express or expose themselves for fear of arousing suspicions about their allegiance and loyalty. Demanding the application of equal rights for all or questioning the government about its alliances with dictators or on political security issues, as should have happened after the 11 September atrocities in the United States and the "natural" retaliation against the people of Afghanistan, raises a critical and autonomous discourse in the midst of the turmoil. Too few Western Muslims are able un–self-consciously to take an intellectual position that, in the end, acknowledges that one is speaking from home, as it were, as an accepted member of a free society, and in full awareness of that—with causes and fundamental values that must be respected.

We must end this incomplete list of deficits with a last difficulty that is often, too often, encountered in Western Muslim communities. Anyone who tries to evaluate the ways in which Muslims are drawn to the discourses offered to them will discover that emotion is the main means of attraction. Discourses that touch the heart, that invoke a supposed communal unity, that relate an often idealized history of Islamic civilization, that "prove" the greatness of Islam through a routine criticism of the West . . . and people's hearts and minds are transported for an hour or so. The truth is saved: we are right, the other side is wrong. There is a patent lack of self-criticism every day, and in the minds of many Muslims "to criticize a Muslim is to criticize Islam," or, even more seriously, "to play the game of the enemy—the West." This skin-deep emotiveness has caused a whole swathe of Muslim communities, in the West as in the East, to lose the faculty of critical response and awareness of the Prophetic tradition we have already referred to: "Help your brother whether he is unjust or the victim of injustice." One of the Companions asked: "Messenger of God, I understand helping someone who is the victim of injustice, but how should I help one who is unjust?" The Prophet replied: "Prevent him from being unjust. That is how you will help him."[6] To look critically and constructively at the action of one's brother in religion or one's community is a requirement of faith, and self-criticism serves the interest, and above all the dignity, of those who attempt it without complacency or exaggeration.[7] It is this critical and self-critical awareness—and its daring to express itself—that is largely lacking in Western Muslim communities.

The sum total of these deficits explains why Muslim discourse in the West today finds it so difficult to be clearly expressed and heard. Much has evolved, as we have seen, but there is much to do. Some immediate objectives clearly arise from this exposition, but it is less easy to set out clear steps by which these objectives may be attained in the longer term. The next section introduces some ideas about this, but it is actually the whole of part II that will shed light on the priorities and concrete stages that will enable us to realize them.

General Objectives

Between the idealism of the principles of the Way and the difficulties of daily life in the West, Muslims owe it to themselves to awaken their faith and their intellect in order to put forward rational and reasonable solutions to the challenges they face. It is also necessary that the injunctions of Islam, with its universality as well as its flexibility and its ability to adapt to times and places, be understood by the majority of Muslims. There is no doubt that this should be the first objective of Western Muslim communities: to disseminate a serious understanding of the Islamic universe of reference, with priority given to teaching ulama, intellectuals, and leaders of organizations. The enthusiasm we have already referred to and consider to be one of the basic assets of the Muslim presence in the West would make it possible for this work to be done effectively. A number of increasingly significant Muslim organizations and institutions are already at work, but it will be necessary to organize this work more effectively. Eventually, a university-style program should emerge in all the Western countries that would be authentically anchored in the Islamic tradition while being in step both with the communities living in Europe and North America and with the realities of their respective environments.

At the present time, it is already possible within the various communities to set up an Islamic educational program that is both demanding and open, respectful of traditions and progressive—in short, a "reformist Islam" that follows the guidance of the Prophetic tradition that we have already referred to and that told us to renew our reading of it in history. Intercommunal dialogue must be established quickly and in depth with all the partners who have a desire for it, and they are many. On the local level, it is already possible to engage in fruitful internal dialogue by avoiding three areas that are unavoidable sources of division: the historical preeminence of one or another train of thought over others, and, above all, leadership and money. The wisest way to begin a dialogue is by concentrating on teaching and on limited shared projects, by collaborating and by achieving at least mutual recognition of the other's right to exist. In some cases, collaboration has even led to a change of direction in the involvement of the parties in order to encourage a healthy complementarity rather than insidious competition.

This endogenous dynamic needs time and patience because it naturally follows the slow rhythm of mentality change. The program therefore requires the development of a calm and confident self-image; this is why it is necessary to construct the future by building on the assets we have spoken of and their inherent dynamics, spreading an adapted program of education while articulating clearly and very audibly a discourse on the necessity of entering fully into citizenship. The emergence of a new Islamic consciousness, Islamically educated and rooted in an assured and active citizenship, embracing women as well as men, will by its nature lead to the development of an increasingly detailed and articulated Islamic discourse, whose objective is to speak out and be understood, not to please and simply be tolerated. In the meantime, Muslims should demand more than toleration. An individual may be tolerated while being ignored. The basic purpose is to achieve respect: one truly respects others only by seeing them and by having an exchange with them through the development of better mutual understanding. Our differences, known and admitted, should call us, which is why Western Muslims must normalize their presence without trivializing it. In every area of life, when they try to find solutions that will make it possible for them to live true to their principles, they can show their fellow-citizens that there are perhaps other ways, and that in any case one must search and never give up but always press on and try with all one's being to build what is to be, to strive for the ideal. At the heart of this interaction, Muslims will inevitably find the universal dimensions of their message and try to bear witness to them. Priority must be given to achieving this opening up of minds and hearts: to be oneself not in opposition to the Other but alongside him, with him, dealing with our differences in active proximity, not in the isolated corners of our intellectual and social ghettos.

With an assured faith, firm teaching, and active dialogue both within and outside their communities, Muslims will acquire a self-awareness that is anything but shriveled and nervous. The critical, and sometimes self-critical, spirit that will be born of this multidimensional process will allow them to become assured as people who know what they hold (a universal message), have a sense of the purpose of life (to travel toward and be faithful to the Source), are aware of their responsibility (to be faithful to the original covenant), and, finally, seek to make their lives a sign, a gift, an enrichment (the meaning of bearing witness).

Contribution

Perhaps that is how this first part should end. So many demands have been made on Muslims to adapt, to integrate, even to be assimilated, that some of them have finally lost even the thought that they could bring something to their society. If Western society has, without any question, positively driven Muslims to reread their sources, to awaken their minds, and to revitalize their imaginations, it must also be said that their presence is, in itself, an enrichment, and we sometimes struggle to remember this in North America and Europe.

Communities of several million souls, of whom a very large number are devoted to faith in God, to spirituality, and to the values of life, justice, and human solidarity, cannot but do good in societies where the consumerist temptation sometimes seems to have taken precedence over every other consideration. When people see alongside them men and women who pray five times a day, are committed to promoting the value of education, control their consumption to the extent of fasting for one-twelfth of each year, avoid alcohol and its excesses, and against all the odds develop strong family and community ties, it cannot all count for nothing. For believers, as for aware humanists, this presence is a testimony and an enrichment. Honesty requires that we say and recognize it.

On a more global level, this presence of Muslims at the heart of Western societies is beginning to make it possible for the citizens of Europe and North America to live in fact the pluralism they often claim to respect in theory. Northern societies are no longer homogeneous, for the population is now made up of individuals who have very different histories, religions, and cultures. We must very quickly take these realities into account, not only at the level of simple discussions about good and tolerant intentions[8] but also at a deeper level in our history and geography syllabuses in dealing with questions about the origin and make-up of nations. The civilizational and cultural richness of the countries of origin and the relations that have existed with them (sometimes based on equal collaboration, sometimes on colonialism or enslavement, often on economic exploitation)—all this must be taken into account from now on if we really want to build the pluralist societies that we call for with our votes.

The Muslim presence, if it stays consistent with itself, is also a reminder of the South. Arriving in Europe and North America as economic or political exiles, immigrants both old and new bear the two stigmas of murderous poverty and ravaging dictatorships. For their fellow-citizens, those Muslim citizens who are the most actively engaged also bear a message about humanity: we cannot extol democracy for ourselves and silently allow our governments to deal with the most sinister dictators. We cannot want peace and denounce violence and at the same time stand passive before the most fearful and deadly terror of an economic order that is responsible for the deaths of forty thousand people every day. We cannot. If Muslims, nourished by their faith, clothed in their values, and enlivened by their awareness of justice, can make it possible for their fellow-citizens to have access to a living and active spirituality, a demanding ethic of solidarity, coming with a real sense of the difference and the awareness of the South to call for economic and political equality, then their presence is an enrichment and a gift. It will challenge, it may even disturb, and in that there is, in some sense, a benefit. As expressed in the words of an American intellectual, "I do not only want my difference to be respected by you. I want it to bother you." It seems to me that both are necessary, and this is really the meaning of our phrase "*normalize our presence without trivializing it.*" Normalization can exist only when there is respect for never becoming "trivial," that is, for continuing to be a witness in all circumstances to the meaning of life, values, and justice, and, when consciences are about to fall asleep and give up, to bother them, niggle them, perturb them. Out of this bother and disturbance positive lessons can always be drawn.

Part II

The Meaning of Engagement

Taking as the starting point the Islamic world of reference presented in part I, I am going to try to present here some perspectives on the future of Muslims in the West. My concern, as I have said, is to try to stay within the "Path to faithfulness" while taking into account all the dimensions and criteria related to our life in modern societies. The Islamic message, with its double nature, both comprehensive and universal, requires that our minds find solutions that allow us both to remain consistent with the essential axis of our being (which is the sense of *tawhid*) and to live in step with our times and our societies.

This search for solutions and the multidimensional engagement of Muslims with the aim of applying concretely the teachings of the "Path to faithfulness" require a *constant and balanced effort*, for which Arabic uses the term *jihad*. The Way, *al-Sharia*, which as we have defined it, is the path toward justice, demands individual and collective efforts, *jihads*, to be made at various levels and in various areas. On the intimate level, it is working on one's self, mastering one's egoisms and one's own violence; on the social level, it is the struggle for greater justice and against various kinds of discrimination, unemployment, and racism; on the political level, it is the defense of civil responsibilities and rights and the promotion of pluralism, freedom of expression, and the democratic processes; on the economic level, it is action against speculation, monopolies, and neocolonialism; on the cultural level, it is the promotion of the arts and forms of expression that respect the dignity of conscience and human values. These are the *jihad*s to be carried out in the name of active and responsible citizenship—*jihad*s that are spiritual as well as social, economic, political, and ecological, that reconcile Muslim participants in Western societies with the deep meaning of Islamic terminology. The global understanding of the meaning of *sharia* as a Way toward justice opens up the new and demanding horizon of *civil jihad.*

The first area of our engagement takes place inwardly: there can be no harmony with the environment without a search for inner peace, though this is not restricted to the aloneness of being. It should, as we shall see in chapter 5, radiate out to all the areas of life. The Islamic teaching on spirituality is, in this sense, very demanding, for it requires the individual to maintain a spirituality that is *responsible, active*, and, above all, *intelligent*. We shall come back to this. Western ways of life make it particularly necessary to begin with this interior dimension. To build our vision of the future and to try to establish its essential aims and priorities also requires that we give thought to some key areas such as education, social and political participation, interreligious dialogue, and alternative cultural and economic models. We shall try to sketch the broad principles of a coherent plan of action in each of these areas so that, by the end of this study, we shall be able to outline a project, a *vision* for Western Muslims. Obviously, we shall draw only the general framework of an approach for the Western environment, which presents certain general characteristics; the concrete plan of action must take into account the specifics of each country and do so at several levels. Each country's history, institutions, memory, psychology, culture, language, social fabric, and political system are all data that must be considered if the establishment process is to succeed. We certainly cannot, in this study, refer in detail to each country, and we shall restrict ourselves to suggesting, on the basis of the characteristics that Western societies have in common, a way forward that will then require thought, given the objective realities of the respective countries.

To begin with, let us summarize some of the fundamental teachings considered in part I that we shall need to draw on constantly in our discussion of the various subjects we shall deal with. The Muslim consciousness, with its faith in God, is linked to *tawhid* by the *shahada* (the declaration of faith that testifies to the fact of *being Muslim*) and refers for its authority to the two "books"—one created (the universe) and the other revealed (the Revelation)—as well as the Prophetic tradition (the Sunna), in order better to proceed on "the path to the source," "the Way of faithfulness," *al-Sharia*, which makes it possible to find out *how to become and remain Muslim*. The activity of reason, which extrapolates from the sources universal principles and primary and secondary regulations, enables us to differentiate between the various fields and methodologies: if the area of religious rite and practice and the area of creed (*al-aqida*), with a certain number of related injunctions, are fixed and essentially unchangeable, there is still a vast area open to human reasoning and creativity. Knowledge of the context and the ability to analyze and to innovate are the key words here. And, in this second part, we shall go to the heart of this area. The scriptural sources, as well as scholarly works, teach us that we have tools at our disposal to help us take up the challenges we inevitably face in the course of history: the evaluation of *maslaha*, the practice of *ijtihad*, and the formulation of detailed *fatawa*. This understanding of fundamental principles and the use of tools for contextualization must be firmly grasped, for they are an essential part of a comprehensive approach that draws on the "principle of integration": all that is not in opposition to an Islamic principle (or a recognized prohibition) on the level of human and social affairs is to be considered Islamic. We have seen that on the social, cultural, and scientific levels, this approach is in direct contradiction with all the binary formulations: the spirit (which is good) against the body (which is bad); one society or culture (where all is good) against another (where all is bad); some sciences (the Islamic ones) against others (the non-Islamic ones), and so on. Using the model of the pilgrimage during which women and men circumambulate the "House of God" (the Kaba), which is the center (the *axis mundi*), everything in Islam seems to take the shape of this paradigmatic image: Muslim identity and the order of the world, as well as the representation of the various sciences of knowledge, are all reflections of this image. If life leads us unmistakably outward, our responsibility is at all times to keep the connection of faith, witness, and ethics with the center, the source. This path, which leads out from the source, leads us on a long journey and then back to the source; this "path toward the source" is the way of spirituality and mysticism: it is the heart of that awareness of the finiteness of life that, if we keep the recollection of it alive in us, brings us back to the meaning of our birth. But, if we forget it, death will always lead us back to the state in which we were before we existed: wherever we go, we shall return, and Muslim tradition calls us to live this experience daily.

5

SPIRITUALITY AND EMOTIONS

In most Western countries, people no longer like to speak much of "religion" (except at the difficult or symbolic moments of life): the word has developed connotations of obligation, compulsion, and sometimes, frankly, of old-fashioned fustiness. Many claim not to belong to any religion, even if they believe "in something." But the fashionable word is "spirituality," which has come to refer to a countless number of different realities, from relationship with God to simply the meaning one may give to life or to "things," including retreat from the world, the search for inner peace, overcoming the traps of the consumerist society, or even diving voluntarily and deliberately into the world of emotions. The Jewish or Christian origins have faded or simply disappeared and the idea of spirituality now covers almost everything imaginable that could "give a breath of life" or "give meaning."

In the confusion of a world of reference like this, the Muslim consciousness, without giving itself the right to stand in judgment, must make an effort to define for itself its own spirituality, its specific qualities, its demands, and its instruments. In order to avoid succumbing to fashion, confusing categories of experience, and finding only a superficial spirituality at the level of discourse, Muslims are called to carry out a real "inner work," conscious that if they lose the source at the center, they will inevitably lose their way further out. This is a statement of the importance of this subject. This is where everything begins, but it is also where everything may stall.

Want and Fashion

Our consumerist societies offer us a home, food, comfort, and free time, and we all know how important these things are if one is to live a dignified and balanced life. In fact, it is not a question of refusing the gifts of industrialized societies but of knowing how to handle them so that they do not give rise in us, at the very moment when we are becoming conscious of *having* so much, to a feeling, deep down, of not *being* at peace, or in harmony, or simply happy. The sense of "want" that is born in this situation is without doubt the most widely shared feeling in the West. It has various causes, but it seems to be summarized in the double reality of *want of time* and *want of dialogue*. The rhythms of life have become such that we have a sense of constantly drowning. It stifles us and drags us along and in the end kills in us the source of vital energy and shuts us up in a world in which we simply function. Habit and routine reinforce in us daily this feeling of unease, which may take on different hues but seems to us to lack emotion, affection, love, and, more generally, humanity. To whom do we *really* speak, who *really* understands us, how many people *really* love us? Who can answer these questions?

The French poet Arthur Rimbaud, in his poem *Les étrennes des orphelins*, describes the world of two children without a mother with this felicitous expression: "On sent dans tout cela qu'il manque quelque chose" (In all this one feels that something is missing). Doubtless he was one of those in the nineteenth century who felt most intensely the voids we are referring to, and in *Une saison en enfer*, he adds: "Ceux que j'ai rencontré ne m'ont peut-être pas *vu*" (Those I met did not *see* me, perhaps). As early as the nineteenth century and in spite of being so young, he expresses this sense of want (which our societies seem constantly to worsen), while his whole life conveyed the birth of a thirst for a solution. In the end, as he recounts, he left Europe.

Developed societies seem to offer us only two choices by which to overcome unease: either to dive into the most intense feelings and emotions, which, even if they are not always real or deep, do give us the sense that we exist, or to go into a sort of exile, which, whether for an hour or a lifetime, takes us away from the world to live inwardly, in psychological or mystical introspection and meditation, listening for one's self, one's being, and/or one's feelings. Though many have become expert at the first option, people who speak of a "spirituality" as distinct from religion often today turn toward the second. It consists of a kind of retreat and distancing from the rhythm of daily life, taking time and giving meaning to things. The secularization of societies has caused a rise in this phenomenon, and people find a great need to be grounded at the private and intimate levels, far from the hubbub of public life.

This retreat-spirituality is today felt to be a necessity, a need, and it sometimes takes the form of not very well considered types of "consumption." Some people practice exotic forms of yoga without really studying or understanding it, others get involved in sugar-coated varieties of Buddhism adapted to their "need for a break," yet others choose undemanding types of Sufism that help them to escape from themselves without hindrance, rather than helping them find themselves by exertion. Some essentially psychological techniques, even treatment by psychoanalysis, are also suggested to help people live "more inwardly," develop "emotional intelligence," or achieve more self-control. The "spiritual" life is often confused with techniques that enable one to find a balance between living out one's emotions and desires to the full and developing in oneself the means to control them.

In fact, these practices often are only superficially associated with long-established and authentic spiritual teachings such as Buddhism, which are, by contrast, built on rigorous disciplined work, control of desires, and denunciation of the "I," which is the object of this spiritual project. Muslim mysticism shares the demanding nature and in-depth work on the "I" of these Far Eastern traditions. But, at the present time, we are witnessing the spread of a curious understanding of Sufism, whose main characteristic is above all that of an individual and private enterprise[1] but one that is basically almost entirely lacking in the very strict methods of initiation into approaching and knowing the Transcendent (*marifat Allah*). There is emphasis on the remembrance of God (*dhikr*), on withdrawing from the world, and, above all, on a semi-invisible practice. Even more serious, in the minds of some, following Sufism ("another Islam," an Islam said to be "enlightened") means less practice and ritual, although the great tradition is to require very demanding spiritual exercises of the initiates (*murid*s). The former endlessly reduce the practice, while the latter have nothing to do but augment and increase it, so important is it that the "wanderer" be aware of his special calling through his efforts (*jihad al-nafs*) and testing (*ibtila*).

In fact, Muslim spirituality has nothing in common with these trends and fashions, and neither is it a simple exercise in managing the emotions. It requires awareness, discipline, and constant effort (*jihad*), because it is the expression of a returning to one's self, which should be a liberation. Today, at the very heart of Western societies, this exercise is a test.

Self-Liberation

We have seen in part I that, according to the Muslim tradition, God in His oneness (*tawhid al-rububiyya*) put into the heart of each human being an original breath, a natural longing (*fitra*) for the Transcendent, for Him. Muslim spirituality is the work the consciousness of the believer does on the self in order to be liberated from all forms of worship of things other than the Transcendent and to find the way to this original breath and its purity. This way toward the One (*tawhid al-uluhiyya*) is difficult and demanding, because human nature also tends to be drawn to the contingent realities of the world. Caught between longing for the Most High and the attraction of the world, the believer's first experience of awareness is of facing an internal conflict. The choice is between liberating one's self or losing one's self and drowning in the vicissitudes of life. The Revelation tells us: "By the *soul in the body* (*al-nafs*) and what has balanced it (given it form) and inspired [both] its licentiousness and its intimate sense of God (its piety). He who purifies it will certainly be happy and he who corrupts it will certainly be lost (crushed)."[2] Doubly inspired, consciousness is free and must make a choice: even though the appearance of faith seems beautiful and naturally attractive in its intimacy—"God has made you love faith and has beautified it in your heart"[3]—this same intimacy may also drive one toward evil: "The *soul in the body* (*al-nafs*) certainly directs (commands you) to evil,"[4] and the world calls one to follow the same way: "The love of desires and pleasures (sexuality, offspring, and money) have been beautified in human eyes."[5] Caught between these two currents, these two postulations, to use Baudelaire's expression, conscience must make a decision and act. With the first deep awareness of the conflict, the need for constant effort must immediately be impressed on the consciousness of the believer. To return to God, to choose good, to turn one's life to face the light, is a real *jihad* in the most absolute sense of the word: the effort that has as its aim to overcome the interior conflict in order to lead the being into peace.[6]

Islamic teaching has given us concrete tools to help us succeed in this work on ourselves and to arrive at balance. In the West, as in the East, to lose them is the same as to lose oneself. Closeness to the Most High and liberation from all sorts of idolatry, whether material or nonmaterial, are not to be confused with maintaining "spiritualizing" emotions, disordered exiles where one may live "sometimes for a few hours," or retreats "to try to get one's bearings." They have nothing to do with it. The daily requirements of Muslim practice give us the direction and the first steps along the way to this freedom. Awareness of the Presence and of the closeness of the Very Near One moves toward the center, the heart of the same community of faith, through the five daily meetings in prayer, the weekly gathering of that community of faith, the purifying tax on one's possessions (*zakat*), the fasting for a full month of the year, and the making of the pilgrimage once in a lifetime (if one has the means). By meditating on these requirements, we discover that they really are demanding and operate on several levels: on the memory (for people are so inclined to forget); on the management of time (the daily rhythm of prayers and other practices throughout the year); on the individual and communal aspects of being before God (communal prayer, giving *zakat*, and so on); and on the division of efforts among the various elements that constitute the human being (heart, spirit, body, possessions). The "comprehensive character of the message of Islam," of which we spoke in part I, is already etched in this elementary level of practice: to be with God is to come back to oneself, manage one's time, control one's love of possessions, develop concern for others, and know how to relativize attachment to one's roots if they are a hindrance to faithfulness.

The lack of spirituality and inner balance that may be felt in the West as well as in the East is, according to Islamic teaching, completely natural if one lives far from the original spark, on the margins of one's being, especially if one does not have a daily and holistic practice of faithfulness to the source. All the principles that we have referred to in part I are concentrated here to direct human beings and to urge them to engage concretely and regularly in the practice of this deep, responsible, and active spirituality. This is the surest way to become free of desires, however well nourished one may have become in one's prisons or in the worship of the idols of ancient and modern times—money, sexuality, consumption, appearance, social status, power. There can be no worthy liberty without clear and constant effort.

But this is not all. At the heart of the West, whose rhythms of life and myriad opportunities for diversion may unsettle even the strongest determination, practice may become a mechanical ritual, lifeless and without spirituality. Memory repeats the invocations and prayers, the lips say the words, the body goes through the motions, the hand gives, but the soul is absent. The ritual is not enough: life must be liberated. The Revelation tells us that our existence should be a constant watchfulness, a continual reading of the Creator's signs. Before our eyes, the natural practice of active spirituality comes through observing the universe and deeply contemplating its signs.[7] "The sun and the moon move in calculated patterns, and the star and the tree bow down in worship."[8] The world speaks to the mind (the calculated patterns) as much as to the heart, to which it reveals its secrets (the bowing down of the elements). Malik Badri is right to point out that this exercise of contemplation works like therapy, insofar as the Muslim does it in remembrance of God. In the same way, to read the written Revelation and to meditate on it are natural ways of arousing the consciousness and infusing it with continuous spiritual energy.[9] So one must develop a way of reading the world to keep the breath alive in one: this exercise then passes into the heart of life, into the daily round cycle. We could say that we need to get used to the unusual, to the breaking point that gives meaning: it is through this breaking point that we move from habit to worship (*min al-ada ila al-ibada*).

So, at the magical moment of sunset: "In the creation of the heavens and the earth and the succession of nights and days there are signs for those who contemplate."[10] The remembrance of this sign, buried in habit, made the Prophet weep for a whole night.

The heart of the message of Islam is that a living spirituality comes at the price of willingly making the effort to come back to what is essential, to contemplate the world and to take the road back toward one's self. In the daily practice, alongside the "book," the Creator has given human beings a model in the person of the Prophet. "His character was the Qur'an," said his wife, Aisha, and he was "like a Qur'an walking on earth." He was the concrete embodiment of the teachings, and his tradition calls us to love him and live close to his memory, his life, his actions, and his silences. The intensity of spirituality can be measured by comparison with the intensity of the presence of the model in each person's heart and life. In Europe and in North America, Islam is still the natural religion of the "books" and the model. It calls for a certain way of being in the world, of contemplating it, of being aware of one's memory, of time, of one's body, of one's behavior and one's actions, and trying as much as possible to live with God "as if one sees Him" and with the Prophet as if one were in his company.

The Prayer of the Mind

Muslim spirituality, as we have said, is demanding and, through the Islamic teaching, touches all the dimensions of life. It begins, at the very moment when one becomes aware of one's human responsibilities before God and among humanity, by finding in oneself "the need of Him" to which we have referred in part I. The return to one's self gives birth to a feeling of humility that characterizes the human being before God. This humility should spread wide and deep through all the areas of life: at every stage of working on one's self there will be a struggle against complacency, pride, and the pretentious human desire to succeed alone, using one's own resources (on the social, professional, political, or intellectual level). This truly spiritual exercise goes beyond the framework of ritual religious practice or rare moments of contemplation, and its effect should be visible in every aspect of life—in the way in which one treats one's body, manages one's possessions, carries out one's professional activities, lives with other people, and interacts with the whole of creation: in everything, those who reflect on the signs and are indwelt by "the need of Him" are invited to distance themselves from forgetfulness and arrogance. In the West, practicing Muslims live uncomfortably with the disjuncture they feel between their religious and spiritual practice and the type of public or professional life into which they are drawn. Theoretical discussion about "the comprehensive character" of the message of Islam struggles to come alive in practice; it is here that a rupture takes place, and people almost lead two parallel existences—one their spiritual practice and the other their active life. People do not understand very well how to make their spirituality truly active and effective in everyday areas. The environment these days seems to impose on us this division between private practice and entry into the public arena. The opposition between them seems complete. The beginnings of a response to this are to be found in what we have just described: indwelt by "the need of Him," strong in that humility in action and at the heart of professional and social life, the Muslim consciousness should build a reciprocity between the state of the heart and the nature of one's acts. The link, the connection between them must be intimate and personal: it is expressed in the way in which our action is inspired, lived, and undertaken—in the recollection of His presence or in forgetting it, in the sight of God or only of human beings, to please Him or to impress them, to be recognized by His love or only to be recognized by them? This is how active spirituality is expressed, and the division between public and private space in secularized societies does not prevent its being exercised, so that our spirituality is able in all circumstances to inspire our way of being and doing.[11]

To this state of recollection and humility must be added another concrete dimension of spiritual teaching that requires the establishment of a constant link between the demands of conscience and life choices. As we have already intimated in part I, it is a matter of ethical teaching and its application. To ask ourselves, in every situation in life, the three fundamental questions (What is my intention in this action? What are the limits set down by my morality? What will be the consequences of the action?) will inevitably change not only our way of being but also our way of living. Our spirituality must be intelligent and question the ethical nature of all our activities, even those that appear to be the most natural and simple. This active, intelligent spirituality makes us attentive to the apparently "neutral" aspects of our life, which may sometimes have serious ethical consequence. It questions our approach to consumption: the source of the food, the way it was produced, the fairness of the commercial aspect, the way in which animals used for food are treated and killed,[12] and the social and economic implications of our consumption. We need to be more and more, and more and more deeply, aware of all these questions: the way in which we answer them transforms spiritual energy, too often shut up in ritual and sometimes imprisoned by a practice that has become mechanical, into a radiant, responsible, active, and intelligent spirituality. If the message of Islam really does have a comprehensive quality, its spiritual message must extend to the horizon where the feeling of humility and the demands of ethics marry in action. The same applies in the exercise of one's profession: to ask the same three questions means never to consider that any work is ethically "neutral," however scientific it may appear to be. To work for a multinational that plunders the planet, or in an armaments industry that produces death, or for banks that fuel a murderous economic order is not "to say nothing." And beyond these basic questions, the way in which one goes about one's work, and identifies with it and carries out one's responsibilities to perform the activity and to follow the rules in the best possible way, is an active and consequential spiritual undertaking with which everyone's conscience must engage. The same can be said of the way we spend our free time and enjoy ourselves. To retain one's humanity and dignity at times of rest is a sign of a lived and serious spirituality. The Prophet said to his Companion Handhala, who felt himself to be a hypocrite because he was not in a sort of permanent state of prayer, that he should match an hour of prayer with an hour of rest: he was implying that the quality of that rest would necessarily influence the spiritual intensity of his prayer. In the West, more than anywhere else, *the use we make of free time and entertainment is a spiritual exercise* that helps keep us in harmony. This comprehensive and multidimensional activity is bound to influence relations between human beings. At the heart of the community of faith, the practice of this spirituality should be *visible*. To foster humility in oneself and to keep one's ethical awareness alive naturally means being attentive to human relations, even in their smallest details. This life, led with the constant intention to be in dialogue with God and with oneself, should lead us to learn to listen and to be in dialogue with others. The calls to brotherhood, solidarity, and companionship are all facets of the spirituality of daily life. Here again, we have to be spiritually responsible, active, and intelligent in learning to make the fundamental distinction between judging an action and judging an individual, between condemning a gesture and condemning a heart. We must have the clarity to engage in the first but resist the temptation of the second. This way of being among people can be achieved only by working at allowing spiritual and ethical teaching to radiate into all our areas of activity. This would naturally reform the kinds of relations that we too often see at work within Muslim communities—relations based on judgment and rejection of the Other, competition, and power struggles. There is little listening, little dialogue, little affective silence: Muslims know this, as they should know that there are not innumerable remedies.

We should add, to end this chapter, that on a broader plane, the spiritual teaching of Islam makes us open to human universality and by its nature creates bridges with men and women of other faiths, and even with all the humanists, agnostics, and atheists who are concerned about human values, ethics, and respect for the universe. There is no doubt that many people, without being Muslims, will recognize themselves in the preceding lines, and it is on the basis of these fundamental considerations that we should try to engage in dialogue and shared action. At this depth, encounter is possible and fruitful, and our societies show us every day that involvement *together* is essential.

Far from fashions and temptations to reclusiveness, we have tried here to describe the demanding characteristics of Muslim spirituality. It radiates out from the axis of *tawhid* and calls human beings, in addition to their religious practice and meditation, to allow the light of the sense of His Presence and His moral precepts to shine on all their areas of activity. This spirituality, which we have called responsible, active, and intelligent, inspires awareness at the heart of life and society and offers itself as an everyday mysticism, an applied Sufism, which leads individuals to learn to manage the direction and content of their actions rather than simply to be acted upon. Humility, which feeds the heart, as well as ethics, which directs the spirit, both make it possible for the mind to be open to another order, a kind of continuous prayer, in which, aware of its limitations, it serves goodness as well as it can—the prayer of the mind.

Many women and men today are leaving the Islamic associations because they reach a point where they feel that something is missing, that there is a real lack of spirituality. This is often the case, and it is by a renewed and constant effort to apply the teachings we have just referred to that things will change. It will not always be a case of deciding to go it alone—all the more given that so many present their humble retreats with such pride and arrogance! On the contrary, Muslim spirituality teaches us fragility, effort, and service: to be with God is to recognize one's limitations, know them, and serve people, among people.

6

TOWARD A REFORM OF
ISLAMIC EDUCATION

At the heart of every family, in every organization, and in Western Muslim communities generally, the same concern and fear are expressed about passing on Islamic values to the children. How can the flame of faith, the light of the spiritual life, and faithfulness to the teachings of Islam be preserved in environments that no longer refer to God and in educational systems that have little to say about religion? Every mother and father who cares about faith are sooner or later confronted by this difficult question. The first generations of migrants, who were frequently families of limited means, were often astonishingly successful at transmitting the faith: without having much religious knowledge to speak of, they transmitted to their children an intuitive understanding of and a respect for faith. They came from countries where God was everywhere referred to—in the vocabulary and in daily life—and, sometimes unconsciously underestimating their influence, they were able to keep the connection so that "the sense of God" passed into their children's consciousness. It is the second generations that have expressed the need to know more, feeling the need to move on from feeling alone to real knowledge. The more educated immigrants quickly understood that there was a need to put structures of "Islamic education" in place for the young. They were naturally inspired by what they had known and experienced in their countries of origin, where the Qur'an, the Prophetic traditions (*ahadith*), the life of the Prophet (*sira*), and something about law and jurisprudence related to religious regulations (*fiqh al-ibadat*) were taught. Classes in Arabic and religion began to be organized in mosques, and *madrasa*-type patterns began to appear in Western Muslim communities, especially among Indo-Pakistanis. These informal structures, which essentially operated on the weekends (and sometimes on Wednesdays and in the evenings), played a decisive role in the first decades of Muslim settlement. With time, more elaborate structures were established, up to the level of Islamic private schools, which have now become widespread, in response to a more and more acute need.

Nevertheless, the impression remains, and is confirmed by numerous indicators, that Islamic education in Western societies needs more effective input and that the solutions being proposed today, even though they may be more or less satisfying for very small minorities within the communities, fall very far short of responding to the needs of most Muslims. The dissatisfaction is of several kinds: although the Islamic message is universal and "comprehensive," and although it should provide the tools everyone needs to face the challenges of the environment, what is now called "Islamic education" is confined to the very technical memorization of Qur'anic verses, Prophetic traditions, and rules without a real spiritual dimension. The learning of ritual spills over into mechanical ritualism, and the teaching that is offered is completely unconnected to American and European realities. It is as if the children still live "there," and if one refers to "here," it is above all to emphasize the defiance that the young should feel toward a society that is not ours, or theirs. So we find in this education the two failings against which the Islamic message has warned us and to which we have referred in part I: the reduction of spirituality to ritual technicalities, and the adoption of a dualistic and Manichean approach based on "us" as opposed to "them." This extends even to the life of the Prophet (in which one might have hoped for a human approach), which is reduced to a series of dates and events without real substance: one would have liked the young to love the "model," but he has been almost completely dehumanized by the content of the teaching.

The educational methods are not much better. While the public school system teaches children to express themselves, give their opinions, and articulate their doubts and hopes, the exact opposite is found in some mosques and Islamic organizations. Here, one must be quiet and listen; there is no room for discussion, exchange, or debate. Many young people are asked to cope with a sort of double personality, an unhealthy schizophrenia, in which they learn to express themselves on every subject with "non-Muslims" and become dumb (by giving the appearance of "religiously" respecting everything they are told) when it comes to speaking about Islam or interacting with their religious teachers. They play the game of an education that has in fact lost its way. If we consider what is usually offered today to generations of young Muslims in the West, we become convinced that what is called "education" (which should be the passing on of knowledge and of knowing how to be) is in fact an ill-administered "instruction," simply a handing on of knowledge based on principles, rules, obligations, and prohibitions, often presented in a cold, rigid, and austere manner, without soul or humanity. Some young people know by heart long *suras* (chapters) of the Qur'an and a dizzying number of verses and *hadiths* that have absolutely no impact on their daily behavior; on the contrary, inevitably, they have taken on the outward form but have no contact with the base. Furthermore, young Muslims are very often taught to fix their "differentness" by means of a critical and deprecatory discourse vis-à-vis the "Other," the Westerner, whom "they must never resemble." This outward value, fed during the weekend by the encouragement of a feeling of absolute Otherness, changes during the week in everyday life, precisely through contact with this "Other," into an uneasiness and an inferiority complex almost impossible to live with. Eventually, the religious and spiritual education that is provided and that should give the young and the not so young the means to confront the challenges of their society pushes them along one of three avenues: to pretend, to lose themselves in silence, or to reject everything and rebel. There are certainly many exceptions, which are evidence of remarkable successes (which should therefore be studied), and we have elsewhere pointed out how much Muslims owe to the educational structures that were put in place in the beginning, but we must nevertheless look reality in the face and think of steps that can be taken toward an in-depth reform.

Meaning and Content

Before beginning a presentation of some concrete and realistic proposals, we should ask how we can discover the basic meaning and content of this "Islamic education," which we keep referring to without explaining exactly what we mean. If the objective is indeed to stop importing pedagogical methods and curricula from the countries of origin and to think of a project adapted to the realities of our societies, we still need to know the aims of this education.

The sum of the reflection we presented in part I gives us substantial help. The heart of the Islamic message rests on the affirmation of faith in God and the diffusion of the spirituality that this is bound to engender. To be able to acquire a healthy practice presupposes that one has some fundamental knowledge of the Qur'an and the Prophetic tradition and of the basics of ritual, law, and jurisprudence. The universality and "comprehensive character" of this message also requires a knowledge of the context in which individuals have to act in order that they may have the means to live consistently with the demands of the morality of their religion. This knowledge of the milieu must be coupled with the constant exercise of a critical spirit able to understand, select, reform, and eventually innovate in order to establish a faithful connection between the universal principles of Islam and the contingencies of the society in which Muslims live.[1]

If we consider all these elements and try to extrapolate the areas with which "Islamic education" is concerned, we might say its first objective is the education of the heart, which links the consciousness with God and should awaken us to an awareness of our responsibilities toward ourselves, our bodies, our relatives, our communities, and the human family at large. The second objective is the education of the mind, which should both be able to understand the message of the scriptural sources and develop a knowledge of the environment and the human beings who live in it in order to make it possible for reason to find the way of faithfulness in everyday life. The third objective, joining the education of the heart with the education of the mind, is to make it possible for all Muslims to enter into personal growth and, consequently to become autonomous in their lives, their choices, and, more generally, in the management of their freedom. The spiritual education that should lead individuals to a conscious awareness of "the primal need of Him" in the depths of their beings should at the same time impress in those same beings the need to be completely independent of people. Faith in God cannot justify any alienation: on the contrary, it calls, as we have seen, for an inalienable freedom and for the search for the complete liberation of heart and spirit.

This reflection on the demands of the message of Islam as we have presented it in part I has made it possible to set three fundamental objectives that give direction to Islamic education as we think of it. We may then go further and establish the content of that education. If the learning of the Qur'an, the tradition, law, and jurisprudence are fixed, according to the model proposed so far by the mosques and related organizations, we must add to it an in-depth knowledge of the environment, adapted for different age groups: mastery of the language, familiarity with the history of the country, knowledge of the institutions, study of the culture, social dynamics, and the political landscape, and so on. It is impossible to flourish independently without having the spiritual and intellectual means to discover who one is, where one lives, and how to plan one's way of faithfulness. The universality of the message of Islam is not adequately served by an intellectual hodgepodge through which students are supposed to acquire the tools they need to face the difficulties and to discover for themselves how to use them. To educate is to provide the tools that will enable individuals to grow into independence by acquiring the capability to look for personal and collective solutions. This is what must be central to the programs we are proposing for Western Muslims. The study of the environment and of people is an essential part of this learning process, and it is the only way to avoid a so-called Islamic education that is completely disconnected from reality and in total contradiction with the principles that it claims to respect. Nevertheless, it must be noted that this study of the environment and of collective psychology will inevitably press teachers into revising the way they teach the Qur'an, the Sunna, and Islam, in general. If things were the same as in the students' countries of origin, the teaching methods and the presentation of the subjects would naturally have to take into account the milieu in which the education was given. We are not talking about teaching a "new Islam," as we have said several times; it is a matter of knowing the objectives or sources and of reading them with new eyes in order to be true to ourselves in the West as in the East, today as yesterday.

Nevertheless, it is clear that the objectives and contents of what we call "Islamic education" are vast, demanding, and operative at various levels. How should we proceed? Have we even the means to achieve these objectives? Is the environment open to the success of this project, or should we redesign everything and think of a parallel school system? Some people have opted for the latter solution and created private Islamic schools; others are trying to work within the public school system. Let us study these alternatives.

Islamic Schools: The Panacea?

In order to win the struggle for a comprehensive education, many Muslims think that the only solution is the creation of private "Islamic schools," subsidized by the state almost totally, partially, or not at all, depending on the systems in force in the United States and the various countries of Europe. For people who are dissatisfied with the educational methods and curricula, and deeply mistrustful of the atmosphere in public schools, which they consider to be lacking in morality, the answer seems to be to consider a parallel system that would integrate the fundamentals of Islamic education and its moral standards with the compulsory traditional and secular subjects from the national curricula. Schools of this type have been in existence for more than twenty years in Britain, the United States, Canada, Sweden, and the Netherlands, as well as in smaller numbers in other countries. How can we assess these experiments, whose achievements in terms of methods and curricula have undergone considerable evolution in recent years?

It is the intention here not to oppose Islamic schools in principle but to note what has been attained by these institutions and what they lack. It goes without saying that offering children a body of teaching in which they have a sense of their Islamic identity through living their education in accordance with the rhythm of the daily prayers and the events of the

Muslim calendar (e.g., the Ramadan fast, the feasts), while immersing them in a school program in which their religious education—learning the Qur'an, tradition, and Arabic—is integrated has an extremely positive effect. In an Islamic school, children understand the essentials of their Muslim identity and the priorities of their upbringing through their relationships with their teachers and fellow-pupils and also acquire the tools that will help them to succeed in the other disciplines. To judge from performance indicators, most Islamic schools produce excellent statistics and are often at the top of regional and national school tables.

However, this is not the complete picture. The first comment to be made is that, taking the Muslim communities living in the West as a whole, these schools take in only a very small percentage of children, and so in this sense they can hardly be regarded as "the solution" for Islamic education in the West. Other approaches have to be found for the other children. It must also be pointed out that in most cases (those in which the schools are not heavily subsidized by the state—that is, up to 75 percent, depending on the country), only the children of affluent parents are able to enroll because fees are high, often above the very limited scholarships. And beyond these measurable realities, we should study the motivations that have often been behind the creation of these schools. In most cases, the purpose has been to protect the children from the bad influence of society, to distance them from an unhealthy environment,[2] and make them live "among Muslims." These motivations often make themselves felt in the way in which these schools are run, with their programs and educational activities all run internally. The result is that "artificially Islamic" closed spaces are created in the West that are almost completely cut off from the surrounding society. We comfort ourselves by asserting that the programs are in line with national requirements, but what is no less a reality is that these young people live in a society surrounded by adolescents who do not share their faith and whom they never meet. The school puts forward a way of life, a space, and a parallel reality that has practically no link with the society around it. Some Islamic schools are in the West but, apart from the compulsory disciplines, live in another dimension: while being not completely "here," neither are they completely from "there," and one would like the child to know who he is . . .

Moreover, teaching staff are often not well educated, and many teachers have no pedagogical background; practice in some disciplines leaves much to be desired. The Arabic language, for example, is taught by women and men who know the language but are not always adequately trained.

With regard to Islamic teaching properly so called, there are some questions worth asking. By adding "Islamic" disciplines (e.g., learning the Qur'an and the traditions) and teaching them in the classical manner (that is to say, usually as it is done "there"), do we really give the pupils the tools they need to live here, pious, self-fulfilled, and aware of their respon-sibilities? After more than twenty years of experiment, it is well worth asking the question. A scattering of Islamic teachings, verses learned by heart, and values idealistically passed on do not necessarily forge a per-sonality whose faith is deep, whose consciousness is alert, and whose mind is active and critical. It is no argument to quote school performance indi-cators in self-satisfaction: the "success" of an Islamic school cannot be measured by success on examinations. If that were the measure, there would be no place for putting so much effort into these projects: it would be enough to look to the "good" public schools. The legitimacy of an Islamic school should be evaluated by its ability to respond to the compre-hensive objectives we have spoken of in the previous section and to provide syllabuses coherent with them. In most cases, we are still far from having achieved even a small part of these aims, and some schools continue to serve up an education that pushes children toward the development of two contradictory personalities—one within a school that tries to provide a happy environment and where Islamic teaching and behavior have been inculcated, and the other outside school, where they end up getting lost without knowing how to use ethical references to establish their own eth-ical guideposts because they have not really been prepared to face life in society and to interact with others in it. Having been given a solid edu-cation in an artificial environment, the students are deeply fragile in real life: how many young people live torn between the two, how many feel "bad" or "guilty" because, having received so much knowledge at school, they feel unworthy because of not knowing how to live an integrated everyday life? Whose fault is it? They have often been instructed in the ideal, but they feel so ill educated and ill equipped in the real world.

Even if we have not yet found an "Islamic" alternative to the crisis of educational systems in the West, we must still refer to some interesting developments and initiatives: a few Islamic schools (a small minority), par-ticularly in Britain, Sweden, and the United States, have been founded in a totally new spirit. They are open to qualified teachers of any origin and are thought of as inner-city schools, so it is not enough for them to pass on ossified Islamic teachings in a protected, artificial environment. They are in touch with the outside and, through a variety of activities, make it possible for their pupils to get a better grasp of their surroundings and to interact with children of the same age and with their fellow-citizens and to put their ethical teaching into practice through visible acts of solidarity grounded in the society in which they live. Their programs have gone through a considerable evolution and allow for more contextualized teach-ing in step with society and with a culture that is Western and not im-ported from the East. These developments are extremely interesting and permit us to think that Islamic schools will be able to provide part of the solution to the problem of Islamic education in the West, if they avoid the mistakes we have mentioned and rise to the criteria of openness, contextualization, and interaction with the surrounding society. It is a long road, because mind-sets still have to undergo a fairly complete evolution: we often feel inclined to discourage some projects to establish Islamic schools because they are so far from a spirit of openness and are not ready to reform and encourage development in the field of education, where too many Muslims behave rigidly and self-consciously and hide behind copying old models (*taqlid*) to prove their faithfulness to principles. But, as we have seen, there is a great difference between historical models and universal principles, and today everything is proving that the formalistic imitation of models in an age other than one's own is in fact the betrayal of principles. In the area of education, this has serious consequences. The investment of time and money involved in establishing an Islamic school is huge, and often it affects only a few hundred children at most. Can these astronomical sums not be used to affect more children? Should we not be more creative in suggesting new initiatives? As I have said before, this is not to oppose the idea of Islamic schools in principle, but it would be better to avoid involvement in such projects if the conditions we have mentioned are not sure to be respected. And, in any case, the question remains: what is to be done for the other children?

What Are the Alternatives?

The aims and contents of a complete educational program in the West become particularly demanding as soon as one starts trying to put them together with a built-in respect for the universality and comprehensiveness of the message of Islam. It is not only a matter, as we have said before, of passing on a knowledge of the scriptural sources that will illumine the heart with faith and build the mind for an understanding of self, humankind; and creation, but it also concerns providing a very deep knowledge of the cultural and social environment, of history and human beings, and, more broadly, mastering the general disciplines and sciences that will give Muslims the means of living at home in their environment. These are the necessary prerequisites for harmony among faith, morality, reason, and life in the world. The most relevant question to ask at this point is whether Muslims in the West have the means to carry out such a program. Do they have the financial resources, and are they yet competent enough in a contextualized approach to the Islamic sources, an in-depth understanding of Western societies, and scientific developments to put forward a completely autonomous alternative educational plan, thought through from within the Western world, for the Western world? Apart from the question of deciding whether a totally separate parallel system is in itself desirable (and I think not), it is appropriate to work out whether, on the basis of their own intellectual and human resources, Muslims have the means to achieve these ambitions, as some people hope.

In our view, the most realistic approach, and the most coherent and wise one in the circumstances, would be to work on a double initiative: on the one hand to build the framework of a *complementary*, not *parallel*, educational approach and on the other hand to concentrate on establishing connections as active as possible between the education provided in the West and the overall philosophy of the Islamic message.

Most Muslim children attend public schools, which provide in most areas (though some cities suffer from clear discrimination on the educational level) a quite complete and often well-thought-out basic education. Why should we reinvent what the public system already provides? Why should we invest so much money and energy in setting up, in most subjects, the same programs with the same outcomes and leading to the same examinations? (The difference in Islamic schools is essentially the framework,[3] the rhythm, and a few additional religious subjects.) Would it not be wiser to think of an approach that proposes a "complementarity" between what society provides for all children and what Muslims want to pass on to their own? The first advantage of this plan is that it would reduce the needed financial investment and would more effectively highlight the requirements of this complementary education in terms of human resources; this would make it possible to reach a more significant number of young people. The second advantage, and actually the more important one, is that it would allow children to live, and have others alongside them, amid the ordinary realities of their society: the environment, the friends, and the moral challenges they would face would be those with which they will build their lives and their futures. The more this education is carried out in permanent interaction with, and at the heart of, a concrete situational context, the more solid (and also the more unpredictable) it will be. Finally, this type of complementary accompanying education would compel us to study in depth the society in which we live, even if only to find out what it has arrived at, and how. This is not the least of its advantages: how many parents and leaders of Islamic associations are completely uninterested in the subjects taught at school, as if they were not really very important and did not concern Muslims?

One approach, in the complementary plan, requires the exact opposite attitude and calls for involvement in the life of public schools in various ways. The first is by studying the various programs to find out what they contain and what the requisite levels of knowledge at the various stages are. This information will be essential when, later, we try to build on a complementary (religious, moral, or even civic) education that must obviously be adapted to the levels of understanding that are naturally deter-mined by the patterns established in school. Another crucial aspect is to encourage parents to be interested in school and in all facets of school life. Contact with teachers, membership on parents' committees, and partici-pation in school activities are all opportunities for understanding, entering into dialogue, and playing a real part in the education of children.[4] It is imperative that every educational project in the West strive to involve fa-thers and mothers in one way or another: Muslim associations working on setting up a complementary education for children should suggest (and sometimes require as a condition of a child's enrollment) parental atten-dance at regular meetings, activities, and evening gatherings for discussion and dialogue. We might even contemplate the establishment of a "school for parents," such as exists today in some towns, with courses that provide basic information but also socialize fathers and mothers in the area of educational concerns.

From another perspective, taking an interest in public school also in-volves taking part in the discussions on the subject that are current in society. Most educational systems in the world go through crises, and everywhere the authorities put forward structural reforms and try to adjust the programs to the evolution of societies. These questions concern all citizens and are not the prerogative of politicians and teachers. What con-cept of settlement in the West says that American and European Muslim citizens have nothing to contribute to these discussions and that they should simply be by-standers? It is vitally important to concern oneself with the place of the school in the city, the reasons for the falling status of teachers, methods of testing and selection, and the timetable and con-tents of programs. On the last point, concerning programs, for example, citizens of immigrant and/or Muslim origin should make suggestions. If one looks at history (and sometimes geography) programs, one finds that they include representations of the world that are open to debate. The history of colonialism, parents' experience of exile, the newly plural nature of Western societies, and some of the information provided about other civilizations as they are presented in most Western educational programs need some serious revision. Being interested in one's children's school also means being concerned about it. In this connection, the experience of Shabbir Mansuri, founder of the Council on Islamic Education (CIE), in California, is edifying: because he found out one day what his child was being told about her religion, he decided to devote himself body and soul to a critical study of the history and geography programs and to suggest alternative syllabuses. His thesis, which was not concerned only with the teaching of Islam and its civilization, is that it is necessary to propose a "paradigm shift" in the study of these two subjects and to revise the ex-isting Eurocentric and Western-oriented approach. He concentrated on this work, drawing on the support of a solid team of specialists, and they came up with very interesting studies on the presentation of world history, particularly concerning the Chinese, Islamic, and African civilizations. Today, thanks to the seriousness of his work, official scholarly bodies in his state and from across the country consult his organization, and editors of school textbooks submit them to him before publication. This interest in the public school system and the inevitable consequent involvement is an important prerequisite for thinking about a complementary education, because the starting point must be the realities lived by young people.

We must revise and reform our whole approach to Islamic education around the school. First, it is right to take time to listen to young people and to analyze as well as possible their expectations, needs, and difficulties. By taking into account this information, the objectives we want to attain with regard to specifically Islamic education, and the need for a balanced life (e.g., intellectual, social, athletic), it becomes possible to build a picture of a coherent complementary approach. The Islamic organizations involved in this work should, more than any others, be characterized by their strength, competence, and seriousness, because this is about working with hearts and minds, and a hodgepodge of contributions and wild experiments have grave consequences, as we have seen too often, and are completely unacceptable. The proposal to create an "after-school school" needs a lot of serious thinking at various levels, because it would be a development that must be adapted to the environment. Taking into account the children's ages, school programs, and life patterns (after listening to them), it should be possible to think about a contextualized religious education program. Apart from the traditional and essential training in learning to recite the Qur'an, the study of Qur'anic passages and commentaries on them should be related to reality, as should the presentation of the life and tradition of the Prophet. We must bring the sources alive (in the awareness of young people and adolescents) by giving priority to their dynamic and practical aspects over the simple accumulation of dry, theoretical information. The teaching of morality is deepest when it is made up of exercises based on real situations. So it is a matter not only of putting forward programs of study that are exclusively intellectual but also of supplementing this with social, cultural, and sporting activities. It is imperative that Islamic education be integrated into the dimensions of real life, at the heart of our towns, in the relationships with women, men, and nature that constitute our environment. In this way, a true "pedagogy of solidarity" can be instilled by organizing activities to support people who are sick, elderly, or disabled, and, for young people above a certain age, work with prisoners and drug addicts. Visits to political and social institutions will help build civic awareness and involve young people in the life of the city.[5] And, finally, suggesting various cultural activities in line with the Western world of reference and connected with the lived experience of the people involved will naturally show them that being a Muslim does not mean having an Eastern and permanently foreign culture but consists in coming from here and learning early on to distinguish between what is consistent with our values and what is not.[6]

Public schools already teach the basic subjects; it is for Muslims to find complementary, alternative, and original ways of providing the knowledge they judge to be essential to comply with the requirements of the message whose followers they are. In the conviction that this message is universal, they must find the means to be faithful to it in the West. It is clear that planning a series of traditional "courses" where young people sit and learn in theory the ideal principles of their religion will not do. Two two-hour sessions, held for example in the late afternoon twice a week, with an additional half-day during the weekend, should be enough over the course of a year to provide appropriate Islamic education with a series of innovative activities of the type suggested earlier.[7] Children can and should be involved in these activities, first because, having been born and now living in the same context, they know better than anyone else what young people need and how it is possible for them to interact positively with society. In addition, such a program is an excellent "school of life" experience for the students themselves, who should under no circumstances forget their duty of solidarity. If they do not have money, they have knowledge and time, which they should, like any other possession, share, give, and offer. This is exactly the meaning of the Qur'anic phrase that defines believers: "[those] who give of the gifts with which [God] has blessed them."

The Islamic associations concerned with education in the West that would like to take the path of complementary action should therefore decide who their partners are and what their human resources (school, parents, students) are; what their precise objectives are for each year; and what is the scope of activities that can be covered in a balanced fashion (religious, community, civic, cultural, and sports education),[8] keeping always in mind the need to integrate their educational project with the life of the city.[9] What is central here is to understand the crucial importance of giving a sense of worth: to educate is to give all persons a sense both of their own value and of the value of what they do. Young Muslims living in the midst of the city who are being taught to remain true to their principles and to live fully in their society must feel that that society recognizes them, respects them, and values their involvement. Acts of solidarity and community service and ethical behavior in itself are a kind of public expression that should ultimately bring them a sense of recognized worth.

At the beginning of this section, we referred to the need to establish working connections between the various educations provided in the West and the overall philosophy of the Islamic message. To be truthful, this particularly concerns university education and professional activities. Many students do not know how to find a link between the object of their study and their belonging to Islam: here, too, we seem to find a division of the personality, and we see Muslim women and men very comfortable with their academic work but suddenly ill at ease and even inconsistent when it comes to their Islamic context and the link between these two areas of their life. The same is true for many professionals, whose competence in a particular field (medicine, engineering, political science, and all kinds of manual and technical employment) feels to them completely disconnected from Islamic teaching and morality, and they regret this. The result is a double impoverishment: on the one hand, Muslim communities cannot benefit from the outstanding abilities of these students and professionals, and on the other hand, the latter, although in the midst of society and with their religious and ethical resources to draw on, have nothing original to offer in the way they use their knowledge and their talents. What is needed here is first the inculcation of a state of mind, a way of engaging with study, while bearing in mind the three major questions we have spoken of before: *What is my intention? What are the limits my tradition imposes on me with regard to the use of knowledge? What are the outcomes of the latter and of my profession?* This awareness, formed too by humility ("the need of Him" in everything), must be wedded to that fundamental precept of Islam: the service of other human beings. The Prophet said: "The best among you is he who is best for people."[10] He did not say "for Muslims" only but spoke of all people, of humankind. Here we find the basis of the universal teaching of Islam concerning the acquisition and use of knowledge, which advocates establishing a virtuous harmony among *knowledge, competence, morality,* and *gift.* Whatever subject one studies, whatever profession one follows, being true to one's principles and at the same time serving one's community and society demands that one aim for the highest levels of competence and mastery in one's field, a fine sense of the ethical boundaries in using them, and a constant concern that they be exercised for the benefit of one's society. In this way, the Muslim presence in the West can become normal without becoming trivial—not by voluntarily clinging to Otherness or by justifying difference but by offering solidarity and moral principles coupled with a confident competence in one's field. One is valued by making a visible contribution, not by being different.

The Birth of an Islamic Feminism

No chapter on the reform of Islamic education in the West would be complete without a reflection on the status of women in Muslim communities and the role that has devolved to them. We have already pointed out that numerous women of the second and later generations (not to mention many converts) have become involved in Muslim organizations, in which they play an increasing part in leadership. This does not mean to say that mentalities have always changed accordingly, and many Muslim men, and women too, submit to these developments rather than accept them. In their heart of hearts they are not convinced that "all this" is really Islamic. The issue of women is a sensitive one in almost all Western Islamic communities, and it sometimes appears that the whole question of faithfulness to Islam centers on it. Moreover, the repeated allusions and questions of our fellow-citizens, intellectuals, and the media about "women in Islam" cause a sort of psychological pressure that drives Muslims to adopt a defensive and often apologetic stance, which is not always objective. To believe that nothing in the message of Islam justifies discrimination against women is one thing; to say that they do not suffer any discrimination in Western (or Eastern) Muslim communities is another. Any look at these communities that could be called objective will reveal that we are far from the ideal of equality before God, complementarity in family and social relations, and financial independence, behind which many ulama and intellectuals hide by quoting verses and Prophetic traditions. This does not reflect the reality and to say otherwise would be a lie.

We saw in the first part that the work of categorizing methodologies in the fundamentals of law and jurisprudence (*usul al-fiqh*) taught us to differentiate between universal principles and commandments and the forms that their implementation take in a given culture. Although, as we have explained, the *principle of integration* allows us to consider as Islamic everything that does not oppose Islam, it is nevertheless erroneous and methodologically incorrect to confuse an Islamic principle a posteriori with the way it has been expressed in a given culture. It is always the principle, extrapolated and based on the scriptural sources, that must be our ultimate source. It is evident that there is so much confusion over the issue of women and their status that it is in this area that we have most often to recall these principles of methodology. In the minds of many Muslims, being faithful to Islamic teachings with regard to education for women, access to mosques, marriage and divorce, social and financial independence, and political participation means doing what was customary in their country of origin or what "the ulama from back there" used to say. Thus, we find parents justifying their unequal treatment of their sons and daughters (clearly discriminating against the latter) with regard to permissiveness, going out, and so on. Some in Europe and in the United States do not allow women to enter mosques, and if, by happy chance, there is a place for them, it is usually dilapidated and often even without a good sound system. Imams find "Islamic" justifications for "fast-track" marriages, without any preparatory official administrative procedures, leaving women without security or rights, abused and deceived by unscrupulous individuals. Divorce is made very difficult, even when it is clear that the woman is defending her most basic rights. Some women, with the knowledge of all around her, suffer violence and degradation while the Muslim community remains culpably silent and complicit, justifying its inaction and cowardice by reference to the Islamic injunction "not to get involved in what does not concern you." But demanding dignified treatment for women has nothing to do with unhealthy curiosity: the first does us honor, the second—to which the Prophetic injunction refers—is unworthy of us. One also finds all sorts of restrictions to do with women, such as the "Islamic" prohibition against their working, having social involvements, speaking in public, and engaging in politics. And what have we not heard about the impossibility of "mixing"! It is true that these practices have sometimes been affirmed and advised in the countries of emigration, and one can certainly find ulama in the traditionalist and literalist schools who declare that these are Islamic teachings. But it is essential that we go back to the scriptural sources to evaluate these practices (and to draw a clear distinction between customs that are culturally based and Islamic principles). We shall discover that there is broad scope for interpretation and that some people, either knowingly or not, have reduced it.

And we must go even further. Cultural influence is not only found after the extrapolation of regulations and in their application. A careful reading of the works of specialists in the fundamentals of law and jurisprudence (*usul al-fiqh*) and in *fiqh* itself shows that they themselves are immersed in a cultural milieu and a society that influence the way they proceed. It is impossible for them, as for any human being, to detach themselves totally from their social and human environment. In one way or another, it shapes their mind and their way of looking at the Qur'an and the world. If our only reference is to be the scriptural sources, then we necessarily must have the right to study and question the readings produced by classical scholars in order to discover whether or not there exists scope for interpretation that our new context may open up. To be in accord with our Islamic principles in these areas means to be willing to follow this thorough study of the fundamentals of law and jurisprudence (*usul al-fiqh*) to its conclusion. One cannot *make* the texts say anything (and there is a great body of standard literature on that subject), but one must be able to say what the text makes it possible to say, even if that shakes our old legal and cultural habits.

This is the level at which we must work with regard to the issue of Muslim women. Their access to education and the revival of their civic involvement is in the process of enabling them to study the Islamic sources more deeply and to engage in a more profound consideration that questions the old evidences born of ancient cultural practices. But this is not a process that will set women against the oppression of men. In fact, we observe a different dynamic: scholars, intellectuals, and women together are now giving birth to a movement of women's liberation within and through Islam itself.[11] Distancing themselves from the most restrictive interpretations, it is in the name of Islam itself that they declare, together with many men, their opposition to discriminatory cultural practices, to the false Islamic identity of certain regulations, and to violence within marriage and their respect for the rights of women in matters of divorce, property, custody, and so on. The first time I used the phrase "Islamic feminism" to describe this movement, many Muslim men and women criticized me, and some non-Muslim critics were not convinced:[12] but a study on the ground, in North America, Europe, and elsewhere in the Muslim world, in Africa and Asia and through the Middle East and Iran, reveals that a movement is afoot that clearly expresses the renewal of the place of women in Islamic societies and an affirmation of a liberation vindicated by complete fidelity to the principles of Islam.

What we see in actuality in the West by way of reform (and there will necessarily be examples of it in the Muslim world) revolves around three essential axes. The first concerns the conception of woman herself: if, until now, most of the classical texts concentrated on the role of woman as "child," "wife," or "mother," woman is now spoken of as "woman." This change of angle is not a mere detail: a real transformation in the conception of woman is at work in the revision of our way of speaking about her. We are now interested in her psychology and her spirituality, and we read the Qur'an with new eyes. We are still a long way from the end of our work in this area, but many men and women are working in this direction in the United States, Britain, France, Germany, and Spain, to name but a few countries. It is also worth noting the influential role of many women converts who are often thoroughly versed in the legal instruments and who carefully question the Muslim legal heritage, into which numerous Arab and Asian features have been surreptitiously introduced.[13] As this work goes on, discussion moves to women's rights, decision making within couples (other than in terms of the confrontation between the rights and the responsibilities of the spouses), social involvement, and female participation in academic and political debate.

The second axis of reform that is in process is the direct consequence of what we have just described. It is the emergence of a new discourse, firmly anchored in the Islamic sources but open to original female perspectives. What is particularly new is that this discourse is increasingly conducted by women themselves, because they study, express themselves and, more and more frequently, teach. They label themselves as Muslims, criticize erroneous interpretations, and use the scope for interpretation provided by the texts and the various opinions of the ulama of the reformist tradition to construct a discourse on Muslim women that calls them to an active, intelligent, and fair faithfulness—an Islamic faithfulness that sets them free before God and does not subject them to the masochistic imagery of either East or West.

The last axis is the consequence of the first two, because it is the recognition of the necessary visibility of women. Their presence in mosques, at conferences and seminars, in Islamic organizations, in the public space, and in universities and places of work has become more and more substantial, and this visibility is a clear vindication as much of their right to be, and to be there, as of their right to express themselves. Many women in the West now indicate their right to be respected in their faith by wearing the headscarf and by giving visible signs of the modesty in which they wish to be approached: but their faithfulness to Islamic rules does not prevent them from having completely Western tastes when it comes to the style or color of their clothing. They are engaged in a liberation movement within and through Islam, and they promote an "Islamic feminism" that does not mean the uncritical acceptance of the fashions and behavior of their Western fellow-citizens. They are fighting for recognition of their status, for equality, for the right to work and to equal pay, but that does not mean that they want to neglect or forget the demands of their faith.[14] They are Western Muslims—they respect the principles of their religion and dress them according to the style and taste of their culture. It is interesting to note that many Muslim women, both veiled and unveiled, work together in several organizations respectful of each other's personal choices: this development is important because it is a step toward acceptance of the opinions of the other and the promotion of a much needed internal dialogue.

This feminism is on the march, even if it is difficult in the West to accept that a Muslim woman can be liberated from within the very confines of the Islamic terms of reference or that a woman who wears a headscarf may in some way be really free and liberated. The visibility of women, and their voices, which are increasingly heard, should eventually change these images and, one hopes, propose another model of a modern, autonomous, Western, and profoundly Muslim woman. This would not be the same as the classical model of the "liberated Western woman," but we have said earlier that what creates freedom is not a particular form of expression in a given historical period, or for a particular population, but the true existence of the principles on which it is based: an autonomous conscience that makes its choices on the basis of its convictions. People in the West would do well to respect this other way of freedom.

For Muslim women and men, it remains to negotiate some shared challenges that are of prime importance in Western societies and that must not be relativized or minimized in the name of the promotion of feminism.

Men, as well as women, must remember that Islamic commandments emphasize the centrality of the family, the role of mothers as well as fathers, the education and support of children, the passing on of knowledge, and all the things discussed in the previous sections. The desire for liberty and rights, for men as well as for women, cannot mean forgetting one's individual, familial, and social responsibilities. Everything leads us to believe that without more vigilance, Western Muslims will increasingly experience the same difficulties as some of their fellow-citizens' families: divorce, violence, desertion of children, generation gaps, abandonment of elderly relatives, and so on. We are not yet there, but all the statistical indicators show that Muslim families tend to settle toward the worse. This state of affairs should make them wake up to the need for a thoughtful and effective social engagement.

Let us say again, at the end of this section, that we must hear and understand the reservations expressed by some Muslim women and men about the term "Islamic feminism" for both historical reasons (the memory of colonialism) and ideological reasons (fear that the phrase will be Westernized). In fact, the intellectual and social movement aimed at promoting a new reading of the scriptural sources and establishing an autonomous status for women is actually of a "feminist" nature (in the sense of vindication of rights) within and through Islam. It will be only a moment, a stage, in the affirmation of women and their rejection of discrimination in Muslim communities in both East and West. Beyond this struggle, we must speak of and promote "Islamic femininity" and encompass all aspects of the matter: the dignity and autonomy of the feminine being, equality before the law, and natural complementarity. This "Islamic femininity" should define a certain way of being and of feeling oneself—and wanting to remain—a woman before God and among other human beings, spiritually, socially, politically, and culturally—free, autonomous, and engaged, as the Texts require and as societies should guarantee.

7

SOCIAL COMMITMENT AND
POLITICAL PARTICIPATION

With the questions of social commitment and political participation, we embark in this chapter on some thinking that is central for at least two reasons. The first is that the treatment of these subjects in the West is beset by a number of recurrent confusions that result in a false representation as much of Islam as of the motivations of Western Muslims. The second is that the Islamic scriptural sources contain an extremely vigorous and demanding social message that inspires believers wherever they are on earth. It is therefore important to build our study on concrete realities, without forgetting the teachings of the Qur'an and the Sunna concerning these two areas of social commitment and political participation. However, presenting things in this way runs the risk of confirming in the minds of some observers and enquirers that Muslims, even in the West, merge the categories of the religious and the political, private and public, and that, in the last analysis, they have not understood and cannot adapt to the principle of separation between Church and State, which is the foundation of the constitutional framework of secularized societies. It is therefore necessary to begin by clarifying the terms of the argument before putting forward concrete suggestions.

Leaving Confusion Behind

The theoretical elements presented in part I will be a great help in clarifying our position regarding the idea that Islam maintains a confusion of categories when it comes to the religious, social, and political aspects of life. Two of the principles we have considered should be recalled here: (a) There is a difference in nature between the Islamic principles related to religious ritual and those that concern the affairs of the world and society: the first are very detailed and precise, while the second are, with very rare exceptions, general and give guidance in a certain direction, rather than fixing a restricting framework; (b) The methodologies in these two areas are the complete opposites of each other: only the text is to be relied on for deciding what is allowed in terms of ritual practice, while the scope for reason and creativity is very wide when it comes to social affairs, which are limited only by the prohibitions found in the scriptural sources, and these are in fact not numerous. Having differentiated the principles and the methodologies, we may take a step toward clarification by stating that although, on the level of ritual, the Islamic message provides a clear, fixed, and, so to speak, unchangeable framework, it is not at all the same on the social and political level, where principles and an awareness of the prohibitions *inspire* the type of commitment that individuals make in these two areas. They must decide what this should be individually and independently, using their reason, their freedom, and, more broadly, their imagination. There is in fact no confusion between the restraining authority of the religious and the civic independence of the individual, between the realm of dogma and that of reason, between the private and the public. Contrary to the widely held idea, Muslims have no particular problem with the principle of distinguishing the various orders of things, even within their sources, because they find these distinctions articulated in the first works of categorization of orders carried out by the ulama as early as the eighth to ninth centuries. In the history of Christianity, arriving at this "distinction of orders" led to the necessary establishment of a clear "separation" between the two spheres of authority (Church and State). This structuring, and the use of space that it assumes, is very accessible to Muslims because it is close to their way of conceiving of the nature of their relationship with God and the modalities of their acting in the world.

What appears to differ, however, is that for Muslims the source of reference remains the same, even if it speaks differently to the heart and mind. With regard to the first, it recalls the dimension of one's dependence on God; with regard to the second, it sketches the paths to independence and freedom in relation to human beings. The original and natural principle of *distinction* in Islam has not had to go as far as separation, even divorce, as in the Christian era, in order to provide humankind with rational autonomy and the ability to confront the temporal evolution of societies. So Muslims continue to find in their scriptural sources principles that inspire their social and political commitment without ever imposing a definitive model, a timeless code, or, more broadly, a dogma for action. In fact, these principles form the body of an ethic that their constantly active reason must seek to respect as much as possible. On thinking about it, we realize that this approach, apparently particular to Muslims, is in fact not so: many Christians, Jews, Buddhists, agnostics, and atheists are inspired in their social and political commitments by their religious, humanist, and ethical convictions and try to act in a coherent manner. They may quote their sources less often, or less directly, than Muslims, but they are perhaps inspired by them just as much.

The difficulties Muslims encounter in social debates in the West arise most with people who confuse "separation" and "conflict" or "mutual rejection" and project onto the secular space a militant ideology opposed to any form of religious expression. There really is a great difference between the normative constitutional order of laicity, or secularism, and the very tendentious and ideologically oriented reading of it that certain radicals, even extremists, would like to impose.[1] To them, in order to be completely "integrated," people should not express their faith at all and should become religiously invisible: any reference to Islam should completely disappear from the public arena, "Islamic" associations should not be so called,[2] and essentially the exercise of one's citizenship should never be inspired by religious convictions. Those who hold these extreme views justify them on the basis of fear of creating religious ghettoes, sectarianism, and the possible return of religious conflicts to the West. These fears are understandable, but we have the right to question the proposed remedies: Western societies have so changed and become so unhomogeneous that wiping out all allegiances in the name of national unity is a measure that maintains only a pretense or hangs on an illusion. Moreover, the feeling of belonging to a community of faith, for example, is not necessarily a withdrawal or an intellectual and/or ethnic isolation and, on the contrary, depending on how it is conceived, may produce extra spiritual energy available to the society as a whole. This is what we will try to demonstrate in what follows. It should provide some answers for those who maintain and nourish distrust of the real intentions of Muslims, which they think are hidden behind deceitful double talk.[3]

The second confusion that must be removed is directly connected with this discussion. It exists as much among Muslims as among their fellow-citizens and concerns the understanding of what Muslims mean by "the community of faith." The overall consideration we gave in part I to the principle of loyalty is needed here to distinguish among the various kinds of belonging and the way in which they are structured. Without repeating the whole idea, let us remember that the community of faith imprints the heart of believers with the collective dimension of their belonging with regard to spirituality, practice, and solidarity; it does not justify taking up a passionate, chauvinistic, or blind stance. Higher ethical principles should inspire the behavior of individuals, sometimes even against their own co-religionists if they are untruthful, treacherous, unjust, or oppressive. Spiritual community is an allegiance to a body of principles and a morality, not to a community united by blood or self-interest. One gets involved in politics not in the name of "my people" but before God and in conscience, in the name of inalienable principles. As a result, the community of faith is essentially opposed to any form of communitarianism.

Something must also be said about a confusion that is in its nature clearly sociological but that often arises in discussion about Islam and causes a disturbance in the debate concerning Muslims in the West. This debate often focuses on a mixture of vague considerations related to the problems of immigration, marginalization, violence, and drugs. First of all, the question of Islam has nothing to do with immigration as such, and many Muslims are now American or European citizens: Islam is a Western religion in the full sense of the word. If these social problems do touch many Muslims, this is obviously not intrinsically because of their religious allegiance. It is a matter of urgency to establish a clear distinction between the nature of the problems, their causes, and their consequences in order not to fuel the simplistic equations: Muslim = immigrant = violence. What should be called into question are the immigration policies of Western countries and their social and urban policies, which have catastrophic effects, spreading very negative images of the Other and giving rise to vexatious, discriminatory, and unjust administrative measures.

These are complex problems, and there are many areas of overlap. They should therefore be dealt with as clearly as possible, and we should work toward reform not as "Muslims" but as citizens, inspired of course by a message and a morality, but above all aware of our responsibilities and determined that the right of every person to be treated justly and fairly (as the common law guarantees) should prevail. Partners are needed in this venture and should become more and more numerous. After all, this will be the best proof that the caricatures lie and that Muslim citizens are today among the men and women who are working against social breakdown and violence. As for those among them who are victims, like all other victims, they suffer the consequences of deficient social policies that become increasingly tight and restrictive the more they refuse to act against the causes of injustice.

The Social Message of Islam

Before thinking further about Muslim social commitment, we should set out the three great principles from which they may draw the inspiration to live in accordance with their convictions. I think the meaning of this "inspiration" is clear enough: it shows the way, but says nothing about the choices, strategies, and priorities to be applied to social action in a given society. It is for the citizens, in the midst of their own realities, to make their choices, work out the stages, and propose realistic and reasonable reforms in each of the societies in which they live.

If there is one area where a basic respect for the universal principles of Islam requires vigilance at every moment, it is the social sphere. At every level, that of religious ritual (*al-ibadat*) and also the broader plane of daily life, Islam is the bearer of a teaching entirely directed toward the collective and social dimension, to the extent that one could say that there is no true religious practice without a personal investment in the human community; the serenity of our solitude before the Creator can exist only if it is nourished daily by our relations with our fellows. So we understand that if each individual bears a responsibility before God, there is, by extension, a vital requirement addressed to the group, or rather to society, at the heart of which the destiny of each person's destiny is decided. It is therefore necessary that people be offered the conditions that will best allow them to respond to their spiritual, moral, and human aspirations. In part I we recalled that humans are above all *responsible* beings—before God, but also before human beings and among their fellows. All human beings must seek to live and to nourish and give meaning to what constitutes their humanity: to acquire knowledge in order to draw closer to the truth; to express their values forcefully in order to achieve good; to listen and participate in order better to respect themselves and to be respected. The Prophet's call to seek for knowledge ("The pursuit of knowledge is obligatory upon every Muslim man and woman"); the Qur'anic requirement to work for good both for oneself and for society ("You command good and forbid evil"); and finally the numerous commandments to observe moderation in all aspects of life, and gentleness, that are found in the Qur'an and the Sunna ("Speak to them in the best way," "Do not forget to observe generosity, kindness, and gentleness toward each other") all point clearly in this direction. So it is impossible to think about a society without beginning with individuals, who must take upon themselves the effort to reform their being. This is the meaning of the much-repeated verse "God does not change the condition of a people unless they themselves change that which is in their inner selves."[4]

The transition from the singular "people" to the plural "individuals" who constitute the people happens without any hesitation in the sense of the injunction. The social dimension finds direction at the spring of the consciousness of each individual who is alone yet strengthened through the effort of the collective. For those who have faith, this understanding is brought about through a constant concern for balance: "Seek instead, by means of what God has granted thee, [the good of] the life to come, without forgetting, withal, thine own [rightful] share in this world, and do good [unto others] as God has done good unto thee; and seek not to spread corruption on earth: for, verily, God does not love the spreaders of corruption!"[5]

So society should allow all persons not to neglect their "rightful portion in the life of this world." Human needs echo the words: society must think of itself as a function of individuals and should provide for them the opportunity to meet fully the needs of their humanity. For their part, as we have said, individuals should know and accept their responsibilities. At the heart of the message of Islam, there is no part of Muslim ritual, from prayer to the pilgrimage to Mecca, that does not emphasize—even prioritize—the collective dimension. To practice one's religion is to participate in the social endeavor, and so there can be no religious consciousness without a social ethic. The first inspires and directs the second. This concept certainly shapes the mind of Muslims in the West. Being responsible before God for one's own person and to respect creation as a whole, one should offer to all people on the social level the means to fulfill their responsibilities and to protect their rights. So the social message of Islam is born in all people's consciousness of their obligations to make it possible on the collective level to organize structurally the protection of the rights of all. Without going into an exhaustive analysis of each of these rights, we may here point to seven for which respect is essential:

1. *The right to life and the minimum necessary to sustain it.* In part I, we have referred to five principles around which all the Islamic injunctions revolve, and it is clear that the first condition needed for them to be applied is respect for life. Every being must have the right, in any society, to the minimum amount of food necessary to live. And we are speaking of *living,* not *surviving.* All the Islamic sources call human beings in general and Muslims in particular to *live* like human beings, in dignity and respect for themselves and for others. A social organization that does not provide its members with this minimum undermines their integrity as created beings who have to give account of themselves before the Creator. To be by nature responsible means that one should have the means by which to carry out the responsibility one bears; otherwise, the innocent become "guilty" and we are blaming the victim. The situation of those from the Fourth World (the poor) in Western societies, following the example of the millions of Americans and Europeans who live below the poverty line, are like permanent tribunals condemning systems guilty of sacrificing lives and human consciences.

2. *The right to family.* Each person has the right to enjoy a family life, and so society, through responsible policies, should make it possible for all people to live with their families in a healthy environment that includes: (1) psychological preparation to assume the responsibility

(e.g., opportunities to meet a suitable spouse, premarital counseling, a support system, role models), (2) caring for children (their physical/mental well-being), and (3) ways to preserve the family during turmoil. The right to family is inseparable from the right to housing, the right to work, and the right to education. We complain about parents who do not know how to bring up their children, who, as we say, "give up on it," when they have not been given the means to live and simply be recognized as a mother or father.

3. *The right to housing.* This right follows directly from the one before. Housing is the first prerequisite for family life, and Islam insists heavily on the sanctity of private space. A society should provide each of its members with a roof; it is a prime responsibility. It is essential to think of adequate local structures: living five or eight to a room is not establishing a household—it is constructing a prison, arranging a suffocation, creating future ruptures and tomorrows full of isolation and marginalization. The state in which suburbs, cities, and inner cities are kept or rather abandoned is truly unacceptable. A man without a home is not a citizen; he is an outcast and a victim. Speeches change nothing. To deprive people of the conditions necessary for their humanity and then make them pay for their vagrancy is doubly unjust. To be before God requires that one be *in oneself, at home,* literally as well as figuratively.

4. *The right to education.* Strong emphasis must be laid on this point, particularly in our time. To be able to read and write, and to find through education the ways to identity and human dignity, is essential. To be Muslim is clearly "to know" and then right away, almost naturally, to make one's way toward greater knowledge. The Qur'an could not be more explicit about this: to know is to gain access to the reading of the signs and to a greater knowledge of the Creator, as we have said in part I. This is what the Prophet continually affirmed: "The pursuit of knowledge is obligatory upon every Muslim man and woman." This means all fields of knowledge, and so it goes without saying that education and basic instruction are imperative. The first verse of the Qur'an to be revealed is "Read, in the name of your Lord who created." This is what is specific to humankind to the extent that it gives people preeminence over the angels in the roll call of creation. A society that does not meet this right has lost its sense of priorities; to put it more clearly, a society that produces illiteracy, whether absolute or functional, scorns the dignity of its members and is fundamentally *inhuman.* A Muslim in the West cannot help being conscious of the dysfunctionality of an education system that, while being increasingly selective, produces throughout the West more and more functionally illiterate people.

5. *The right to work.* People must be able to provide for their needs. For this reason, work, like education, is one of the inalienable rights of a social being, and all people should be able to find their place in the

society in which they live. According to Islam, humans are by virtue of their action and work. It is clear, then, that a society that prevents people from working is one that does not respond to the elementary social contract. We know the saying of the Prophet: "It is better for one of you to take his ropes, go to the mountain and carry a bundle of fire wood on his back and then sell it, than to beg of people, who will either give him or deny him charity!"[6] Work is a sacred command that goes beyond cultural custom; but it appears to be a burdensome duty. The struggle against all kinds of unemployment should be a political priority. It is imperative; it is humane.

6. *The right to justice.* Justice is the foundation of life in society after being, in Islam, the strongest determinant for courses of action: "Certainly, God commands justice,"[7] we read in the Qur'an. This principle of justice applies to all—rich and poor, presidents and populace, Muslims and non-Muslims. Eight verses of *Surat al-Nisa* (Women) were revealed to exonerate a Jew and cast the responsibility for the event on a Muslim. The verse that associates bearing witness to the faith with doing justice makes the idea explicit: "O you who have attained to faith! Be ever steadfast in upholding equity, bearing witness to the truth for the sake of God, even though it be against your own selves or your parents and kinsfolk. Whether the person concerned is rich or poor, God's claim takes precedence over [the claims of] either of them. Do not, then, follow your own desire, lest you swerve from justice: for if you distort [the truth], behold, God is indeed aware of all that you do!"[8] It is essential that the social structure guarantee respect for the rights of each person, and this must be expressed in two ways: obviously, judicial power must apply the laws fairly to every member of society, but it is equally important that society stretch itself to meet all the organizational requirements necessary for the provision of the rights we have already mentioned. Thinking of social justice means deciding on a project, setting priorities, and building a dynamic that will guide social, political, and economic action on the basis of fundamental principles. A poor man in the West does not benefit from the same justice as a rich man; a black man in the United States is found guilty much more quickly than a white man—and this is not acceptable.

7. *The right to solidarity.* One cannot have a sense of the Islamic *religious* world without directly encountering a concept that makes the duty of solidarity central to a living expression of the faith. To be before God is to be in solidarity. The third pillar of Islam, the purifying social tax (*zakat*), is situated at the center of the vertical and horizontal axes of religious and social practice: one's *duty* before God is to respond to the *right* of human beings. The Qur'an is clear in referring to sincere believers: "And [would assign] in all that they possessed a due share unto such as might ask [for help] or such as might suffer privation."[9] The Qur'anic injunction resounds forcefully: "You will not

attain piety until you expend of what you love."[10] It is the responsibility of each person to participate actively in the life of society. The obligation to give *zakat* is only one aspect of a much wider conception of social solidarity. Commitment on the personal and family level, which seems to be self-generating, should be accompanied by attention to one's neighbors, the life of the community, and national and international concerns. Of course, Islam has thought of an institutionalized way to fight poverty (through *zakat*), but it is apparent that the solution is not to be found primarily in structures: it is a matter of awareness and morality. The strength of this awareness of human fraternity and solidarity is the living source of the struggle against social injustice, poverty, and misery. Whoever is a bearer of faith bears the duty to undertake this commitment; whoever is a bearer of faith knows the right to claim it.

The various rights referred to do not cover all the factors involved in the individual and social arenas, but they give a clear enough idea of the basic directions that social action should take. At the source and heart of our reflection, we find, with the knowledge of the creator God, some ultimate considerations all of which center on the notion of justice. The "way of faithfulness" on the social level is a path that should take us daily a little closer to the ideal of justice, which is essential and foremost, and the whole of human activity, in all its parts, must hold to it steadfastly. To achieve this, it is best to analyze situations one by one and not to apply absolute rules; for the context can make the most legitimate or the most logical law unjust or feeble so that it betrays in fact what it meant in spirit to defend.

The Sense of a Presence

The general presentation in part I, together with the social message of Islam, provides the framework and direction that should inspire the commitment of Muslim citizens in the West. Here we shall put forward five points that should take priority in our consideration so that the way can be opened up for relevant and coherent thinking and action on the social level: the idea of moral responsibility, defense of rights, solidarity, partnerships, and, finally, common projects.

Moral Responsibility

Muslims who want to remain faithful to their Islamic terms of reference and who, as members of Western societies, are set completely apart, are called to develop civic awareness founded on their sense of moral responsibility. The "way of faithfulness," in the sense we have given to the concept of *Sharia*, clearly establishes ideals that must be aimed at and that are universal, as we have just seen in the presentation of the social message of Islam. Social commitment is a moral commandment, and reform is an obligation of conscience that, in the mind of the Muslim citizen, determines a "moral responsibility." It is important to state here that, when we refer to the "social" we begin not by formulating a list of rights but by describing a state of mind formed by a *sense of responsibility*. As we have said, the whole of Islamic teaching is based on this order of priorities: an awareness of responsibility by each person is the only way to protect the rights of all.

So, the first stone in the edifice of social action is laid at the individual level. The way one lives, consumes, spends, treats one's neighbors, votes or not, and serves one's fellows is within the order of social action. Many citizens are surprised to see the energy put into Islamic associations by their members, and their concern to commit themselves, to serve, to "promote what is good" and "reform what is bad" and to labor for justice and solidarity. They are particularly surprised to see them encouraging their coreligionists to vote because it is a "duty," which is something that has appeared in print in leaflets and brochures produced by Muslim associations in Britain, France, and the United States. Some see this as a disguised form of proselytism, others as an unfortunate confusion between religion and politics, and yet others as the promotion of an ethnic approach to politics. Even if some association, or some of its members, may actually show signs of these dangerous attitudes, the reasons for this movement should be perceived differently and at a deeper level: Muslim morality is entirely based on awareness of one's responsibility before the Creator and among humankind. To be with the One is to serve one's fellows. In the Muslim mind, this is the root of the idea that Muslims have a mission of social reform to accomplish, wherever they are, in their society, with their fellow-citizens. There is a great difference between social mission and missionary activity that seeks to make converts: the first is a human obligation, but the second (converting people) is the province of God, who alone holds the key to people's hearts.[11]

Rights

This intellectual position, beginning with oneself and one's responsibilities, should immediately commit the Muslim citizen to promoting respect for the rights of every person in Western societies. If we count the dysfunctions occurring in our societies in terms of unemployment, homelessness, discrimination, violence, racism, and xenophobia, we might well wonder how a conscience informed by a sense of moral responsibility can remain passive. This is a matter of claiming rights in the name of Right: many

Muslims passively submit to harassment, racist remarks, and discrimination that are unacceptable. All people, as citizens, are responsible for claiming their rights and gaining respect. Society does not hand out rights as one offers privileges: they are a matter of law, respect, even compulsion. Standing between the bureaucracy that does not do its work, officials who allow themselves to make unwarranted insinuations, police officers who are rough and impolite, and those who suffer this treatment, there is the law, and it is sometimes right to fight for it to be respected. In all circumstances it is right to resist the victim mentality by refusing to sink into emotional complaining that brings isolation or a blind rebellion that brings exclusion.

This must be done for oneself, as well as for others. Associations such as CAIR (the Council of American Islamic Relations) in the United States and Canada and FAIR (Forum against Islamophobia and Racism) in Britain have emerged that defend the rights of Muslim citizens (by fighting against all kinds of discrimination) because they are often silent if not consenting victims and many of them do not know what action to take. These are important developments: the Anglo-Saxon system naturally supports this kind of community defense, but it is still necessary to resist the temptation to shut oneself away in a minority enclave that may give the sense that "one's community" is against the system. It is for this reason that it is urgent to create partnerships with other organizations that work more widely in the same areas so that a plural front can be established against injustice, discrimination, and xenophobia in the name of all citizens without differentiation. We shall return to this later.

On a broader scale, commitment to the rights of the most disadvantaged social classes and the social spaces that have been left out of the economic prosperity in Western societies must also not be neglected. Within the community, this will be a good way of re-establishing links between affluent Muslims and those who have been left out of the general prosperity. This refers not to a merely "charitable" solidarity (we shall come to this in the next section) but rather to the development of a dynamic of resistance so that legitimate social and economic rights can be claimed. Although associations of this type have been created in the United States and in France, we are clearly taking only the first, faltering steps toward this essential commitment. The social commitment of Muslims should not be restricted to a patronizing and good-natured solidarity. If Western societies are our societies—and they are—and if glaring injustices are visible and sometimes institutionalized, then we must say so and reject them and fight, with all the others who are fighting, to demand our rights, and not simply hope for kindness or say compassion.

Solidarity

This does not mean that all activities expressing solidarity should come to an end. On the contrary. Our thought is that they are insufficient, not that they are useless. Over the past two decades, acts of solidarity have multiplied in Western Muslim communities. After being at first expressions of solidarity only with Muslims, they have little by little extended to all groups in society. The "couscous de l'amitié" in France and the food provided on university campuses during Ramadan (in the United States and some European countries) to vulnerable people (e.g., the unemployed, the homeless) are examples of this. These actions have not always been welcomed as they should be by local political authorities and the media, who are often suspicious that there may be hidden motives (proselytism, fundamentalism), but they have nevertheless developed in the Muslim consciousness a sense of being at home in the West and of serving society. They have also given an opportunity for some citizens to come into contact with Muslims in a different way and to become aware of some of the social values of their religion.

From a more long-term perspective, we must point out the work carried out by some Muslim groups in deprived areas and in prisons. Although generally directed toward the Muslim community, these activities have sometimes touched non-Muslim citizens, too. It is a matter of improving the quality of life, fighting against drugs, violence, marginalization, and illiteracy. The work carried out by Afro-Americans in this area is exemplary: the struggle against violence, drugs, and illiteracy has been effective in many parts of the country, and the commitment of the imam Siraj Wahhaj in the area around his Al-Taqwa Mosque in Brooklyn has been well known for years. This initiative from within has become more visible as more and more Muslim citizens have chosen to become social activists and to get involved in working alongside young people in deprived areas. But separation between the affluent and the poor is, nevertheless, the rule, and the social commitment of the former is starkly inadequate compared with the needs of the latter. On a broader front, a commitment to solidarity toward the whole of society, with non-Muslim partners, remains an exception in the United States and Europe, for two reasons: such activities are often, as we have said, misinterpreted, and the possibility of working openly with non-Muslims remains something of which only a minority are aware.

Partnerships

If we are to try to be faithful to the message and act in harmony with the direction it gives, we must take the process of putting down roots to its conclusion in order to serve "all humankind" and to know better those with whom we are living. If the nations and tribes were first constituted, as the Qur'an says, in order that people should seek to know one another better, it seems evident that the people who make up one society should acquire an even deeper mutual knowledge. Moreover, if the message of Islam is really universal, many of the values it promotes should inevitably be accessible to and shared by human beings of other traditions who live with other convictions. On the level of values, of morality, of the demand for social justice and resistance to discrimination of all kinds, Muslim citizens find a great number of potential partners in all Western societies. After all, their values are shared by the vast *majority* of the population, even if committed Muslims find themselves engaged on the ground with only the small, actively resistant *minority*. It is because of this, and because of the clearly understood sense of the universality of the values to which they subscribe, that Muslims should, as we have said, avoid the trap of the minority temptation. Establishing partnerships at the local level is the best way of allowing this transformation of their state of mind to take place.

These actions must be considered at several levels: the promotion of an ethic of responsibility can take place with partners of other religions, ecological groups (as in France, Belgium, and Switzerland), alternative movements, and so on. Commitment to respect for human rights is already expressed through innumerable bodies with which Muslim citizens in all the Western countries are too little in contact. Fear, and sometimes mutual suspicion, has long prevented the formation of links with bodies such as the League of Human Rights, ATTAC, Globalize Resistance, and the alternative banks, but things evolve, and Muslim associations are increasingly establishing connections beyond "the community." Groups of associations, such as "Divers-Cité" in the Lyon region (and other towns in France, such as Maintes-la-Jolie and Roubaix) and local partnerships in some cities in the United States (such as Washington, D.C., Chicago, and Los Angeles) and in Canada (Toronto, Ottawa) show that the process is slowly moving forward and that new and essential perspectives are opening up with regard to the settlement of Muslims in their society. The creation of multi-dimensional partnerships is one of the keys to the future: not only will it confirm to Muslims that their values are shared, but it will make it possible for their fellow-citizens better to gauge how and why the presence of Muslims in the West, with the vitality of their organizations and their convictions regarding social mission, is a source of enrichment for the society they share in common.

The World of Associations

In the course of their settlement in the West, Muslims have passed through several stages in the creation of associations. In the first period, it was a question of gathering together either on the basis of a common origin (by creating organizations for people coming from the same country) or, more often, with the aim of carrying out a project such as the establishment of a mosque. These were the two axes that most attracted new arrivals. Slowly, new kinds of structures came into being, more oriented toward education, social work, and more specialized activities (e.g., for young people, students, women) or toward Muslim representation at local and national levels. It is organizations of this type that characterize the general landscape of Muslim communities today both in Europe and in the United States. They are all the fruit of the initiatives of Muslims who wanted to become involved in one field or another, and all refer in their titles to the "Islamic" character of their approach. They have become part of the national picture of voluntary associations in practically all Western countries, even those where the Muslim presence is a recent phenomenon and even if there is sometimes no structure of representation at the national level. The number of such Muslim associations has multiplied exponentially in the past few years.

These organizations are essential, and they must remain present and active in Western countries because they help to normalize the presence of Muslims in the West. However, it is important, at least in those countries where the Muslim presence is the most long-standing, to consider embarking on a new phase in the type of organizations invented and founded by Western Muslims. This *third stage* of associational structures for Muslims should make it possible for them to create new organizations that, while complementing what is already being done in the field, will be set up around shared values, social projects, and causes and will not be based simply on the Muslim identity of its founders. These will not be partnerships with other associations but, taking one step further, will represent shared commitments within one association. If necessary, new structures could be created, or they could quite simply be integrated into existing organizations (as numerous Muslims have already done in the United States and Europe): the important thing is to establish places of real encounter, dialogue, and commitment "together" in the name of values held in common by virtue of sharing a citizenship lived in an egalitarian fashion. This type of involvement is more complex on the ethical level because, in a situation where we are not "among our own," we must sometimes face situations or behavior that are not in harmony with our values or codes of conduct. By making time for dialogue and explanation, by defining clearly the boundaries of commitment, it is possible to find areas of agreement. It takes time: creating an atmosphere of trust and respect requires that we talk to each other, listen to each other, and do not refuse to respond to any question, provided it is asked with respect and with the intention of seeking understanding. This is what is lacking these days between Muslims and their fellow-citizens—joint meetings; frank, deep, and sincere discussion; and partnerships that alone can build the mutual trust that is so wanting. This third age of associational structures should make it possible for Muslims to achieve part of this objective, which, beyond its practical results, reminds us that we have numerous values in common that invite us to enter into commitments side by side.

Many Muslims, still unsure of their identity and of what people think of them, are afraid of going too far in this direction. And we are still far from reaching this point in many European countries, but in the end this is the direction in which the Islamic association landscape in the West is bound to evolve—Muslim citizens distributed among cultural networks, working in specialized "Islamic associations," and ultimately participating in bodies that unite those with pluralistic beliefs and common values. In the end, this is the universal dimension of Islam, integrating pluralism and human diversity and inviting everyone in the sense suggested by the saying: *Know who you are and commit yourself with the Other for dignity, justice, and peace, for the Other as well as for yourself.*

The Basics of Political Involvement

There have been numerous and lively debates among the ulama and among Muslims more generally on the question of whether it is possible for them to participate in the political life of their countries in Europe or the United States. On the basis of both general principles declared by the Islamic sources and the works of the classical scholars, some have replied in the negative and others in the positive. Most of the thinking of the ulama throughout history has been about situations in which Muslims were in the majority, with a legal system inspired more or less by their own sources. The minority position is not new (e.g., in India and Africa), and many scholars have given attention to the question, but what is new is the nature of the societies that are receiving Muslims today (democratic, secularized societies based on law) and that give them a status as citizens, which entails extensive prerogatives and requires a serious reflection on the implications of that status in the light of the Islamic sources.

Some ulama and thinkers from the traditionalist and literalist schools of thought[12] refuse any kind of contextualized approach on the basis that the Islamic principles are not open to interpretation and can be summarized in five main points: (1) There are no "elections" in Islam (it is not a Qur'anic term, and the relation between the individual and the political leader is a contract of allegiance [*baya*]); (2) One may not desire [political] office, on the basis of the Prophetic tradition (among others) "We do not give (political) authority to those who ask for it or ardently desire it"; (3) A Muslim can give allegiance only to a Muslim and must otherwise abstain from all political involvement; (4) A Muslim must respect the political authority exercised by a Muslim, even if it is not ideal, on the basis of the Qur'anic verse that commands Muslims to obey God, his Prophet, and "those who exercise (political) authority"; (5) The democratic system (not a Qur'anic concept) does not respect Islamic criteria (the criteria of *shura*[13]), and a Muslim in the United States or Europe, outside his natural home (*dar al-islam*), must distance himself from any support for a system opposed to Islamic values.

We can see how completely restrictive and out of context this approach is. Trends of thought present in the West and strongly supported by the petromonarchies (particularly Saudi Arabia) sustain these theses and pressure young people to cut themselves off from all relations with their social and political environment in order to observe a ritualistic and very literalist practice. Other scholars have considered the question from the point of view of exceptional situation (*hala istithnaiyya*), necessity (*darura*), or need (*haja*): in their view, the basic rules are known but need to be reconsidered in light of the actual situation (*al-waqi*). This means engaging in *ijtihad* to make it possible to draw a broad outline for Muslim involvement in Western societies, and, if necessary, issuing circumstantial *fatwas*. All the responses put forward by reformist scholars are aimed at encouraging Muslims to participate in the political life of their countries, but with a greater or lesser degree of reservation with regard to the way the Islamic frame of reference should be defined. As far as almost all the ulama are concerned, reading between the lines of their constant reference to "necessity" or "need," one feels that they have not completely come to terms with and assimilated the idea that Muslims are at home and must live with this reality and find responses that are not responses to *exceptional* circumstances.

It must be noted here that there is today in the practice of *fiqh* (law and jurisprudence) and among the most reformist scholars a tendency to make constant, and in my view abusive, use of the concepts of *exception*, *need*, and *necessity*. If, in the first instance, this approach allows for the declaration of new *fatawa* (plural of *fatwa*) that offer Muslims the possibility of living better tuned in to their time, it is appropriate to study the logic that underpins this development and the consequences that may ensue. In practice, scholars observe the situation in societies in light of an ideal Islamic order (and principles related to it) and pronounce legal opinions

that allow the closest possible adherence to these principles in given situations or the choice of the least evil option. To perpetuate and encourage
without reservation this kind of approach, which is necessary at first, nevertheless produces two unfortunate and serious consequences: far from the
ideal, law and jurisprudence are thought of in terms of temporal or partial
adaptations to a global system to which one feels in permanent subjection;
by approaching Western societies through concepts of exception or constraint, individuals are given the means to survive in the global system
and thereby affirm it but not to participate in its reform. By avoiding the
contradictions of daily life in this way, this development fuels another difficulty that is clearly more fundamental, which lies in the feeling that this
work of adaptation (this *ijtihad*) ends up by giving in to a world political
and economic order that our conscience is actually calling us to transform.
In this way, the sense that we are constantly in a sort of legal patchwork
because we are in situations of necessity (*darura*) or need (*haja*) has the
perverse effect of teaching us to learn to protect ourselves without giving
us the means to work out a global strategy for resistance and alternative
solutions. Here Muslims seem to be stalled: their concern to veer as little
as possible from the "path to the spring" seems to deprive them of the
means of building a global vision of that "way to justice" that rejects
injustice and is not content simply to compromise with reality. So, even
though this work of adaptation is necessary, it is appropriate to think of
the forms it should take. To think and to assess the reality on the scale of
a supposed "ideal of society" may provide points of reference in the elaboration of legal opinions, but, as we have said, this is in fact paralyzing. It
would be better, in my view, in the political and economic fields,[14] to go
back to the universal and global principles of the message of Islam (rather
than to the ideal models that have developed from them[15]) in order to be
able to consider both the normality of one's "life here" and the ways in
which one might make a global commitment for the sake of justice and
goodness. The liberating dimension of Islam insistently demands, on the
basis of the universal principles, that reality be challenged in order that it
be reformed, not that its deficiencies be added up in the hope that we may
at best adapt to them or at worst successfully protect ourselves from them.
It is a question of going much further than simply changing our way of
approaching *ijtihad* or juridical adaptation. It is about getting out of the
logic of *exception* and *necessity* and thinking of our presence in terms of
faithfulness to principles in the strict sense. In practice, it is a question of
acquiring means of adaptation that will enliven people's minds and give
them the tools with which to resist and reform rather than those that
make it possible to survive, protect oneself, and ultimately act politically
only in the name of the interests of "the Muslim minority community." If
badly handled, reformist religious thought may produce a dangerously re-

actionary and conservative intellectual and political attitude: the evidence already gives reason to fear the worst among Western Muslims.

This reflection, which has taken us a little away from the question without completely straying from the subject, finds its place here because it influences the way we tackle the political issue, and also, in the next chapter, the economic issue. The paradigm on the basis of which links are made between Islamic principles and reality (particularly the Western reality) has, as we shall see, important consequences for Muslim involvement. As we have said, we are here very clearly facing a contextual situation vastly different from that which inspired classical Islamic thought up to the twentieth century, that it requires a rereading of the Texts and the relativization of the works of the scholars. Let us try, using the general principles discussed in part I and the tools supplied by the work of the jurists, to fix a framework of reference for political involvement and the criteria for its application.

The Framework of Reference

We have seen that the universal message of Islam directed human intelligence toward the quest for justice and provided the faithful with an ethical teaching so that they could follow the "way of faithfulness" (al-Sharia). In new situations, not envisaged by the sources, the establishment of a political strategy has been defined by some ulama in the course of history as arising from al-siyasa al-shariyya or from fiqh al-muwazanat; the first concept refers to the elaboration of political reflection faithful to the general requirements of Islam, while the second relies on studying and weighing the options on the basis of their faithfulness to the sources, their adaptability to the situation, and so on. If we look at them more closely, we can see that both approaches are directly linked to the study of the common good (al-maslaha), which we have already considered. When the sources are silent on a specific issue (maslaha mursala), it is for the experts to study the details of the situation in order to make a statement of legal opinions that must both respect the objective of the message (and of justice) and be faithful to its ethical content (to achieve the common good—tahqiq al-masalih—and resist all that may oppose it (daf al-madar). All the revealed Islamic teachings have been understood as possessing this double quality, and there is a well-known scholarly formula: "Maqasid al-ahkam masali al-anam" (the objective of the Islamic legal rulings is the well-being—the common interest—of human beings). So this is the spirit in which our thinking should be pursued.

Scholars of the fundamental principles of law and jurisprudence (usul al-fiqh) have added a second fundamental recommendation: in real situations, as opposed to the ideal model, one must strive when making choices to give preference to the better of two goods, or, in difficult circumstances, to the lesser of two evils. The measure of which is the better of two goods or the lesser of two evils is established on the basis of the moral teaching of Islam, which should inspire scholars in the formulation of directives as it inspires citizens or politicians in the framework of their actions. And, beyond this, the causes and conditions that could bring moral improvement or degeneration to concrete situations should be considered. We find in the works of specialists in the foundations of law and jurisprudence a series of rules that stress not the character of the action itself but the objective conditions that lead to it or encourage it and that therefore themselves take on the same positive or negative moral quality *(al-dharai)*.

Finally, it must be added that a specific legal injunction may also be utilized to preserve the general public interest, and one must be careful not to rush to judgment, as some literalists do, if the injunction or action appears at first glance to contradict an explicit text. In the area of social affairs in the broad sense, as in virtually all matters of religious ritual, faithfulness to the principles is measured not by equating the literal meaning of a text with the apparent meaning of a given action, but, more subtly, on the basis of its intention *(qasd)* and the means it employs *(wasail)*, keeping the comprehensive message in mind. So, taking into account the ultimate objective of an action in light of the general message requires that we go beyond a restrictive interpretation based on literal faithfulness to a text with no consideration to the context and with no sense of priorities. It is incontestable that we should refer to ethics, but that makes sense only if we also apply an active intelligence well versed in the affairs of the world and capable of understanding the situation, judging the extent to which the action is to be measured on the scale of moral faithfulness, setting priorities, and establishing the objectives of the action according to the ultimate aims of the message. All these considerations are implicit in the scholastic formula *"al-umur bi-maqasidiha"* (matters are to be judged by their final objectives), which informs us that we must be aware of our responsibility to know the objectives of the message to which we are committed in order to set the direction for our lives and, in light of moral teaching, choose actions and methods that are in harmony with our conscience.

Western Muslims can profit from these overall theoretical and specialized considerations. Bearing in mind the general message and its ethic, which directs their conscience, wherever they are, to defend justice, promote the good, and reform their society, Muslims have a duty to make an appropriate study of their society in order to determine the features of the common good *(al-maslaha)*, the main achievements to be preserved, the injustices to be fought as a priority, and the means at their disposal and, at the same time, to identify the actors and the key points in the social and political dynamics of their society. It is then a matter of applying concretely the body of directions put forward by scholars: to work for justice and against every form of injustice, to choose the best possible of the good things available and the least evil, and never to forget ethics when evaluating the causes, consequences, and means of carrying out an action and in all circumstances to evaluate the ultimate purpose of one's deeds.

Even if the legal instruments we have used to present this frame of reference are the same as those used by the Muslim jurists in ancient or recent times, the way things are presented here is quite different: we want to read the reality of the world from the starting point of the requirements of the universal message of Islam, with the idea not that, in case of difficulty, under domination or in minority, we have to compromise (though it goes without saying that this is sometimes necessary) but that it is necessary in all circumstances to understand, master, choose, and reform. This is not simply a difference of style.

This critical effort to understand the scriptural sources and the world, this *ijtihad*, cannot be the work only of the ulama and of specialists in law and jurisprudence. The world has become too complex, in every area, for us to be satisfied with theoretical studies "outside real life." It is time to promote councils that would bring together on an equal footing ulama and experts from various fields (the human sciences as well as the natural sciences) to make it possible to formulate legal positions in step with our time. On the level of political involvement, on the basis of the general [Islamic] principles, it is for the Muslim communities in each country to open up an internal debate bringing together ulama, intellectuals, associational bodies, and [ordinary] citizens in order better to study their political environment, taking their Islamic frame of reference as the starting point and then, as appropriate, deciding on one or more general and/or specific strategies that make it possible to be faithful to both the essential principles and ethics. We are here in the realm of social and political action, and each organization, even each individual, can, while respecting the common Islamic frame of reference (if one feels connected with it), freely determine its priorities and civic and political choices. It is not for the community of faith to come up with a uniform communal political commitment.[16]

Conditions

Most contemporary reformist scholars hold the view that political involvement is legitimate, and even a duty, for Muslims in the West. In addition to the fact that they all refer to the exceptional situation (of Muslims being outside a Muslim majority society), their conclusions all point in the same direction: it is necessary to be socially and politically active in the West by trying to bear witness to one's spirituality and, essentially, by adapting one's presence to one's ethics. Of course, the first general principle (al-asl) is not to become involved in a system that is not totally in accord with the demands of Islamic spirituality, values, and morals, but in fact Muslims still have to respond to an ethical requirement: to limit injustice and evil as much as possible,[17] to be committed in all circumstances to choosing the least evil option,[18] to find solutions that will ease people's lives,[19] and to work in stages.[20] And people often point to the Qur'anic story of Joseph (Yusuf), who asked the governor of Egypt, who was a polytheist, to make him responsible for what might today be called the national treasury and who therefore had a political responsibility under a non-Muslim political authority, which he carried out with dignity, morality, and faithfulness.[21]

This is far from the literalist interpretation described earlier; here the field is open to thoughtful, contextualized participation on an individual and collective level. However, it would still be good to consider some conditions that, if one wishes to be consistent with the ethical message of Islam, must, in my understanding, be respected: "the way of faithfulness" is a way that leads toward more justice, and civic and political involvement in a society of whatever kind must move in the same direction. So, individuals should in their own hearts and consciences, according to their own understanding of the world and their own opinions, weigh their involvement according to this criterion and note the scope for maneuver that their society allows them. This first condition assumes two others that are fundamental: one is to refuse absolutely to serve or collaborate with a dictatorial government that imposes a society that lacks rights. In this situation, when it comes to citizenship and political involvement, a stance of determined resistance is required, not of caution in the face of a dictatorial system. The last condition is to avoid being used and to treat with caution interests that are not always expressed. This may be true in an autocratic system, but it is also a risk in a democratic system. We see politicians, at election time, playing on the community solidarity of "immigrants" and "Blacks," for which read "Muslims," by putting on their list the name of a very "representative" candidate or putting forward projects calculated to gain support (such as mosques and cemeteries). We have then not only to be awake but also to have a conscience and principles: the aim is to promote a more dignified society, not to accept indignity under the pretext that this will protect one's interests. The "electoral communitarianism" of some candidates is in itself unacceptable. In the end, it must be clear, whatever the nature of our civic or political involvement, that one is not compelled to follow all the chosen views of a party, an elected representative, or even the population at large. Involvement in a free society should guarantee the right to act on one's conscientious objections, to have moral reservations, and to be able to express them when appropriate. This requires the development of a critical observation of oneself and the nature of one's political involvement, as much as of the society in general: this is the price to be paid for effective political involvement.

An Ethic of Citizenship

The concept of citizenship is fashionable. People want to vindicate it, defend it, promote it, and extend it. It is the banner of the progressives and the badge of "integrated" people. To be honest, the concept of "citizens" is used to speak of everything and nothing with the understanding that, in the end, there must come into being a European/American-born Muslim citizen. Nevertheless, if we look more closely, we find on the level of civic awareness and political participation that the picture, as far as Muslims are concerned, is very variable. For nearly ten years, increasing numbers of Muslim associations, especially in Britain, France, and the United States, have constantly called on their coreligionists to vote and to take part in the political life of their country. More and more young activists and students have certainly understood the important of the political game, but in the poorest areas the level of participation in elections remains much lower than expected. Like all citizens who experience the same objective living conditions, Western Muslims vote rarely, if at all. It must also be said that although the "call to vote" may be simple and clear in itself, the messages that go with it are not always so accessible: some call on people to vote to "take on their responsibilities as citizens," others in order to show the growing weight of the "community," still others mainly to "defend the interests" of the community. An observer can no longer tell what it is that minds and hearts are being mobilized for: principles? which principles? an identity? which identity? interests? what are they? Most Islamic organizations legitimize their appeals by the accepted reference to Islamic principles but sometimes seem to forget in fact the requirements of the body of reference to which they call themselves to be faithful (and which we have just presented in the previous section): so, in practice, they end up by forming the idea of a "community," whose members should think about political participation in the sense that they should get involved above all in order to protect the specific needs and interests of the community. One hears many voices in the United States, Britain, Germany, and France legitimizing this position by insisting on the fact that Muslims are "a minority," "in a weak (political and financial) position," "without great means" of influence on the society at large. The universal message of Islam that should move Muslims' civic conscience to promote justice, right, and goodness everywhere is reduced to this: "since we are a feeble minority"—a defensive, self-pitying discourse, narrowly concerned with the protection of self and "the community."

On a broader plane, these repeated and almost incantational calls for civic and political participation by Muslims seem to just float in the breeze. There seems to be no awareness of the conditions for bringing people together to make participation possible, unless it be a show or a pageant. There can be no authentic civic involvement if a solid program of citizenship education has not been developed and proposed in advance. Calls and slogans and singing the praises of "the good fortune of being a citizen" will change nothing: understanding one's society, its history, and its institutions, developing one's intelligence, and building an independent spirit—these are the things that will teach us, and everyone should be given the means to undergo this training. Without these prerequisites, and others, it is actually impossible to escape from this defensive and self-pitying attitude that in fact prevents us from acquiring a true citizenship ethic that not only proposes protection but also makes a commitment to the way of resistance and reform.

The Prerequisites

Here we must insist on the absolute necessity of making available to Muslims in each of the Western countries a deep knowledge of their environment. We have already referred to this in the chapter on education, but it is even more important when it comes to access to citizenship. We must profit fully from what is provided by the public (state) school system in these areas—knowledge of history, geography, language, culture, and traditions. All these elements make it possible to comprehend, from within, the frame of reference of the society on the regional, national, and even continental levels. And we must add to all these disciplines a subject on which there is much variation in public education in the different countries—civic education. It is important to reconnect with the tradition in which this training was given, because young people know less and less about the functioning of the institutions and the whole political system of their countries and show a growing disinterest in voting and participation. All citizens need this civic education/citizenship training, which today is full of gaps, and Muslim citizens have to understand it as an integral part of their personal and collective development if they want to remain faithful to their principles and also become actors in their societies.

The world has become complex, and political implications are sometimes not explicit. In order to form an independent and serious opinion requires, beyond a proper civic education/citizenship training, the capacity to listen, understand, express oneself, and engage in dialogue with others. It is of prime importance to cultivate a genuine culture of debate among citizens. To go beyond the very shallow consensus of fashionable ideas and to keep a critical distance from the unhealthy and incessant administration of "opinion polls" and make one's choices freely requires taking time to admit the complexity of things, to exchange ideas, discuss theories, and meet the other—one's fellow citizen. This culture of authentic, searching, honest, and guileless debate is a real school for citizenship. Some parents manage to achieve this in the home, and some teachers bring it to life in their courses. It is for all Islamic organizations, both within their own groups and vis-à-vis the world around them, to develop this attitude and love of exchange and debate, this intelligence that learns to listen and this critical mind that knows how to ask questions.

The third prerequisite is learning through concrete participation in the life of the city. Citizens must gain, or regain, a taste for public issues. Nothing is more formative than close involvement, in one's own area or town, in public service projects, social politics, or, more broadly, human solidarity. A civic awareness begins when we have the feeling that our human and social environment concerns us and that we are active participants in our own lives and our own society, and not the objects of other people's decisions. Perpetual criticism of political authority or of the police is futile and meaningless when, alongside it, we as citizens do nothing to change things. Posing always as victims is a kind of cowardice. To be up in arms at every police blunder when we have become passive observers of the breakdown of the social fabric and watch silently (without showing any inclination toward concrete involvement) when young people display unspeakable violence and steal and assault and insult adults in their communities (particularly the police) does not make much sense and is, above all, unworthy. Obviously, there are police failures, but they increase in number as public resignation increases. Close involvement is a school for prevention and development: we do not perceive key features of national life in the same way when we find out how people who are really excluded from the system live with us and alongside us. A citizenry whose discourse and commitment forgets these people is a contradiction in terms: it should speak of justice and equal rights but actually promote social and economic oppression.

It may appear that calling on people to vote is a positive thing and a sign of open and progressive thinking, but to do it without providing for the concrete prerequisites for civic commitment is dangerous. Without education, a culture of debate, and practical involvement, any individual, particularly the young, may be drawn into "fashionable" movements or groups that lobby for or defend special interests rather than putting forward a social policy. Muslim citizens, inspired by their spiritual and ethical message, have a major responsibility to take these prerequisites into account: to be true to their conscience in the Western environment absolutely requires it. This is the way that will lead to the growth of a responsible, active, and intelligent citizenship—three qualities that are already part of their spirituality.

Civic Ethics

It is no good to become citizens by any means and at any price. This is where the Islamic principles of human actions and the constitutional principles of civic commitment connect in their universality: they all rest on the dignity of the human being, and they all require an ethical basis. That is why we speak here of promoting a true "civic ethics." In practice, in addition to a watchful respect for the prerequisites mentioned earlier, we have to find a particular way of becoming committed and acting politically. We have noted that, to our way of thinking, *normalizing our presence without trivializing it* means insisting, for Muslims, not on sustaining a sense of Otherness but rather on an awareness of their belonging and commitment to society in general. The universal principles of Islam concerning the brotherhood of mankind, the necessity for justice and equality before the law, the need for involvement, and, last, service to others requires that attention be given constantly in society to the evaluation of the moral quality of actions, the motivations and abilities of the significant actors, and the ultimate nature of the dynamics that are set in motion. Quite apart from competence in the use of the tools of citizenship, when these principles feed the individual's conscience, they lead to a certain way of being, deciding, and acting, whether alone or collectively.

Promoting an ethic to be applied to the citizenry demands first of all that one feel entrusted with a mission that consists in reminding one's fellow citizens of the demanding responsibility they have, on both the individual and collective levels, to respect their fellows and the creation as a whole: this also means commitment to enforcing the elementary principles of respect for the rights of human persons—their integrity, freedom (of conscience and worship), right to equality, and so on[22]—for all people in all circumstances. It is true that these rights sometimes have to be defended on behalf of a particular community that is facing discrimination, but, as we have said, that does not mean perverting one's civic action by reducing it to a mere defense of "my religion," "my culture," or "my ethnic group." The principles that undergird the "community of faith" require that we act against communitarianism and the thinking of the ghetto and sectarianism. The natural isolation that Muslims have endured during the first years of their presence in the West must today give way to a commitment that, if it is inspired and fed by the principles and ethical message of Islam, must be put at the service of all, for the good of all.

Some suggest that Muslims should follow the example of the Jews in the United States. As an extremely well-organized lobby, very active and extremely influential in the corridors of power in Washington, they are characterized by continuous activity, with the aim either of protecting the interests of the Jewish community or of supporting the state of Israel. This should be, some argue, the model of communal political commitment by Muslims in the West: to form a sort of lobby and defend "their" interests. Even if the lobbying tradition is different on the different sides of the Atlantic, it is still true that each national political culture has determined, for the various community, economic, and religious groupings, a particular way in which it can bring pressure to bear and influence the political life of the country. The practices of lobbying and exerting pressure, while they go on in the full light of day in the United States and cause no shock, are employed differently, or simply more discreetly, in European countries. New Muslim citizens should go with the flow and follow suit.

Perhaps we should begin by comparing like with like. Muslims do not have the same history or experience as Jews living in the United States and Europe, and the great majority of Muslims do not know the territory or the political culture and do not have at their disposal the means available to the Jewish community in the West. The idea of acting in the same way or even moving in the same direction is ill considered and has little chance of success. More fundamentally, quite apart from the possibility or impossibility of such a strategy, the crucial question is whether Muslim communities in Europe and the United States should organize themselves into pressure groups or get into lobbying on the political level. Is this the way they should see their role? The whole of our analysis leads to the conclusion that this question must be answered in the negative. The role of Muslim communities in the West is to defend principles, not interests, and if it transpires that it is in their interest to have their universal principles respected, it should be clear that their fight for these principles serves society as a whole. Raising high the standard of right, justice, and ethics cannot stop at the boundaries of the community of faith: the universality of the principles calls us back to the meaning of the brotherhood of mankind, which consists in serving the whole community and all human beings. The "way of faithfulness" compels us not only to respect plurality but also to step outside the ghettos, know each other better and act together for the common good if we are to reach the end of the "way." If, on the basis of their own specificity, which is well understood, Muslim communities could allow political action to become once again a more noble, worthy, and transparent activity to serve the people rather than to serve itself, their presence would have some use and would have carried out part of their witness among their fellow citizens.

This is the understanding that must rise from now on in the political consciousness of Western Muslims. It would benefit the whole of society to restore a little morality to political activity. Politicians in contact with Muslims at a local or national level should be able to "feel the difference": they should notice that the concern of Muslim citizens is to respect certain principles; that their satisfaction lies in justice being applied to everyone, black and white, "native" citizens and immigrants, and that if they are engaged in a forceful relationship with local authorities, it is with the aim of fighting corruption, discrimination, and violence, or, more fundamentally, social policies that protect the rich and their privileges. They cannot be bought because they refuse to be sold!

At election time, candidates should receive a clear message without political contortions. Some of these elected representatives, or prospective elected representatives, promise the "Muslim communities" a mosque, or a center, or a hall, or a cemetery, or even a place for ritual slaughter or some other privilege in order to get their support and their votes,[23] and unfortunately they find Muslim citizens ready to play their game. These same politicians do not hesitate to criticize ghettos, social separation, and communitarianism, even when they have themselves fueled a perverted communitarianism for electoral purposes. Muslim citizens then get only what they deserve: they have to realize that those who are capable of buying them before the elections have no scruples about selling them afterward. Small compromises follow their own rules and their own logic: that has to be accepted.

Voting is too important an action to be negotiated for so mean a price. The ethics of citizenship here comes into its full meaning: it is not about voting for a candidate capable of protecting our interests or of voting only for a Muslim; it is clearly a question of establishing objective criteria for making choices on the basis of conscience. The best candidate, at whatever political level, is the one who brings together the three most essential qualities when it comes to seeking a political mandate (which essentially consists in serving the community): integrity, ability, and willingness to serve. Do such candidates do what they say? Do they have the abilities necessary for the post in question? Are they present on the ground and engaged with and on behalf of their constituents? These are the questions that Western Muslim citizens should ask, and they should make their choices as responsible and independent citizens. It is for them to evaluate, consider, and finally decide, case by case, in favor of the best, or sometimes the "least bad," candidate. A citizenship that never wants to betray an ethic of life is demanding and depends on a permanently and deliberately critical mind that, on the political level, is the condition for wisdom.

As we have said, we should not necessarily choose a candidate who is a member of "the community": one can be a Muslim and dishonest, politically incompetent, and more concerned with titles than with serving people. To choose such a person, for example (and such do exist), would be a betrayal of principles. Did not the Prophet say: "Anyone who appoints to a position an individual from a community when there is someone else more competent betrays God, his Prophet, and all Muslims"?[24] The choice should be based on the balance between the three qualities referred to earlier and not on the religion or community membership of the person.[25] In the two situations, the act of electing and the hope of being elected, a civic ethic operates in the same way and makes the same demands: it calls upon responsible and independent individuals to know their principles, ethics, and environment, to decide on the ultimate aim of their commitment, and, in all circumstances, to be responsible for their actions. If politics has a meaning and political action has any worth, they should be found somewhere at the heart of these dilemmas, at the precise moment when each person's conscience is looking for the point of balance that marks the intersection between means and ends, ethics and effectiveness.

The Voice of the Voiceless and Popular Action

Western Muslims, who are still for the most part of immigrant origin, must not forget where they come from and the road that has led them to Northern societies, in the name of their principles and their history. They must indeed be concerned with the affairs of their society, as we have said—with justice, law, unemployment, violence, and so on—but, at the heart of industrialized societies, they must also remain the *conscience of the South*. Dictatorships, the state of total decay of societies and economies, endemic poverty, illiteracy, and the daily death of millions of human beings as a result of a world order that sows terror are the realities that bear evidence against the way the planet is currently managed. We have to be the friends and partners of anyone in the West who denounces the horror, and we must call for the world to be changed.

It is said that it is necessary to develop a critical mind capable of taking account of things. The West is neither monolithic nor demonic, and its phenomenal achievements in terms of rights, knowledge, culture, and civilization are realities that it would be unreasonable to minimize or reject. At the same time, we must think clearly and know how to be critical of economic or strategic policies imposed by the North that are suffocating whole societies, compromising with heartless torturers, and promoting the veritable cultural colonization of underdeveloped countries with the help of the demeaning products of modern Western culture. To be a Western Muslim and speak these truths is to run the risk, almost systematically, of being considered not completely "integrated," giving rise to suspicions about one's true loyalty: it's as if Muslims have to buy "integration" with their silence. This kind of intellectual cant must be rejected. To be a free citizen in Northern societies means having the means and the right to make critical choices, assessments, and evaluations from within the heart of the Western frame of reference. It means recognizing and fighting for the achievements of democracy and challenging one's own government (be it American, French, British, or any other) by making it understood that it is not acceptable to betray our principles through complicity with dictatorships. It means congratulating ourselves on the level of development and material well-being that we enjoy *here*, while fighting with all our might against the economic policies of the World Trade Organization, the International Monetary Fund, and the World Bank, which, by means of international agreements and structural changes, support terrible and chronic suffering *there*. And how many other battles, too!

To be *the voice of the voiceless* today is a moral imperative. Defending all the forgotten people of the continent of Africa, the Palestinian resistance, the rights of the Chechens and the Tibetans and all the oppressed peoples of the world is the most explicit expression of our fidelity to our principles and our ethic. In our time we must also reject the establishment of a kind of frontier of law between the North and South that would operate unilaterally against the victims of economic injustice; policies proposed to combat immigration are dreadful and assume that the clandestine immigrant is a liar, a thief, even a bandit. With their inability to call their economic policies into question, Northern governments, our governments, apply repressive policies against the victims of their own regulations. All political thinking and planning that do not take migration into account impose a double sanction on the victims—by imposing on them a shameful way of life in their own countries and by imprisoning them there or expelling them "in the name of law" when they have the dignity and courage to refuse inhuman treatment.

New security policies are all moving in the same direction: in the name of the war against terrorism, anything, or almost anything, goes. Hundreds of Muslims are imprisoned without trial in the United States, antiglobalization activists are under surveillance, cross-border travel is restricted, civil liberties are curtailed, and, on the international level, the repressive policies of Sharon and Putin are met with silence and eyes are closed to the behavior of our Saudi and Pakistani allies. This is all said to be to protect us from "those who do not like our civilization and our freedom." Muslims of conscience living within the West must have the courage to say that this is not true and that if terrorism really is unacceptable, war must be declared on all forms of terrorism, particularly state terrorism, and priority must be given to dealing with its causes. Condemning without a moment's hesitation the atrocities of 11 September 2001, for example, cannot mean that we have to accept all and any reprisals and policies because we might be in danger. This kind of diversion has serious consequences: by putting citizens in a state of siege and feeding their fear, the government prevents them from thinking and critiquing the world order and its injustices. Citizens who are afraid do not go out to change the world; first of all they protect themselves and what belongs to them. They become dangerously distracted as a natural reflex.

Here again, it is not a question of being interested only in international situations in which Muslims are implicated, as it may appear today. We have seen that all situations are interconnected and that international politics have an immediate impact on domestic realities. So we now need to build a global vision of problems, and it is more important than ever to decide who our partners are in this struggle. The international popular movement that has recently developed across the world (which must not be confused with the violent tendency of some groups and individuals) expresses critical theses and demands reforms that for the most part are completely in accord with the Muslim ethic. Organizations that call for the establishment of fairer trade (of the type proposed by Max Havelaar or development cooperatives); those that want to promote more responsible management of the economy and the financial markets (in the manner of the ATTAC movement or, more locally, of institutions committed to ethical investment); the Peasant Confederation and the supporters of a Christian theology of liberation and resistance (now found throughout the world) must become in time, with many other resisters on the local level, the objective allies of this plural front for which we long. It is the responsibility of Muslims to commit themselves to this way, to decide what kinds of alliances are possible, taking into account their limits as well as their demands. The globalization with which we are presented and that is imposed upon us today sanctions above all the absolute primacy of the logic of economics over every other consideration, and the efficiency of communication networks and highways seems to draw us more and more into becoming better consumers. The picture would be very dark were it not for a widespread movement of resistance: when faced with neoliberal economics, the message of Islam offers no way out but resistance. In the West, as in the East, we are summoned to use our minds, our imaginations, and our creative abilities to think of an alternative—using our sources in partnership with all those who resist and mobilize for "alternative ways."

8

ECONOMIC RESISTANCE

The age of globalization is an age of upheaval, or more accurately of reversal, that condones the domination of economics and financial markets over all other areas of human activity. Globalization is first and foremost economic, rather than political, cultural, or technological. It has become impossible to formulate a serious critique of the world order, the policies of the industrialized nations, or the decisions of the G8 without referring to a minute study of the neoliberal economic system, the institutions that sustain it (the World Trade Organization, the International Monetary Fund, and the World Bank), the formidable power of a handful of multinationals, and the functioning of the banks and financial markets.

Strictly political approaches and discourses concerning states that observe the rule of law, effective citizenship, the end of colonialism, national independence, aid toward development, and autonomy have become meaningless: in a time of world markets, speculation on every front, and virtual financial transactions, the old realities of domination, the subjugation of the Southern nations, and colonialism have changed in nature and in name but have not disappeared. It is now no longer necessary to be present in Caracas, Bamako, or Jakarta in order to make decisions; the dominant powers operate from offices in Washington, London, and Paris and from stock exchanges in New York and Tokyo following the new division of labor, which condones a "new look" colonialism and a veritable "long-distance" slavery. These dominating powers have no heart and oppress and kill children, women, and men every day under a reign of terror and with unheard-of violence, with the cynical advantage of attracting no media attention but acting slowly, silently, and unadvertised. Two years ago, well before the events of 11 September 2001, in Burkina Faso, a scholar friend, disheartened by so much hypocrisy, confided: "If terrorism consists in seizing innocent people and killing them, this world order is sanctioning a cynical, silent, global terrorism." Rising from the heart of one of the poorest countries on the planet, this voice has some legitimacy.

The world has changed, and all these transformations have serious consequences. But it all happens as if the thinking of Muslim ulama and intellectuals had stalled, particularly in the field of economics. We observe, like everyone else, the phenomenon of globalization; we study its basic precepts and its logic; we perceive its serious ethical shortcomings; but we hardly offer an alternative, or at least a critical perspective on the basis of the scriptural sources and an understanding of the context. In the meantime, the opposite phenomenon is emerging: the Islamic world has produced economic and financial institutions that, by trying to arrange, within but on the fringes of the system on a small scale, so-called Islamic transactions, without *riba* (usury), condone and affirm the logic of the global system because they do not resist it. We propose structural adaptations to protect ourselves, but in fact the system is accepted for what it is and we "deal with it." Observing the world economic order and its injustices objectively and realistically is one thing, but coming to terms with it by adapting to it is another.

The whole of the Islamic world is in subjection to the market economy. The most overtly Islamic states on the level of law (which are overwhelmingly repressive) and government, such as those of Saudi Arabia and other petromonarchies, are the most economically integrated into the neoliberal system, which is based on speculation and tied into interest-bearing transactions. It is impossible to draw a dividing line between the world that keeps Islamic rules and that in which they are broken: the connections and interactions between them are such that it is the globality of the economic order that must be questioned. It is now in the area of economics more than in any other that the old categories of *dar al-harb* (the abode of war) and *dar al-islam* (the abode of Islam), of which we have spoken in part I, have fundamentally collapsed and become totally inoperative. When economic practices were restricted to the local or national level and when they gave priority to respect for the legal codes of nation states, distinction on the basis of geographical areas was legitimate. None of this now holds true, but we continue to hear ulama making distinctions between the "two worlds" and consequently legislating on the basis of obsolete criteria. The world has changed, but their eyes are fixed on realities and on systems of reference that have today been completely overtaken, with the very serious consequence that their legal opinions (*fatawa*) advising adaptation in fact prevent the emergence of an alternative way of thinking.

Geography is not and can no longer be the criterion for distinguishing between Islamic and non-Islamic areas. We have to change completely the way we look at the world order and its logic. Here again, as we have said in part I, we need to live out a true intellectual revolution. At this time of globalization, it is no longer geographical areas but areas of activity that we can evaluate as being more or less close to our principles and ethics of life. Because Western countries, at the level of constitutions and law, protect freedom of conscience and religion and the rights and integrity of their citizens, we have been able to refer to them as an "abode of testimony" (*dar al-shahada*). Wherever in the world we are guaranteed these rights, this *abode of testimony* comes into being as far as Muslim consciousness is concerned.[1] But if we look at the neoliberal system as a whole and the logic that underpins it, we see that we are very clearly in the *alam al-harb* (world of war), or *dar al-harb*, if we use the old terminology.[2] Whether it is Washington, London, Tokyo, Riyadh, Cairo, Casablanca, Kuala Lumpur, or Singapore, the whole world, as far as economic activity is concerned, lives by speculation and interest-bearing transactions, surrounded by the most complex and sophisticated financial and banking logics.[3] We know that these practices are in total material contradiction to Islamic principles on which the Qur'anic revelation is explicit: whoever engages in speculation or the practice of usury is at war with the Transcendent.[4] But is there the potential for an alternative?

Western Muslims live at the heart of the system. For decades, their communities have suffered from deeply disturbed consciences because it is so difficult, and often impossible, to live in industrialized societies and avoid interest-bearing financial transactions. How should we grasp the situation, and what adaptations can be proposed? Many ulama based in Muslim-majority countries have contributed to the debate, and their legal advice ranges from forbidding all involvement in the system to taking into account, as they arise, situations of necessity (*darurat*) and need (*hajat*). A small minority of scholars have freed Muslims from these concerns by stating, for example, that bank interest is not the same as the usury (*riba*) referred to in the Qur'an. This technique of changing what things are called in order to avoid a prohibition is well known: in the same way, beer is not regarded as included in the alcohol (*khamr*) referred to in the Qur'an, and so on! Traditions of the Prophet have warned us against this way of dealing with things, and the great majority of Muslims do not follow this advice. It remains for them, in practice, to make new rulings on a daily basis, and the solutions—from prohibitions to adaptations—considered objectively, are neither evident nor clear. Either we depend permanently on the mitigation of necessity (*darura*), need (*haja*), and exception (*istithna*); or we simply fall back (without real contextualization) on the view of Abu Hanifa and his school, which long ago allowed the practice of usury within *dar al-harb*;[5] or we turn for credit to Islamic financial institutions based in the West; or, to avoid all difficulties, we ask for the charitable support of a wealthy organization or individual in the Gulf. In these circumstances, it is difficult to live an open, independent, and, above all, harmonious life; a heart torn between principles and the economic environment endlessly finds and cobbles together solutions that, while they may pacify the conscience a little, are not capable of changing either the situation or the world.

The global perspective we need invites us to return to our universal principles and to understand their basic objectives. It will then be possible, in light of our specific context, to assess the areas of conflict and the scope for adaptation. It will be necessary above all to propose guidelines (at the local level) that, even if they do not provide solutions that are immediately completely satisfactory (because the problems are so complex), may nevertheless make it possible to begin to think differently about our involvement in the economic sphere, with an awareness of the need and the imperative to search for an alternative that is as much local as global. Islamic teachings are intrinsically opposed to the basic premises and the logic of the neoliberal capitalist system, and Muslims who live in "the system's head" have a greater responsibility, with others who are working toward the same goal, to propose solutions that could create a way out and lead to a more just economy and more equitable trade.

Fundamental Principles in Economics

By way of introduction, we must repeat here that the particular characteristic of Islamic rules in economic matters is the total, continuous, and inclusive link between this area and the moral sphere of reference. In fact, commercial and financial transactions between people are included and fed by the basic teaching of *tawhid*—the principle of the oneness of God—and they cannot be considered in the abstract, apart from their relation with it. Just as one turns toward God, just as one tries not to lie, not to deceive, so in the same way the rule is not to steal, to work for the good of humankind in the sight of God, to do good in the sight of God—always. It is impossible, from this perspective, to conceive of people as cogs in a machine, definable without reference to any ethical qualities, motivated only by their own interest, either producing or consuming, their actions assessed only quantitatively. Economic *science*, which considers itself as *positive* and has concentrated on the study of the famous *homo economicus*, is thus cut off from the Islamic point of view. To reduce a person to the mechanics of how, without any consideration of the ultimate why, is inconceivable, unless people are to be confused with "things," simple tools, just links in the chain that constitutes society.

The Moral Framework: From the Individual to the Collective

In fact, even the most everyday, simple, and natural economic activity always contains a moral quality. Whether we look at production or consumption, it is the moral quality from which it derives its value, not in the first instance from performance in terms of productivity, profitability, or benefit in the broad sense. Every Qur'anic teaching in the sphere of economics revolves around this axis: production of evil, against the humanity of humankind, production leading to terror and the brutalization of the masses, is production at a loss, with no profitability before God, whatever the financial profits that may be achieved. The same is true of consumption: it goes into deficit if it forgets itself. There are innumerable verses in the Qur'an that link "economic" activity with the moral dimension of its ultimate purpose (through which it is linked with mindfulness of the Creator), and we may here cite three kinds of economic action:

Zakat.   This is the third pillar of Islam, and its very essence reveals the importance of social involvement in the Muslim worldview. *Zakat* is clearly a tax on possessions and property, which must first be understood as an obligation before God. This levy "purifies" one's goods on the religious, sacred, and moral levels. So the link with God, with Transcendence, with remembrance of the meaning and finiteness of life, is inscribed and actualized not only in being but in having, and in the relation each human being establishes with that fact. After the two declarations of faith (in the oneness of God, *tawhid*, and in the Prophet), and after the obligation of prayer, which establishes the link between the believer and the Creator, the social purification tax (*zakat*) projects the believer into the sphere of the community, which is thus permeated by Transcendence and the sacred. At the same time, what underpins *zakat* is a full and ethical conception of social organization and human relations: those who have possessions have duties; those who are unprovided for have rights before God and among men. Islam does not conceive of poverty as a normal feature of the social arena and does not envisage that the remedy for this distortion should be the free generosity of some toward others in the hope that the wealth of the rich and the destitution of the poor may somehow miraculously find a point of balance. The obligation of *zakat* puts this question into the realm of law and morality and cannot be left to anyone's discretion. Social solidarity is part of the faith and is its most concrete testimony: to be with God is to be with people; this is the essence of the teaching of the third pillar of Islam.

Abu Bakr, the first successor of the Prophet, decided, against the advice of Umar, to fight the southern tribes who no longer wanted to fulfill the obligation of *zakat*. There can be no compromise on a question that arises, before God, from the right of the poor and hence from the responsibility of every society with a constitution. It cannot simply be a question of generosity; it is clearly a question of justice, and this notion must be defended in every human transaction. The point is that the rich, those who have possessions, must never forget, for in their property, as the Qur'an says, is "the right of the beggar and the disinherited."

Personal Expenditure. Beyond the obligation of *zakat*, we find in Islamic teaching a large number of recommendations about the moral significance of personal expenditure. The management of one's possessions can never be thought of as outside the meaning of being. We may distinguish in the Qur'an at least four aspects of the moral meaning of expenditure: to please God and make gifts along the way He sets us; to give fair measure; to struggle against egoism and acquisitiveness; and to learn discreetness.

TO PLEASE GOD AND MAKE GIFTS ALONG THE WAY HE SETS US. In the Qur'anic Revelation are numerous references with this kind of reminder, among the most significant verses in this connection: "The [the believers] feed the poor, the orphan, the captive for the love of God, saying: 'We feed you to please God alone (for the sake of his face); we do not expect any recompense or gratitude from you.' "[6] In the next two verses, images that compare the "benefit" of giving in the way of God with the abundant life of nature, which offers its fruits without calculating: "The parable of those who spend their possessions for the sake of God is that of grain out of which grow seven ears, in every ear a hundred grains: for God grants manifold increase unto whom He wills; and God is infinite, all-knowing."[7] Further on: "The parable of those who spend their possessions out of a longing to please God, and out of their own inner certainty, is that of a garden on high fertile ground: a rainstorm smites it, and thereupon it brings forth its fruit; and if no rainstorm smites it, soft rain [falls upon it]. And God sees all that you do."[8] Faith is that intimate conviction that God sees what we *do* and knows the intention behind the way we dispose of our possessions. Maintaining this link with the Creator means directing all our financial activity toward goodness, transparency, and justice. It is to give and give again from our plenty, over and above *zakat*, in order to live with our rights in harmony with those of others.

GIVING FAIR MEASURE. It is not necessary to live like a hermit and to give everything without any sort of account. It cannot be right that we should make ourselves poor in order to achieve justice. A true gift is one that is motivated by moderation and awareness of limitations, as well as by responsibility. It is essential that a gift should be in fair measure: "Neither allow thy hand to remain shackled to thy neck, nor stretch it forth to the utmost limit [of thy capacity], lest thou find thyself blamed [by thy dependents] or even destitute";[9] "(The servants of the Merciful are) those who, when they spend on others, are neither lavish nor miserly and who find a fair measure between the two."[10] To give part of one's time and one's possessions is to give the means of a permanent commitment for one's own sake and for the sake of others. Our spirit, our body, those close to us—all have rightful claims upon us to which we must respond, and out of this response is born the true gift of oneself to the other and to society as a whole: fair measure makes it possible to maintain what we need to sustain our own center in order better to be [in solidarity] with other people.

THE STRUGGLE AGAINST EGOISM AND ACQUISITIVENESS. The Qur'anic commandments on this point aim in the same direction and complement what has just been said. To neglect giving and to protect one's possessions to the point of burying them is to forget God and to treat one's possessions like an idol. It means that one is preoccupied with *counting*, when what is needed is prayer and purifying oneself from this natural tendency to egoism: "Those who guard themselves from their own greed, those are they who succeed."[11] The Revelation has some hard words for acquisitive people. The image of a hereafter of suffering is meant to awaken the conscience to the seriousness of an attitude that borders on idolatry and whose consequences we see every day: "as for all who lay up treasures of gold and silver and do not spend them for the sake of God—give them the tiding of grievous suffering [in the life to come]: on the Day when that [hoarded wealth] shall be heated in the fire of hell and their foreheads and their sides and their backs branded therewith, [those sinners shall be told] 'these are the treasures which you have laid up for yourselves! Taste, then, [the evil of] your hoarded treasures!' "[12]

LEARNING DISCRETION. There is a constant reminder of this in the Qur'an. Humankind is asked to find the measure in which it will give and to remain discreet and respectful of others. Indeed, one's way of giving is in itself a testimony of faith: if you have no need to be seen by others, it is a sign that you know God is always with you. Discretion also safeguards the dignity of those you help: "If you do deeds of charity openly, it is well; but if you bestow it upon the needy in secret, it will be even better for you, and it will atone for some of your bad deeds. And God is aware of all that you do."[13] Again we find an image drawn from nature to express the perversity and vanity of giving alms in order to be noticed: "O you who have attained to faith! Do not deprive your charitable deeds of all worth by stressing your own benevolence and hurting [the feeling of the needy], as does he who spends his wealth only to be seen and praised by men, and believes not in God and the Last Day: for his parable is that of a smooth rock with [a little] earth upon it—and then a rainstorm smites it and leaves it hard and bare."[14] This should be the attitude of humankind: to struggle for the rights of all to be respected and to make gifts of one's possessions silently and discreetly. This duty to be discreet is more important than it may appear: it bears the mark of respect for people's dignity in all circumstances, even the most intimate. The aim is to prevent evil, to give before the poor need to beg, and to try to avoid being seen by anyone so that no one has to be embarrassed or look the other way for no reason. When society does not give what its members are entitled to have, the more affluent among them must express the greatness of this principle of dignified generosity. The Qur'an constantly paints this landscape, which must not be forgotten in our personal economic management.

These four aspects of personal expenditure are moral qualities that give direction to human action. When we are mindful of God, we can discern easily that this action takes place in a sacred dimension because it expresses immediately—in the sense of without mediation—the link with Transcendence. It embodies an ultimate purpose, a meaning, and this meaning is clearly the expression of *the morality of the action and thus of elementary, normal, everyday economic activity.*

Collectivity. The teaching that can be deduced concerning the individual and the collective flows from what has just been said about *zakat* and personal expenditure. It is impossible to live, to bear witness, to pray, to fast, to make the pilgrimage alone, apart from other people and thinking only of oneself. Once again, *to be with God is to be with other people*: to bear the faith is to bear responsibility for social commitment at every moment. The teaching that must be understood from *zakat* could not be more explicit: to possess is to have the duty to share. It is impossible shamelessly to accumulate possessions in the name of personal freedom when it leads to exploitation and social injustices; it is impossible, too, to forget the interests of society as a whole and consider only one's own. Of course, people are free, but they are responsible for this freedom before God and other people. This responsibility is undeniably moral: according to this morality, *to be free means to protect the freedom and dignity of others.*

The four practical pillars of Islam have, as we have seen, this double dimension—individual and communal. The essence of Islamic teaching lies along this path between these two extremes: either to put first individuals and their own interests and so create a social space that may turn into a jungle, no matter how lofty the speeches that may be made, or to give priority to the group and to the society and to deny the specificity, the hopes, and desires of each individual by creating a structure that binds and alienates, no matter how many plans there may be for development. A difficult balance, but it is the only way to respond to the demand of the Creator, who expects each person *alone* to bear responsibility for his or her *community* life. On the economic level, it is the only way that allows one to live humanly, taking into account the exchanges we cannot do without. Here, as in other areas, there are rights, and so there are also duties. Islam claims, with all the moral energy of its message, that a human economy without duties is an inhumane economy that organizes, produces, and structures injustice, discrimination, exploitation, and famine. No jungle on earth is home to such horror.[15]

General Economic Principles

Many works have been written on this subject, and many Muslim intellectuals since the beginning of the twentieth century have expounded the broad outlines of Islamic economics. We shall limit ourselves here to indicating by way of summary three principles that explain economic activity without bringing in overwhelming amounts of legal detail.

Tawhid *and Vicegerency.* We have referred in part I to the relationship that exists between the owner—God—and the vicegerent—the human being— in Islam. There is absolutely no doubt that in the realm of economics, this relationship has a profound impact. The teaching of *tawhid* is fundamental: God alone has ownership in the absolute sense, and He has put the earth at the disposal of humankind. "What is in heaven and on earth belongs to God."[16] "Are you not aware that God has made subservient to you all that is in the heavens and all that is on earth, and has lavished upon you His blessing, both outward and inward?"[17] The idea of vicegerency (*khilafa*) gives duties priority over rights. Everyone may, and has the inalienable right to enjoy all natural resources, since they are put at our disposal by the Creator; but this enjoyment cannot extend to disturbing the natural order by savage exploitation of the elements and disrespect for the "signs." Ecological considerations are inherent in the Islamic philosophy of action: to enjoy resources before God, requires that we respect them. There is, of course, the original permission, but there are limits to respect. Thus, all the elements are signs (*ayat*) in creation, sacred in themselves; this point alone has important consequences.

The Creator desires the good of humankind, and we should not forget that desire. What is true on the ecological plane, with regard to use of resources, is also true in the sphere of production. We have already said that what makes a good product is its moral quality: the parameters of productivity, profitability, cost, and so on are nothing in themselves and are void of meaning if they are used to measure the production of what is useless, worthless, or, more broadly, destructive. Clearly, humankind must produce, but never simply for profit; humankind must indeed consume, but always commensurately with its real needs. We must not forget the need to take into account the higher interest of society, which, echoing the divine values, limits all egoistical and thoughtless exploitation. This is the problem contained in the recognition of private property.

Private Property. Ownership and enjoyment of material possessions are permitted in Islam and have a place in the framework that we have referred to many times: the use of goods must respect revealed moral guidance and, further, must take into account the interest of the society as a whole. In this philosophy of the existence and management of possessions, the right and freedom of people to enjoy goods and to acquire property are considerable. The principle for acquisition is found in the Qur'an: "One part of what men acquire through their work is their own; one part of what women acquire through their work is their own."[18] The first teaching to be deduced from this verse is the recognition of property acquired through work. This is what the majority of Muslim jurists point to. We have already referred to the fundamental right to work, and the possibility of acquiring goods is a logical consequence: it may be the salaried work of employees, agriculture, commerce, fishing, hunting, or other work. The only condition, the fundamental condition, is that the work be within the bounds of what is considered legal (which means *for Muslims* the avoidance of dealing in forbidden merchandise, gambling in all its forms, monopolies, usury, and speculation). There are other means of acquiring property: inheritance, capital, *zakat* (for the poor), *awqaf* (endowments), and gifts, and we find in the standard works of law and Islamic jurisprudence commentaries and detailed analyses of each of these means.

The recognition of property assumes the social organization to protect it. This protection is fundamental in Islamic law: in the classification proposed by the scholars, which we have already mentioned with reference to al-Shatibi, it forms part of the *daruriyyat* (essential needs) alongside the protection of religion, of the person, of intellect, and of family ties. So property is inalienable. But it must be stated that its management is subject to conditions whose absence calls for the intervention of the public authorities. Without going into detail, here are three situations that would require intervention on the basis of the principles expounded: (1) management involving corruption, theft, unjust exploitation of employees, trade in illegal products, financial fraud; (2) management that goes against the common interest, which might mean anything from the creation of a monopoly to irresponsible squandering; (3) a case of *force majeure*: natural disaster, wars, or higher demands of the community. Clearly, all these exceptions have to be codified and must adhere to the rules of due process of law to which every citizen is entitled. Even if all these means of intervention do not exist in the West, it is good to remember what situations are defined as abusive or exceptional.

The general principle is expressed by a sort of contract between society and its property-owning members. In exchange for protection, and well in advance of any intervention, which should be the exception rather than the rule, property owners have a duty to society to manage their belongings in a moral way. The basis of their social and economic freedom is not put at risk, but each of them is required to respect the community as a whole. Similarly, society will encourage economic activity, and people's efforts to multiply their goods will contribute to the success of the social strategy. The state, as happens almost everywhere, must guarantee respect for the areas of maneuver that are essential for economic activity and investments. The limitations are necessary for ethical reasons, because people always lose the sense of moderation and well-doing when there is too great a temptation to profit. It is unjust not to trust in people's good qualities, but it is madness to turn a blind eye to their weaknesses.

Requiring people of faith to take care to retain the moral quality in the management of their affairs and to observe the principles of law and Islamic jurisprudence concerning property has two more aspects whose nature is to ward off excess. The first is the obligation to pay *zakat*, to which we have already referred. This purifying social tax is a tax on property and not only on income. Muslims have to give a percentage of their goods to an institution, an organization, or directly to the poor, usually on the basis of a reckoning of their material situation over the period of a year. We have mentioned the religious importance of this payment and its profoundly moral implication. It also has explicit significance for social justice and solidarity between the rich and the poor. It must be added, however, that *zakat* is in itself an invitation to put one's possessions to work and to profit from them without the hoarding that would otherwise be possible. The second limitation concerning management of property is one of the most rigorous Islamic prohibitions in the area of social affairs. We often simply say and recall that Islam is against usury, or against interest, without going into the consequences of this statement. However, it is essential to analyze it so that we may look at concrete solutions that could be brought to bear in response to the failing current economic system. The prohibition of *riba* (which we shall define next) is contained in the economic philosophy that underlies it, whose broad outlines we have traced here; it implicitly demands that we consider an alternative economic system. It cannot remain simply theoretical, and we shall see later that it requires very determined local commitment.

The Prohibition of Riba. There are several definitions of the term *riba*, depending on whether the intention is to restrict or extend the scope of its prohibition in the realm of economic activity. The Arabic word *riba* is derived from the verb *raba*, which means to "increase" or "augment." There are various legal opinions on the nature of the prohibition itself, but the ulama of the past and of today are almost unanimous in understanding that it formally prohibits any rate of interest and any form of usury, because the idea that underlies the notion of *riba* is one of profit that is not in exchange for any service rendered or work performed: it is a growth of capital through and upon capital itself. It is also considered that a form of *riba* exists in situations of unequal exchange: "this is usury on exchanges" or "on unequal exchanges," which relies on the famous *hadith* of the Prophet: "Wheat for wheat in equal parts and from hand to hand; any surplus is usury. Barley for barley in equal parts and from hand to hand; any surplus is usury. Dates for dates in equal parts and from hand to hand; any surplus is usury. Salt for salt in equal parts and from hand to hand; any surplus is usury. Silver for silver in equal parts and from hand to hand; any surplus is usury. Gold for gold in equal parts and from hand to hand; any surplus is usury."[19] The idea that emerges from this *hadith* is one of equality and simultaneity in exchange, with the intention that the terms of exchange should be very clear to both parties. Many *hadith* introduce precise details that insist on the importance of the conditions of exchange, and jurists of all the Sunni schools have deduced from them a formal prohibition against speculation, although there is some diversity of interpretation regarding certain types of economic and financial procedures. The conclusion drawn by Hamid Algabid, former prime minister of the Republic of Niger and former secretary general of the Organization of the Islamic Conference (OIC), is clear and legally precise: "Whether we refer to usury on loans of money or on exchanges, the minuteness of the detail of the prohibitions and obligations in the Sunna shows that hoarding in all its forms is rigorously condemned, and is pursued in all circumstances, no matter how improbable. The clear definition of what is lent and what is restored, what is sold and the price paid for it is an absolute rule—clear definition of the object itself and of the time frame. Speculation is banned as acquisition of wealth without justification; that is to say increasing the value of the object of the exchange without anything legitimate being added to it in return (such as work, treatment, transport, preparation)."[20]

So what emerges on the strictly economic level is a double prohibition contained in the notion of *riba* when one understands it in the Qur'anic sense of increasing the value of goods without performing any service: (1) the prohibition of interest on capital; (2) the prohibition of interest on exchanges that, being based on speculation, monopoly, or other "unequal conditions," is not a profit derived from honest trade. These are the general principles of the prohibition, and every epoch must consider the current economic practicalities in order to measure how far they comply with the principles and the ethics. It is in fact clear that the very definition of *riba* is a function of the type of activities that arise in historical situations and of the extent of the application of the definition. The inclusion of this notion in the ethical order that reminds us of the transcendent and collective dimensions is of prime importance, and there is no doubt that this is the essential point of the prohibition. It is not a question of suffocating human activity—quite the reverse—but it is a question of making it just and equitable, of "separating the good grain from the weeds." The progression in the order of the Revelations that led to this prohibition is very eloquent. The first verse revealed is a kind of allusion and brings out the moral deficiency implicit in paying interest on personal transactions: "Whatever you may give out in usury so that it might increase through [other] people's possessions will bring [you] no increase in the sight of God—whereas all that you give out in charity, seeking God's countenance, [will be blessed by Him] for it is they, they [who thus seek his countenance] that shall have their recompense multiplied."[21] This thought is addressed to debtors who are asked, implicitly and from a moral point of view, not to undertake this kind of borrowing. The verses of the second Revelation dealing with usury speak of the example of the Jews, who had broken the prohibition: they are the creditors who are focused on here and, in their practice of usury, they are said to "consume people's goods unjustly."[22] The notion of justice takes priority: "We have forbidden the Jews excellent foods which were formerly permitted to them; this is because of their prevarication, because they have often strayed from the way of God, because they have practiced usury which had been forbidden to them, because they have consumed people's goods unjustly." The third stage is an exclamation addressed to the Muslims and restricted to a specific practice: "O you who have attained to faith! Do not gorge yourselves on usury, doubling and redoubling it—but remain conscious of God, so that you may attain to a happy state."[23] The verses containing the formal prohibition are among the last revealed to the Prophet, and Umar later expressed regret that the Prophet had not been able to make its meaning more precise for his Companions. Nevertheless, it is explicit, and it makes it clear that it is a matter of distinguishing between good and bad practices in a purely moral sense: trade that can legitimately produce profit is founded on justice if it follows criteria that will prevent it becoming an unequal exchange leading to exploitation of some by others: "Those who gorge themselves on usury behave but as he might behave whom Satan has confounded with his touch; for they say, 'Buying and selling is but a kind of usury'—while God has made buying and selling lawful and usury unlawful. Hence, whoever becomes aware of his Sustainer's admonition, and thereupon desists [from usury], may keep his past gains, and it will be for God to judge him; but as for those who return to it—they are destined for the fire therein to abide! God deprives usurious gains of all blessing, whereas He blesses charitable deeds with manifold increase. And God does not love anyone who is stubbornly ingrate and persists in sinful ways. Verily, those who have attained to faith and do good works, and are constant in prayer, and dispense charity—they shall have their reward with their Sustainer, and no fear need they have, and neither shall they grieve. O you who have attained to faith! Remain conscious of God, and give up all outstanding gains from usury, if you are [truly] believers; for if you do it not, then know that you are at war with God and His Apostle. But if you repent, then you shall be entitled to [the return of] your principal: you will do no wrong, and neither will you be wronged. If, however, [the debtor] is in straitened circumstances, [grant him] a delay until a time of ease; and it would be for your own good—if you but knew it—to remit [the debt entirely] by way of charity. And be conscious of the Day on which you shall be brought back unto God, whereupon every human being shall be repaid in full for what he has earned, and none shall be wronged."[24]

Usury, which appears to bring in money and increase one's capital, and almsgiving, or the purifying social tax, which appears to diminish it, stand face to face: in the divine balance, by the measure of conscience and the gauge of human benefit, they are ultimately the opposite of what they seem: usury is a loss and almsgiving is a gain. The purpose of the prohibition is to put people in a relation of transparence, equity, and humanity: "Do not treat anyone unjustly and you will not be unjustly treated." So it is a matter of refusing all forms of exploitation and of encouraging fair trade. The rich at the time of Muhammad could react only negatively to the meaning of this message directed to them, as people have always reacted to prophetic revelations, from Noah to Jesus: "Whenever We sent a prophet to any community, those of its people who had lost themselves entirely in the pursuit of pleasures would declare, 'Behold, we deny that there is any truth in [what you claim to be] your message.' "[25] In the same way, this message cannot but arouse the disapproval of the richest people today because it is essentially a determined rejection of economic servitude, financial slavery, and all humiliation. There is no scope for distorting its meaning: it charges people to find the most appropriate system for their time, provided that it respects the foundational principle of expressing an economy with a human face, inevitably opposed to interest, speculation, and monopolies.

We are well and truly on the way to opposing the world economic order. It could not be clearer. The rich countries, like the wealthy merchants of Mecca in times past, cannot fail to see a danger in local and national movements whose aim is to remove themselves from the "classical" economic system. Nothing could be more normal. But we now know that the Northern model of development is unexportable: a billion and a half human beings live in comfort *because* almost four billion do not have the means to survive. The terms of exchange are unequal, exploitation is permanent, speculation is extreme, monopolies are murderous. The prohibition of *riba*, which is the moral axis around which the economic thought of Islam revolves, calls believers to reject categorically an order that respects only profit and scoffs at the values of justice and humanity. By the same token, the prohibition obliges them to consider and to work out a model that comes closer to respecting the prohibition. In the West, as in the East, we must think of a global alternative, and local projects must be implemented with the idea of leaving the system to the extent possible and not affirming it through blindness, incompetence, or laziness.

In the West: Patchworks and Adaptations

The preceding lines make it easier to perceive the disturbances and difficulties that cannot fail to arise in the mind of the conscience of Muslims who would like to live faithful to these principles in the West. In their daily lives, with every financial action, at the smallest attempt to invest or launch a commercial project, the question arises: am I true to my principles? What should I do? Is it even possible not to be complicit with the capitalist system, speculation, and interest? Some give up out of fear. Some cobble together more or less viable solutions. Some proceed in resignation, almost convinced that they have to steel themselves to work within the system and adapt to it. In spite of the seriousness of these concerns, the daily difficulties and the importance of the hindrance they present for sound economic activity, no solution seems to be in sight. Most of the ulama are fixed on the classical opinions and reaffirm the prohibitions, some Islamic financial institutions suggest arrangements for some organizations and individuals, but on the whole everyone knows that we are at an impasse, and no alternative for Western Muslims is proposed. It is true that there are specific responses to particular situations, but radical thinking is glaringly absent. So far, Muslims in the West who want to be true to their principles are clearly stalled, condemned either to betray themselves or to marginalize themselves. Ultimately, like it or not, they can be nothing but observers on the economic scene. The very people whose first responsibility should have been to propose "something else" from within the system find themselves forced to give in or to dream, like those who reassure themselves by predicting the imminent implosion of the system "on its own," "from the inside." Now, at a time when "anything economic" is preeminent, losing this battle and refusing to take the risk needed to create an alternative means losing practically everything. This is both irresponsible and senseless. It is first and foremost wrong.

We have recalled that the two fundamental principles of Islamic guidelines in economic matters are an obligation and a prohibition: the obligation of *zakat* on the one hand and the prohibition of *riba* on the other. If we try to evaluate the current situation in the West regarding the concrete application of these two principles, we cannot fail to notice important deficiencies (as much in thinking as in practice) and the more or less endemic dysfunctions within Muslim communities. It is true that the situation has improved somewhat in the past few years, but we are still very wide of the mark. For example, many Muslims are committed to paying the *zakat* that is due, but the way these things are considered and organized leaves them confused. Once the annual calculations are made, the money is either paid to institutions that specialize in collecting *zakat*, or it is sent off for humanitarian works or mosque projects, or it is given directly to people in need in the West or, more often, in the home countries. In fact, the money collected as *zakat* represents phenomenal amounts, and there is almost no local or national body today thinking about or directing the careful and appropriate use of it, even though this is essential if the fundamental purposes are to be achieved. It all simply happens as if *zakat* is just a widow's mite to be paid out of duty and distributed as charity. But *zakat* is anything but that: the levying of this *purifying social tax*, in response to precise requirements set out long ago by the ulama, must be considered within the purpose of establishing a real *system* of collective solidarity and social security, woven into the very fabric of society, that aims at freeing the poor from their dependence so that eventually they themselves will pay *zakat*.

This system can come into being only by applying a thorough knowledge of the social context in which the *zakat* payments are made. This is the more important because it is an absolute priority that the payments should be dispersed in the area in which they are collected.[26] The least that one can say is that nothing seems to be being done today about a system thought out and conceived in and for Western societies: we are not far from a general chaos in which each organization and individual goes its own sweet way. Local, national, and international institutions are set up (such as *bayt al-mal* or *dar al-awqaf*),[27] but strategies for expenditure and distribution are not always clear and are often unrelated to the realities and needs of the area. Moreover, the funds are very often used to finance building projects (e.g., mosques, centers), rather than to provide direct support to people, who are then helped in a very perfunctory way, with no precise consideration and no purpose beyond alleviating a financial difficulty here and there. Ultimately, it is the social philosophy as a whole that leads to this way of acting and maintaining only the outward form of *zakat*, which is thus undermined and even betrayed. As we have said, *zakat* is first and foremost an obligation that requires a systematic approach: to respect the "rights of the poor" in a given society is to limit the dysfunctions of that society in a specific way (e.g., unemployment, homelessness, disability, causes of instability and marginalization); one must start from these factors and decide on a logical strategy that will lead to autonomy rather than dependence; it is a matter of acquiring an in-depth knowledge of one's community, its needs and its priorities, through close involvement or, in other words, thinking through the framework of a real social policy with principles, vision, and inner consistency. We are at present a long way from taking this approach.

With regard to the other principle—the prohibition of *riba*—we have already said that there is a formal prohibition against interest, and Muslims are called to distance themselves from anything that resembles it in any way. In this area, one single exception is made (by the Hanafis), and, curiously, is presented as one of the priorities in Muslim communities in the West. This is borrowing from banks with interest in order to buy houses. The European Council for Research and Fatwas, and the League of Scholars of Sharia in the United States, by a majority rather than unanimously, have pronounced legal opinions that allow the use of this kind of credit. In brief, we may say that they rely in their pronouncements on two main considerations:

1. The particular situation of Muslims concerning their need for secure accommodation as well as for financial security (the ownership of a house is in itself a considerable gain), which implies that the acquisition of a dwelling must be considered a constraining necessity (*dar-ura*), or, more precisely a need (*haja*), which in the nature of things becomes a constraining necessity;[28]
2. The legal opinion of some scholars of note (among the most prominent is Abu Hanifa and his student Muhammad ibn Hasan al-Shaybani) who allowed the use of *riba* in *dar al-harb* in dealings with non-Muslims on the double condition that one is using this practice to protect the goods of Muslims and at the same time neither betraying nor deceiving the said partner to the transaction.[29]

Not all scholars are in agreement with this view. The literalists and the great majority of the traditionalists (apart from those who follow the school of Abu Hanifa, who for the most part accept this ruling[30]) reject this ruling and do not allow any departure from the absolute ban on *riba*. Among those who subscribe to the reformist school,[31] reservations have been expressed as to whether the need to buy property is really "constraining" (since it is possible to rent), and also, with some reason, with regard to the basic contradiction implicit in referring to *dar al-harb* (abode of war) in these specific circumstances when these same bodies (the European Council and the American Fiqh Council) have generally (with regard to citizenship and patriotic allegiance) stated forcefully that the West is not an "abode of war."

What is disturbing, beyond this immediate debate on what is always a very sensitive subject among Muslims, is that people are interested primarily in buying houses, while it is the whole relationship with the dominant economic system that poses the deeper and more complex problem. To allow borrowing from banks on the ground that there is a "constraining necessity" in the matter of housing while keeping silent about financial and economic considerations that are so much more serious and that touch the daily lives of a much more significant number of Muslims than those who would like to buy a property is surprising and in the end illogical. What Muslims in the West are in painful need of today is a global approach that would make it possible for them not only to live but also to develop a spirit of economic initiative and creativity capable of putting forward concrete alternatives aimed at extricating them from the system through financial independence, rather than remaining spectators resigned to their own powerlessness. This is the level at which urgent commitment is needed. Constant ad hoc solutions and adaptations are methods that, as we have said, affirm the dominant system of speculation and interest more than they resist it. Our ethics require us to commit ourselves to an in-depth and radical resistance.

Considering an Alternative

If we recall our approach in part I and try to stay loyal to the general principles of Islam in the area of economics and finance, it becomes clear that Western Muslims are going to have to develop a fundamentally new approach. As we see it, the principle of integration and reform, the requirement to respect ethics in financial management, respect for private property alongside the obligation to pay *zakat*, and the prohibition of *riba* have to be applied in the West by developing a dynamic global concept. The very general nature of the [Islamic] guidelines makes this possible on condition that we study seriously the societies in which we live and try to think on the basis of the realities we find there. It must also be added that the classical *fiqh* tradition, although it incorporates the idea of stages of development of regulations (on the very basis of the circumstances of their revelation in the Qur'an), remains very structured and necessarily compartmentalized, founded on rules for what is legitimate (*halal*) and what is illegitimate (*haram*). But economics and finance, by their own nature and especially today because of the complexity of the factors in play and the constant interaction of practices, are areas that require thinking that is aware of the dynamics, the logics of accumulation, and always the time factor. This is not where *fiqh* (law and jurisprudence) and jurists (*fuqaha*) are naturally at home, and it is often the awareness of this complexity and incompatibility of natures that causes some jurists to avoid pronouncing legal opinions on these subjects, so complex is the situation and so significant the risks. Observance of the formal obligations concerning *zakat* and the undisputed prohibitions concerning *riba* is naturally the best form of protection, even if it cannot claim to be the best solution. There is no other area in which we are more in need of going back to the principles in our sources and to put forward a detailed study of the *maslaha* (public interest) of Western Muslims in the matter, of the *ijtihad* that needs to be developed, and of the *fatawa* that need to be pronounced.[32] Many routes can be explored that will make changes in Western communities possible.

Management of Zakat *and Rethinking Social Solidarity*

Zadaqat (voluntary alms) are a welcome means of supporting an organization on occasion, or a family or individual in [temporary] need, but *zakat* and its management require that a real philosophy of social action be worked out, with a strategy, conditions, and priorities. If we read the legal pronouncements on the question of *zakat* and then study the debates and divergences of opinion among scholars, we understand that this obligation, contrary to the view widely held among Muslims, does not have as its purpose the provision of occasional help for the poor and needy but is clearly aimed at giving them the means to escape from their economic dependence. Whether one grants to the poor an amount that brings them up to the minimal taxable income (like Abu Hanifa) or an amount sufficient to cover their needs for a year (like the Malikite school and most of the Hanbalis) or for the whole of their life (like al-Shafii), the objective is to make it possible for them to take control of their lives and one day reach the level of being themselves taxable. Thus, we find that a number of scholars (al-Shafii, Ahmad, al-Mawardi, and Ibn Hazm among others) have profound ideas about the use of *zakat* consistent with being able to give to individuals not only grants for basic needs (such as food, housing, and clothing) but also the means to enable them to work: tools, land, animals, goods for trade, and so on.[33] We know the story reported by Anas ibn Malik: the Prophet asked a man who was asking for support what possessions he had left. He replied that he had an earthenware jar and a brush mat, and the Prophet asked him to go and fetch them. The Prophet sold them for him for two dirhams and told him to buy food with one dirham and to buy a hatchet with the other. He asked him to cut wood with this hatchet and to sell it for fifteen days and then to come back to see him. By that time the man had earned ten dirhams and no longer had need of help. The teaching of this story is clear: the aim of social solidarity in general and of *zakat* in particular is ultimately to make the needy self-sufficient, and it is to this that *zakat* is first directed.

Rather than continuing to manage *zakat* in a scattered and incoherent way, both locally and nationally by distributing money to institutions and individuals without planning, it is urgent that women and men take a genuine special interest in the social field[34] and develop, wherever possible, authentic solidarity programs that will help women and men toward social and economic autonomy: different kinds of support are needed for unemployed people and disabled people, for educated people and people with no education, and so on. In order to build such programs, it is necessary to study one's society and one's community, to get close to the poor, the unemployed, the disabled, to understand the logic of marginalization, the various kinds of social and financial breakdowns, and the range of difficulties and to work *with a view of the whole picture*. The philosophy of the "right of the poor" and solidarity that is written at the heart of the requirement of *zakat* requires a long-term global vision that will set in motion a dynamic for socialization through employment, economic participation, and financial independence.[35]

With the money raised from *zakat*, one should be able to think about supplementary local social programs for basic education, employment, and technical training. Providing the means to buy tools or to rent land or buildings for economic activities in line with the abilities of individuals is an approach that should be explored as a matter of priority. In the longer term, granting microcredits should be looked at as a means of supporting and acting in solidarity with the recipients in their investment projects. Clearly, the management of *zakat* demands an excellent knowledge of the environment, the community, and the social and economic situation in general. In Western societies, this requires specialists, who would not be bureaucrats but people trained for fieldwork and capable of proposing strategies for acting in solidarity and for training people for responsibility. When we consider the amounts that can accrue from the collection of *zakat* in the West, it is clear that serious, planned management could help guarantee relative financial autonomy for basic economic and social projects. This is the purpose *awqaf* institutions should serve in the West.

Money raised from *zakat* should, of course, be used to help the six or seven categories of people specified (such as debtors and travelers), but the principle of acting from an overview remains the same: it is about the fight against dependence and about understanding, when all is said and done, that, since *zakat* is the inalienable right of the poor, it should translate in our minds into one of the fundamental aspects of our struggle for justice. At the level of Muslim communities in the West, this approach would inevitably change completely the relationship of indifference that is increasingly taking root between rich and poor. Rich and affluent Muslims in New York, Washington, Los Angeles, London, Paris, and other cities send their money all around the world, while sometimes their coreligionists who live a few hundred yards away get no support from them. Even more serious are the scornful remarks we hear from the mouths of these rich people about the laziness, ignorance, and coarseness of these "so-called" poor and unemployed ("almost always voluntarily"). To speak or act in this way is to neglect two express instructions of the Prophet: to respect the poor and on the one hand to take care of them and on the other hand to distribute *zakat* equitably. Working out a global strategy involving, as far as possible, donors (by providing information about the realities around them and about the projects implemented) and all partners would naturally develop local synergies that would be very innovative and that, above all, would be rooted in the life of the community. There are very interesting examples of developments in some American, English, and French towns, but these are exceptions rather than the rule, while the place of *zakat* in the Islamic religion—the third pillar—requires that we work steadily and seriously and that this become the rule.

In conclusion, let us add that it is all the more imperative to study and understand how the social services function in the countries in which we live—on the one hand to make it possible for people in difficulties to receive their rights and on the other to inspire initiatives relevant to the system that will work in a spirit of partnership on the ground, as well as avoiding duplication of efforts by assisting people for whom measures already exist, to provide social and financial assistance. On another level, intracommunal information is vital: many people prefer to give their money for the building of mosques rather than to help human beings become independent. An effort to explain the social realities, the current difficulties and the projects currently under way, is therefore necessary. If one visits the United States, for example, one is surprised, and unfortunately shocked, to find out that well-off immigrants know nothing of the living conditions of their Afro-American or *Latino* "brothers" and that, deep down, they have a vague sense that it is none of their business. One sees how the formal understanding of the command to pay *zakat* may be a betrayal of its deep meaning and fundamental purpose: people who are overlooked in our society are our responsibility—they have an economic claim on us, and they must be given, as Umar ibn al-Khattab said, "a sufficiency" so that they can acquire dignity and liberty. It is really a question of working out a hands-on philosophy of social and economic action, adapted to our reality, with women and men professionally engaged full time in this area of work.

Economic Activity and Riba

The sum total of our reflections on what to call the West is important when it comes to economic affairs and the scope given to us to propose alternatives. We have said that the geographic approach is clearly no longer relevant and introduces confusion into our way of looking at the world. Globalization has shifted all the markers, and even more concretely since the beginning of the 1980s. We have here suggested an alternative way of looking at things that is more global and based on the nature of the actual situation and fields of activity and their relation to the universal principles and ethic of Islam. So, even if it has become possible, in the legal, social, and political fields (since the development of states under the rule of law, the protection of rights of conscience and worship, and the acquisition of citizenship), to consider the West as *dar al-shahada*, the abode of testimony (without distinguishing it from other parts of the world where these developments have come into effect), we see the position quite differently with regard to the field of contemporary economics. Economic and financial activity no longer respects national frontiers, and it is other characteristics to which we should refer, notably compatibility or incompatibility with our ethics. And the neoliberal capitalist system that has been imposed on the whole world represents a universe in the face of which Muslims must resist and propose an alternative: this is for us an *alam al-harb*, a sphere of war, which promotes an economic logic responsible for the deaths of tens of thousands of human beings every day.

Western Muslims live at the eye of the storm, and it is surprising, and more, we would say, very serious, that so far the legal opinions that have been declared on the subject of their relations with economic activity are concerned only with details (e.g., credit cards, purchase of houses, insurance), even though we are aware of how numerous and piercing the problems are—restrictions on economic activities, limitations on relations with the banking systems, the virtual impossibility of establishing capital funds, blocked financial investment projects, the unfeasibility of the development of small and medium initiatives, and so on. The activity of Western Muslims who want to respect their religion is marginal, and, as far as competition is concerned, derisory. No global vision has been proposed, and—whether by adaptation after adaptation, exception after exception, passive spectating and self-marginalization—all the legal opinions, and even the attitude of

Muslims themselves as economics actors, succeed only in confirming the dominant system. A global and detailed approach is required.

In 1965, an engineer living in South Africa used the visit of two scholars from India to explain to them the nature of the problems faced by Muslims in that country with regard to economic activity. In an eight-page summary, he explained that, taking into account the small number of Muslims, their relation to the White separatists (who held political and economic power), and new factors relevant to the development of the country, Muslims risked losing everything—both the advantages they had acquired and economic opportunities—if they continued to marginalize themselves economically and not comply with the dominant system. Moreover, he stated that, in spite of the racial policies that directly affected Muslims, interesting possibilities were opening up for them, particularly in the fields of agriculture and industry, which might allow significant economic development and strongly protect their interests. It took a year for a legal opinion based on the scholars' visit and on the summary document to be pronounced by the *dar al-ulum* (house of sciences) in Deoband and signed by the *mufti*, Ahmad Muhammad Siddiqu. After referring to the illegality of usury, interest, and speculation, the document, relying on the opinions of, among others, Abu Hanifa, al-Shaybani, Sufyan al-Thawri, and Sarkhasi (as well as more recent scholars), found that it is permissible for Muslims to benefit from or pay interest in the economic and financial activities in order to protect their situation and to strengthen their independence within South African society. The statement of the *fatwa* recalls the conditions for this tolerance: that it be practiced in *dar al-harb*, that the ultimate aim be the protection of the property of Muslims, and that these dealings be undertaken only with non-Muslims and on a basis understood and accepted by them (which should not be such as to deceive them). It is finally recalled that this was already the opinion of the scholar Qasim Nanutfi for Muslims living in India.

This *fatwa*, dating from 1965,[36] relies on the same argument that was used by the European Council and the American League, with the difference that here it is general: the permission applies to all economic activities, as long as it is a question of protecting the interests of Muslims (*maslaha*) and that constraint is implicit because the scale of the risks of loss of assets (as a result of economic marginalization) is clear. South African Muslims, like the Muslims of India and of the island of Reunion, succeeded over time not only in protecting their interests but also in strengthening their status in their respective societies, and it is this to which their role and the nature of their economic significance bears witness in these three countries and elsewhere. However, it is not appropriate today, in my view, to take the *fatwa* as it stands and open wide the doors for the involvement of Western Muslims in the capitalist system on the assumption that the prohibition has been lifted with no other consideration. The demands of a global vision and the principles on which it is based compel us to go further and to make clear decisions on the stages that might lead us to viable alternatives.

To enter into economic life and activity on the margins of the contemporary neoliberal system is a trap, and to continue to approach this area with the structural logic of classical *fiqh* is, in my view, a mistake. Moreover, to lift the prohibitions only because we are in *dar al-harb* is dangerous and would inevitably assuage the consciences of all those involved indiscriminately in complying with a system that has lost all ethical concerns. In my opinion, there exists a middle way, which, while referring to previous legal opinions, fixes clear and strict conditions for involvement in the dominant economic system. Western Muslims are well and truly drowning in *alam al-harb*, and they have to decide on the shape of their collective interest (*maslaha*) in order both to protect themselves and to play an active part in economic and financial reform on the local, national, and international levels. What do they need? How should they proceed? *Ijtihad*, and the *fatawa* that are bound to result from it, must take these realities into account.

American and European Muslims have an urgent need today to develop their economic structures within the Western landscape. They need to create enterprises, businesses, and insurance and other companies that will make it possible for them to live and develop in their respective societies. At the same time, they need to acquire a financial autonomy that will put an end to their dependence on funds from abroad whenever they undertake any project for expansion (e.g., a mosque, center, school, bank, businesses). This dependence on the Gulf States and elsewhere, whether on their institutions or on wealthy individuals, is doubly catastrophic: first, because these states are clearly economic links in the chain of the system (and its perversions), and second, because this dependence creates in the Muslim mind the feeling of being maintained beggars, which is unacceptable. The so-called Islamic institutions based in the West are not sufficient to meet their needs for credit and cash, and they are also often remote from the grass-roots level, preoccupied almost exclusively with big projects and rarely with the needs of the private individuals.

It is precisely when we confront these problems that we understand how much we still need all the creativity of Muslim economists, entrepreneurs, managers, business leaders, and association leaders. We need to reflect and take action that takes into account three factors that have appeared in our presentation, giving them the priority that is appropriate within the global approach:

1. To think about a viable alternative to the dominant system (beginning at the local level) and to take into account the time factor when working out an economic strategy.
2. To protect the possessions and independence of Muslims in their society.
3. To comply with the dominant system with regard to financial interest (while respecting the conditions set out earlier), taking care to remember the first factor (to seek to be free of the capitalist logic of speculation and interest).

By way of example, this would mean in practice that people would engage in economic projects (small and medium-size initiatives) by obtaining bank credit in order to assemble the founding capital but would work out business plans that would seek to establish, in three to five years (or some other realistic time frame), a system of financial management that respected Muslim ethics. Muslims today are often hindered because they fail to assemble the capital that would enable them to engage in economic activities: at the heart of the capitalist system, *maslaha* as well as *darura* (necessity) requires, in our view, that we free ourselves from this impasse. But that does not mean that we should bind ourselves only to this exceptional provision: the will to leave the system also requires that Muslims be invited to think of economic and commercial structures and management systems that will make it possible for them, in time, to extricate themselves from the logic with which the system and its dominating power force them for a while to comply.

In other words, this global vision of the necessary alternative must be wedded to the precise legal opinions that allow compliance with the system. Western Muslims could then engage in economic activities, protecting their interests, providing employment, preserving their independence, and, above all, participating from within in resistance to the neoliberal system (on a larger scale, this commitment could appear as the Muslims' contribution to the global resistance thought and promoted by all the people unhappy with this so-called economic order). The development of a stock of small and medium-size complementary initiatives, businesses that interact with one another on an ethical basis, is possible if we put a spirit of initiative and creativity to the test. In Asian societies, in Malaysia and Indonesia, and in South Africa we see Muslims today engaging and succeeding in surprising things by creating economic structures, sometimes far-reaching, that are viable, diversified, and complementary and that function in a way that offers a real alternative. The time factor is crucial: if it is impossible to get involved outside the system, unless one is very wealthy, one must find liberation by stages. In economics, radical and reasonable resistance is a road, a process—it cannot be satisfied by the structural boundary of *haram*, set up like a wall, nor by the senseless, naïve, and idealistic expression of a complete break thought of as "an uncompromised rejection of the system."

By going further than the European Council and the American League, it seems to me that a new alternative based in the West must be put forward and that patchwork solutions and ad hoc adaptations must come to an end. In the *alam al-harb* (world of war) of the neoliberal economy, we shall first have to comply if we are to hope to propose a thought-out alternative that will break with the dominant model; as we understand it, this is the only way of overcoming the paradoxical fact that our total refusal to participate in the system has today become its best guarantee of survival.[37] This must mean that it is absolutely vital that Muslims study closely and deeply the dynamics of resistance that are already in process in the United States and Europe. They are neither the first nor the only ones to reject the dominant economic system: many studies have been published, and development cooperatives, alternative banks, and ethical businesses and investment funds are functioning and putting forward "something else." Muslim citizens should take inspiration from these writings and experiences and get involved in multidimensional, complementary, and long-term partnerships. We have spoken of civil movements, the new approaches proposed by ATTAC, and the reflections on ethics and economics produced by Christian liberation theologians (and other Catholic and Protestant intellectuals); to live in the West and ignore these developments and achievements is madness, and it is going to be necessary for Muslims to emerge from their intellectual isolation into direct engagement with the debates that are stirring their society and from which they are currently largely absent. Few of their fellow-citizens know that the principles held by Muslims are essentially opposed to the economic logic of today's world and that they are, in heart and mind, opposed to its dominance. It is for Muslims to explain and make themselves heard. Overall, they need to develop a global vision of the stakes involved in their presence on the economic scene and to make sure that the adaptations proposed to them by scholars from here and there do not become a safeguard that allows the emergence of a new caste of "highly integrated" Muslim citizens in the style of new capitalists interested primarily in owning houses or shining financially in the world of productivity and returns. We know how many legal opinions (*fatawa*) have sanctioned treacherous behavior, and this is why our acceptance in principle of *riba* is accompanied by a very strong ethical reservation: in *alam al-harb*, compliance with the system is allowed only if the express intention and commitment is to acquire the means (strategically and temporally) of leaving it. Contrary to the old theories, there are no longer two separate worlds, and, whether here or there, our rejection of the dominant economic system is radical *by nature*. The reality that may force us to interact does not in any way force us to give up.

9

INTERRELIGIOUS DIALOGUE

There is a very long tradition of interreligious dialogue. At various times in history, in very diverse contexts, people of various religions have engaged in interreligious exchanges to try to understand one another better; they have succeeded in gaining one another's respect and have managed not only to live but also to work together on shared endeavors. Today, we feel the need to engage even more in this process: Western societies' religious pluralism makes mutual knowledge essential. At the same time, technical developments have changed our view of the world, and daily images of societies and customs different from our own arouse our curiosity. More dramatically, acts of violence perpetrated in the name of religion challenge our awareness: how can such horror be justified in the name of religion? How can we understand it? How can we prevent it?

Many groups of specialists have been formed in recent years. At colloquia, conferences, and seminars, they meet to try to build bridges, discuss sensitive subjects, and prevent conflicts. With time, these specialists in dialogue have come to know one another and to enjoy excellent relationships founded on courtesy and respect. This is an important gain. Nevertheless, the problem remains that these are fairly closed circles whose members are not always in real contact with their own religious groups, and this makes it difficult to convey to the heart of each religious community the advances made in these numerous meetings. Moreover, whole sections of these communities are neither concerned with nor touched by the various dialogues that are taking place. Those who meet do not represent the various denominations, schools of thought, or tendencies of the adherents of their religion. Those who hold the most closed opinions, which in daily life are the cause of the real problem, never meet. Thus, we have, on both the national and international levels, a very uneven picture: dialogue is well under way between specialists from each religion who are more or less open-minded, while ordinary believers meet only rarely[1] and the most entrenched and radical views are never voiced. Common sense and logic would encourage us to hope for the opposite: the specialists do not, or no longer, really need dialogue, and it is within religious communities and between those with the most radical views that the debate should take place. It is a vicious circle: it is precisely because people do not know one another, or reject one another, that dialogue is impossible.

The responsibility of people involved in dialogue between religions is in fact doubly important: whether they have become specialists or are simply members of an interreligious group, it is vital that they play the role of mediators between their partners in dialogue and their coreligionists. It is a question of listening to the other side, challenging it and questioning it in order to increase understanding and then of getting involved in working within one's own community, informing, explaining, even teaching. At the same time, participants in dialogue should express their own convictions, clarify the place of their own sense of religion among other views held within their religious family, and respond as well as they can to the questions of their partners in dialogue. By acting in this way they create, between the various traditions, areas of trust, sustained by shared convictions and values that, even though they certainly do not bring the extremes together, do open real horizons for living together and at least allow ruptures to be avoided and conflicts better managed.

The need for interreligious dialogue is not doubted, but some people still do not understand its real usefulness and purpose. What exactly is it about? Does one want to convert the other? Can one get involved with a clear conscience? What is the real impact of these fine words about respect and living together when we look at how believers from each religion behave? Is there not a place for being doubtful or suspicious about the intentions of one or the other side if we take the time to read the scriptural sources? These questions cannot simply be swept under the carpet. They are of primary importance, because, unless they are clearly and succinctly answered, we run the risk of having an outwardly agreeable dialogue that does not eliminate the mistrust and suspicion and that in the end leads nowhere. Let us try, from within the Muslim tradition, to suggest possible answers to these questions, beginning with the last.

The Islamic Tradition and Interreligious Dialogue

We recalled in part I that, according to Muslims, the last Revelation taught them to recognize all the books of the prophets who had gone before. They all had the same purpose: to remind human beings of the presence of the Creator and the finiteness of life on earth. The Islamic tradition's concept of humankind emerged through this teaching: after forgiving Adam his sin, God told men: "A guidance will certainly come to you from me. Those who follow my guidance will have nothing to fear and will not grieve."[2] This guidance is the series of Revelations that came throughout human history, each to confirm, complete, and correct the preceding.

Necessary Diversity

So individuals, innocent and free, have to make their choices (either to accept or to reject the Revelation); there will necessarily be diversity among people, and so these three seemingly similar verses contain teachings that augment and complete each other: "Had God so willed, He would have united them [human beings] in guidance, so do not be among the ignorant";[3] "If your Lord had so willed, everyone on earth would have believed. Is it for you to compel people to be believers?";[4] "If God had willed, He would have made you one community but things are as they are to test you in what He has given you. So compete with each other in doing good."[5] The first verse instructs us that diversity is willed by the Transcendent, the second makes clear that, in the name of that will, compulsion in matters of religion is forbidden,[6] and the Revelation teaches that the purpose of these differences is to *test* us in order to discover what we are going to do with what has been revealed to us: the last commandment is to use these differences to "compete in doing good." Diversity of religions, nations, and peoples is a test because it requires that we learn to manage difference, which is in itself essential: "If God did not enable some men to keep back others, the world would be corrupt. But God is the One who gives grace to the worlds";[7] "If God did not enable some men to keep back others, hermitages, synagogues, chapels and mosques where the name of God is often called upon, would have been demolished."[8] These two verses give complementary information that is of prime importance: if there were no differences between people, if power were in the hands of one group alone (one nation, one race, or one religion), the earth would be corrupt because human beings need others to limit their impulsive desire for expansion and domination. The last verse is more precise with regard to our present discussion; it refers to places of worship to indicate that if there is to be a diversity of religions, the purpose is to safeguard them all: the fact that the list of places begins with hermitages, synagogues, and chapels before referring to mosques shows recognition of all these places of worship and their inviolability and, of course, respect for those who pray there. So, just as diversity is the source of our test, the balance of power is a requirement for our destiny.

Difference might naturally lead to conflict; therefore, the responsibility of humankind is to make use of difference by establishing a relationship based on excelling one another in doing good. It is vital that the balance of power is based not on a tension born of rejection or mutual ignorance but fundamentally on knowledge: "O people, we have created you from a male and a female, we have divided you into nations and tribes so that you might know one another."[9] Knowing the other is a process that is unavoidable if fear of difference is to be overcome and mutual respect is to be attained. So human beings live a test that is necessary for their nature but that they can—and must—master by making the effort to know and recognize those who are not of their tribe, their country, their race, or their religion.[10] Dialogue, particularly interreligious dialogue, is indispensable.

General Principles of Dialogue

All believers who participate in interreligious dialogue do so having been nourished by a faith or a conviction on the basis of which they understand themselves, perceive the world, and build relations with those around them. Their connection with Truth, with the beliefs of others, and with diversity in general is directly influenced by the content and nature of that faith or conviction. The centrality of *tawhid* in the message of Islam has been strongly emphasized in part I. It is the principle on which the whole of Islamic teaching rests and is the axis and point of reference on which Muslims rely in dialogue. The intimate awareness of *tawhid* forms the perception of the believer, who understands that plurality has been chosen by the One, that He is the God of all beings, and that He requires that each be respected: ". . . and say: 'We believe in what has been revealed to us and what has been revealed to you; our God and your God is the One.' "[11] It is out of this conviction that Muslims engage in dialogue, and this is assumed in forming relations with the other. What establishes difference from the other, and consequently the direction and terms of the dialogue that is to be built, is whether or not there is commitment to the expression of an absolute monotheism.[12] This is why the Qur'anic call to the Jews and Christians begins with: "O people of the book, come to agreed terms between us and you: that we worship none but God, that we do not attribute any associate to Him and that none of us takes other divinities apart from Him. If they turn away, say: 'Be witnesses that we are submitting ourselves [*muslimun*].' "[13] Firmly asserting this principle indicates that *tawhid* is the point of reference on the basis of which a Muslim engages in discussion: if there are differences on this central point, it is then necessary that dialogue be entered into and developed on the basis of shared values and teachings, since the last Revelation recognizes those that came before:[14] "God, there is no god but God. It is He who sent down the Book [the Qur'an] upon you [Muhammad] in all truth confirming what came before. And He sent down the Torah and the Gospel before as a guidance for people, and He sent down the Discernment [*al-furqan*] the Qur'an."[15] This recognition is fundamental and opens up the way for dialogue, which, although it forces us to see our differences, is bound to establish bridges between convictions and traditions.

The Qur'an not only issues a call to dialogue but is also insistent about the form it should take and the way in which it should be conducted. It should not simply be an exchange of information; it should also be a way of being and of speaking, an attitude: "And discuss with them in the best way,"[16] and again: "Do not discuss with the people of the Book except in the best of ways, apart from those who are unjust among themselves."[17] In this last verse, the restriction is not at all upon dialogue as such, but as it pertains to the repressive attitude some Jews and Christians adopted toward the Muslim community, which was at that time facing serious adversity. This contextualized approach is what gives meaning to the often quoted verse "You will certainly see that those most hardened in hostility toward the Muslims are the Jews and the polytheists and you will certainly see that those closest to you in affection are those who say: 'We are Christians,' because there are among them priests and monks who are not swollen with pride."[18] Here again, it is the attitude of people and potential partners in dialogue that is at issue, and not dialogue in itself. To those who choose to understand this contextualized teaching (warning us to be concerned about injustice, adversity, and the pride of human beings) as an absolute prohibition on dialogue, the Revelation replies clearly: "God does not forbid you from establishing relations of generosity and just behavior with those who have not fought against you over your religion and who have not evicted you from your dwellings. God loves those who act fairly."[19] This verse goes even further than all the others: if dialogue is necessary and if the way of speaking about oneself is important, we are here clearly called to establish relations of generosity and justice with all who respect our freedom of conscience and our human dignity. Dialogue is an act of conviction, of listening, of self-awareness, of self-knowledge, and of the heart: together, these qualities constitute wisdom.

Verses Interpreted Variously

When we speak of interreligious dialogue, it would not be honest to refer only to the verses we have quoted without mentioning a series of other passages in the Qur'an that can be equivocal and that are moreover variously interpreted by Muslim scholars. Some of the ulama of the literalist traditions read them restrictively, which basically does not leave any real room for discussion. A sincere involvement in dialogue must stop to consider these verses. Thus, one finds in the Qur'an verses that define Jews and Christians, even though they are among the "people of the Book," as *kuffar* (plural of *kafir*), most often translated as "infidels" or "miscreants": "They are certainly *in a state of denial*[20] [*kafara*], those who have said that God was the Messiah the son of Mary"[21] or again, "Those among the people of the Book and the polytheists who *have denied* [*kafaru*]."[22] According to the perspective of the majority of literalist scholars, this leaves no doubt as to their fate, especially since the Qur'an says explicitly: "Religion in the sight of God is Islam"[23] and again: "He who desires religion other than Islam will not find himself accepted and in the hereafter he will be among the losers."[24] Other verses seem to tell us that we should not trust Jews and Christians: "And the Jews and Christians will not be pleased with you unless you follow their religion"[25] or take them as allies except in extreme circumstances: "Let the believers [Muslims] not take as allies the deniers [*kafirin*] rather than believers; those who do so will receive no help from God, unless you feel yourselves to be in danger from them."[26] Such an avalanche of verses has the effect of causing perplexity and raises questions about whether any real place for dialogue remains, the more so since these same scholars clearly explain that they do not believe there is any virtue in discussion unless the intention is to convince the other party of the strength and truth of our arguments. Interreligious dialogue would then become a call to our truth, a *dawa* (call, invitation, preaching), with no meaning beyond that.

Here we are at the heart of the problem of the types of "reading" to which we referred in part I where the various schools of thought were described. The advantage of the literalist reading over all the others is that it stops at the primary meaning of the text that, as soon as it is quoted, seems to make immediate sense and gives weight to the argument. No trouble is taken to work out a reading based on critical distance, contextualized interpretation, or determination of the meaning of a verse in light of the message as a whole. As a literalist, what I read is what was said, and God speaks through me as long as my quotations are from His word. It is nevertheless advisable to take each of the verses mentioned earlier and to try to discover whether the literalist reading is the only appropriate one.

It must be said, to begin with, that the Arabic notion of *kufr* or *kafir* has often been mistranslated, quite apart from the fact that many Muslims in the West use it as a definite insult. But the word has a neutral sense in the Islamic sciences, and it is clearly perceived at various levels. Without going into technical details here, we may say that, according to the root, the general meaning of *kafir* could be rendered as "a denier with a veiled heart": this refers to those whose original longing for the Transcendent[27] has been stifled, veiled, shut off in their hearts to the extent that they deny the presence of the Creator. But *kafir* may also indicate one who denies the evidence of the truth, like the satanic figure of Iblis in the Qur'an, who *knows* that God is, since he speaks to Him, but refuses to obey: "He [Iblis] refused, became proud and was among the deniers [*min al-kafirin*]."[28] To this must be added various kinds of negation, *kufr*, which are determined according to what is denied: God, the truth of the message, one of the pillars of faith, the nature of a particular commandment, and so on. So to apply the term *kafir* to Jews and Christians in a neutral sense is justified in that, in a quite natural way, they do not recognize the Qur'an as the last revealed book. They deny [*yakfuru*] the truth of the message and its Prophet, but this does not mean we may call them "miscreants" in the sense that their faith in God is not recognized, which would be an inaccurate assertion: this would be as senseless as to say that Iblis, who had a dialogue with the Most High, did not *believe* in Him and was a *miscreant*. This is neither logical understanding nor a consistent translation. We must add that it is never legitimate to use the word as an insult.

The verse indicating that the religion in the sight of God is Islam has caused a lot of ink to flow. Here again we are dealing with a question of interpretation. We know that in the Qur'an the word *islam* has two meanings. The first is universal and generic: all the elements, as we have said in part I, are in "submission" to God because they respect the order of creation; in the same sense, all the revelations and prophets came with a message of the oneness of God and the need to "submit oneself" to Him. Thus, Abraham, well before the revelation of the Qur'an, is commanded by God: "And when his Lord said to him: 'Submit [*aslim*]!' he replied: 'I submit [*aslamtu*] to the Lord of the worlds.' "[29] The words *aslim* and *aslamtu* come from *islam* in the sense of recognition of the one God and acceptance of the obedience due to Him. The second meaning of the word *islam* is the religion whose text is the Qur'an and whose prophet is Muhammad. Literalist scholars have interpreted these verses giving the word the restricted meaning of the second definition, while the generic definition makes better sense of the Islamic message as a whole, which, apart from being the final revelation, identifies natural religion, one and unique throughout history, as the recognition of the existence of a Creator and conformance to His messages. This is also confirmed by the verse "Certainly those who have believed, the Jews, the Christians, and the Sabaeans, all those who have believed in God and in the last day of judgment and who have done good—they will have their reward from God. They will not be afraid and they will not grieve."[30] The generic meaning is clear here, and those scholars who have claimed that this verse has been abrogated [*mansukh*][31] pay no regard to the rule of abrogation, which specifies that only verses stipulating obligations or prohibitions (which may change in the course of revelation) can be abrogated but not information, which cannot be true one day and untrue the next. This verse is clearly giving information.[32]

The verse "The Jews and the Christians will not be pleased with you unless you follow their religion [milla]" is quoted at will in times of trouble or simply when people want to justify mistrusting some Jews or Christians. The verse is heard from mosque pulpits, in conferences, and at seminars, with the implication that it explains the attitude of Jews and Christians toward Muslims: their rejection of Islam, their double dealing, not to say deceitfulness, and colonization, proselytism, wars, Bosnia, Palestine, and so on. But that is not what the verse says: the phrase "will not be pleased with you" [lan tarda anka] translates here the idea of full and absolute satisfaction, expressed with the heart as well as the mind. For Jews and Christians convinced, like a Muslim, of the truth of their own message, complete satisfaction with the other is attained when the experience of faith and truth is shared. One has the feeling of living and sharing this essential element that gives meaning and light to one's life. This does not imply that in the absence of this full satisfaction one can live in and express only rejection, mistrust, and conflict. One can feel and manifest deep and sincere respect toward a human being with whom one does not share this full spiritual communion. It is a matter of being sincere and of recognizing the states of our souls and hearts. It is within our communities of faith that we live most deeply the fullness of the meaning of (rida) with the other who shares our truth, even if it is possible (though it is the exception rather than the rule) that we might experience a unique spiritual relationship with a woman or a man from another tradition. The Qur'an here is speaking only of the intimate and very natural inclination of people of faith toward one another.[33] At a deeper level, believers must be conscious that ultimately what they must seek before all else is to please God [rida Allah], not other people. It is good for believers to remember that the full satisfaction shared with their coreligionists is still only a stage along the way. Seeking the pleasure of God is a demanding path punctuated by testing stations, but this initiation is ultimately the only way that it is possible to become, in humility, fully content with oneself.

With regard to the verse referring to the seemingly impossible alliance with Jews and Christians, we have already referred to it. From the context of the verse, and others like it, we derive that Muslims are commanded in situations of potential conflict not to take deniers as allies against Muslims [min dun al-muminin],[34] that is to say, to make an alliance unjustly or treacherously in opposition to their spiritual community. It does not apply absolutely, and the following verse specifies clearly those with whom relations are banned: "God forbids you to turn in friendship toward [or take as allies] only such as fight against you because of your faith, and drive you forth from your homelands, or aid [others] in driving you forth: and as for those [from among you] who turn toward them in friendship [or alliance], it is they, they who are truly wrongdoers!"[35]

Here a word is needed on that concept of *dawa*, often translated as "preaching," "call," or "invitation to Islam" and which has thus come to express the missionary character of Islam. It cannot be denied that some Muslims, on the basis of a certain number of verses, are engaged in straightforward missionary activity, and in their minds dialogue is only a form of mission. To deny this would be a dishonest. One must then look at how the Qur'an presents the act of "inviting" or "calling" to Islam. The verse that follows is well known: "Call [invite] to the path of your Lord using wisdom and good exhortation, and debate with them in the best of manner."[36] If we meditate on this verse, we understand that emphasis is put first on the Muslim who "invites." He has to have acquired a certain wisdom, know to speak well, and have mastered the best way of expressing things: three injunctions bring together the requirements related to being a good speaker, the content of the message, and the way in which it must be delivered. In other words, to "invite" is first to "bear witness," as much by one's behavior as by the content and form of what one says, what the message of Islam is. It is not a matter of wanting to convert, because people's hearts are God's domain and secret. It is a matter of bearing witness, which is an invitation to remember and meditate. This meaning also is captured by another verse: "And thus have We willed you to be a community of the middle way, so that [with your lives] you might bear witness to the truth before mankind."[37] Interreligious dialogue should be a meeting of "witnesses" who are seeking to live their faiths, to share their convictions, and to engage with one another for a more humane, more just world, closer to what God expects of humanity.

At the end of this section, we note that the verses mentioned earlier are indeed variously interpreted. All religious traditions experience these differences, and, depending on the type of reading that is accepted, one may be open to dialogue or absolutely opposed to it. The nature of these difficulties has to be taken into account in order to avoid any illusions about the possible results of our meetings.

Toward Exacting and Constructive Dialogue

The dialogue we engage in must be anything but complaisant. The lack of trust that permeates our Western societies and the situations of religious conflict throughout the world mean that our task must be far-reaching, exacting, and rigorous. First of all, dialogue must be based on mutual knowledge achieved by our seeking to make clear our shared convictions, values, and hopes, while clearly defining and circumscribing our specificities, our differences, and what may even be our disagreements. This is what is done in most interreligious groups, and I believe it is necessary to move in this direction. But this will not be enough: we have already said that the majority of women and men engaged in this kind of meetings are rather open and ready for the encounter. It is crucial that they describe and explain what they really represent in their religious families—what trend, the extent of it, their relations with the community as a whole, and so forth. It is important to know to whom one is speaking; it is no less essential to know to whom one is not speaking, and why. Interreligious dialogue should make it possible for each partner better to understand the various theories, the points shared, the differences and conflicts that are present in other traditions. It is a matter first of not deluding oneself that the other "represents," for example, the *whole* of Hinduism, the *whole* of Buddhism, the *whole* of Judaism, the *whole* of Christianity, or the *whole* of Islam, and second of knowing what links and types of relations our partners have with their coreligionists.

To be involved in dialogue between religions while being completely cut off from the believers of one's own religion is problematic and can be illusory. Many "specialists" in interreligious dialogue, who go from conference to conference, are totally disconnected from their religious community, as well as from grass-roots realities. This might be conceivable if it were a matter of purely theological discussions, but in most cases, unfortunately, that is not the case.[38] How is it possible to have a real understanding of religious traditions and the dynamics that permeate them on the ground if those who dialogue are not actively involved in their communities? Again, how can one hope to influence believers more widely if the specialists' circle is isolated in an ivory tower and does not report back on the nature of its work to each of the respective religious communities?

So, two fundamental conditions for dialogue with the other emerge: first, to commit oneself, as far as possible, to giving an account of the shared work to one's own faith community and second, in order to achieve that, to devote part of one's energy to opening up intracommunal dialogue, which will make possible the advancement of real pluralism. This dialogue is extremely difficult, sometimes much more difficult than interreligious dialogue itself, because discussion with one's nearest and dearest is so risky. This commitment is nevertheless essential if we want to break down internal ghettoes and sectarianism and try, within manageable limits, to respect one another more. It can never be said enough that intracommunal dialogue between Muslims is virtually nonexistent. Groups know one another, know how to identify one another, and work out where they are in relation to one another, but then they immediately ignore one another, exclude one another, or insult one another, without any attempt at discussion. Within one religious understanding, one current of thought, divisions are maintained by intervening organizations. The culture of dialogue has practically abandoned Muslim communities and the respect for diversity, which always has been and should have continued to be their source of richness, has been replaced by dueling disagreements that contribute to maintaining the division, which causes their weakness. Some still tentative initiatives have taken off, but the movement must become more general and must naturally go alongside involvement in dialogue with other traditions.

Apart from getting to know one another, it is also necessary to establish relationships of trust and respect. Trust is lacking today: we meet often, listen sometimes, and distrust each other often. Trust needs time and support. The frequency and quality of meetings and the nature of the exchanges certainly help to create spaces for sincere encounter. However, it seems to me that four rules should be applied which may be quite demanding as preliminaries, but which are fundamentally constructive:

1. Recognition of the legitimacy of each other's convictions and respect for them;
2. Listening to what people say about their own scriptural sources and not what we understand (or want to understand) from them;
3. The right, in the name of trust and respect, to ask all possible questions, sometimes even the most embarrassing;
4. The practice of self-criticism, which consists in knowing how to discern the difference between what the texts say and what our coreligionists make of them, and deciding clearly what our personal position is.

These rules are essential. One cannot enter into dialogue if one does not recognize the legitimacy of other people's convictions. Not to share them is one thing, but not to recognize, deep in one's heart, their right to be is another. Nor is it fitting to try to become an exegete of one's partner's scriptures. This is not our role or our area of expertise. It is for our partners to tell us what they understand or what their coreligionists understand, from such and such a text. Reading the Torah or the Bible for a Muslim, the Qur'an for a Jew or a Christian, or the Bhagavad Gita for all three is certainly useful and necessary in order to try to understand others' convictions, but these readings should inspire meditation and questions, not a simplistic accusation. We must also give ourselves the right to dare to ask all the questions that occur to us. The answers may or may not be satisfying, they may or may not suit us, but they will have been clearly stated. Trust can be born only from this frankness and clarity: in the meantime, without the latter, courtesy is artificial or even a masquerade. At a deeper level, these are all questions that help people to go further in understanding their own traditions. Looking for a way to give a deep explanation means making the effort to understand better. The relevance of the question to my partner in dialogue is a gift, an intellectual and spiritual tonic, because I learn to express better what I believe and so to understand more deeply the meaning of what I am. Finally, dialogue involves clarity and courage: our scriptural sources have sometimes been used, or have legitimized (and still legitimize) discourses, behavior, and actions toward others about which we need to make clear statements. This is not always easy, but it is nevertheless vital, and all the religious traditions should be involved in this self-criticism. Some see it as a kind of disloyalty toward their own community; it should instead be a matter of self-respect and dignity before God and each person's conscience.

Shared Involvement

Dialogue is not enough. Even if it is rigorous, even if it is necessary to give time to knowing, trusting, and respecting each other, even if we should take on ourselves the widest possible responsibility to report back, it is only one stage or one aspect of the encounter among the various religious traditions. In Western societies, it is urgent that we commit ourselves to joint action.

In dialogue, we soon realize that we hold a great number of convictions and values in common. We understand very quickly that we are facing the same difficulties and challenges. But we very rarely move outside these circles of reflection. Together we say "God," awareness, spirituality, responsibility, ethics, solidarity, but we live and experience, each one on one's own, the problems of education, transmission of spirituality, individualism, consumerism, and moral bankruptcy. In philosophical terms, we could say that we know one another in words but not *in action*. Our experience of fifteen years of joint action in South America, Africa, and Asia has convinced us not only that this path is necessary but also that it is the only way to eventually change minds and build mutual respect and trust.

In the West, there are many shared challenges, first among them being education. How can we pass on to our children the sense of the divine, for the monotheistic faiths, or of spiritual practice for Buddhism, for example? In a society that pushes people to own, how are we to form individuals whose awareness of being illumines and guides their mastery of possession? Again, how are we to explain morality and boundaries, to pass on principles of life that do not confuse liberty with carelessness and that consider neither fashion nor quantity of possessions as the measure of goodness? All the religious and spiritual traditions are experiencing these difficulties, but we still see few examples of shared commitment to proposing alternatives. And there is so much to do—working together, as parents and as citizens, so that schools will provide more and more courses on the religions; suggesting ways of providing educational modules outside the school structures to teach the general population about the religions—their fundamental beliefs, particular topics, and social realities. Such modules need to be thought out together, not only by inviting a partner from the other religion to come to give a course as part of a program we have put together for and by ourselves. By way of example, the Interreligious Platform in Geneva has launched an interesting "school of religions," and there is the Center for Muslim-Christian Studies, in Copenhagen, which, under the leadership of Lissi Rasmussen, has scored a first in Europe in establishing a real partnership within an institution promoting and practicing dialogue.

Acts of solidarity take place from within each religious family, but the examples of shared initiatives are rare. People sometimes invite others, but do not act in collaboration. One of the best testimonies that a religious or spiritual tradition can give of itself lies in acts of solidarity between its adherents and others. To defend the dignity of the latter, to fight so that our societies do not produce indignity, to work together to support marginalized and neglected people, will certainly help us know one another better, but it will, above all, make known the essential message that shines at the heart of our traditions: never neglect your brother in humanity and learn to love him or at least to serve him.

More broadly, we have to act together so that the body of values that forms the basis of our ethics is not relegated to such a private and secluded sphere that it becomes inoperative and socially dead. Our philosophies of life must continue to inspire our civil commitment, with all due respect to the supporters of a postmodernism whose aim seems to be to deny any legitimacy to all reference to a universal ethic. We need to find together a civil role, inspired by our convictions, in which we will work to demand that the rights of all be respected, that discriminations be outlawed, that dignity be protected, and that economic efficiency cease to be the measure of what is right. Differentiating between public and private space does not mean that women and men of faith, or women and men of conscience, have to shrink to the point of disappearance and fear to express themselves publicly in the name of what they believe. When a society has gone so far as to disqualify, in public debate, faith and what it inspires, the odds are that its system is founded only on materialism and ruled only by materialist logic—the self-centered accumulation of goods and profit.

We must dare to express our faith, its demands, and its ethics, to involve ourselves as citizens in order to make known our human concerns, our desire for justice and dignity, our moral standards, our fears as consumers and televiewers, our hopes as mothers and fathers—to commit ourselves to do the best possible, together, to reform what might be. All our religious traditions have a social message that invites us to work together on a practical level. We are still far from this. In spite of thousands of dialogue circles and meetings, we still seem to know one another very little and to be very lacking in trust. Perhaps we must reconsider our methods and formulate a mutual demand: to behave in such a way that our actions, as much as possible, mirror our words, and then to act together.

10

THE CULTURAL ALTERNATIVE

Islam is not a culture. Whether we like it or not, the essence of Islam is religious. The central principle of *tawhid*, which we have often referred to, the foundations of faith and practice, the general guidance we find in the scriptural sources, leave no room for doubt about the reality of this. To speak of Islam is first of all to speak of faith, spirituality, and ethics, which together make up a conception of humankind and of life. This is what it is first and foremost, but that is not all it is. Being aware of the existence of different methodologies in worship and social affairs, which we have spoken of in part I, makes it possible for us better to understand the Islamic universe in its relation to culture. Around the body of principles that define the fundamentals of allegiance to Islam, the area of social affairs is a field that is open to the cultures, customs, discoveries, and creativity of humankind as long as they do not violate a prohibition that is specific and explicit and recognized as such. The "way of faithfulness" integrates all the knowledge, arts, and skills for people's well-being that humankind has been able to produce. This principle of integration, as we have defined it, has made it possible for Muslims to live in very varied cultural environments and to feel at home. This principle provided the particular quality that makes it possible to distinguish between Islamic "religion" and Islamic "civilization": Islam stands as a civilization as a result of this singular ability to express its universal and fundamental principles across the spread of history and geography while integrating the diversity and taking on the customs, tastes, and styles that belong to the various cultural contexts.

So, if one does not perceive, from within, the expressions and the various logics of the Islamic terms of reference, one can scarcely understand this curious mixture of unity and diversity. Faced by this difficulty, one may end up either by emphasizing the unity and referring to "Islam" without knowing exactly what is meant—religion, culture, or civilization—or one may use the plural "Islams" and, thinking to clarify the subject by using sociotheological categories (usually borrowed from other religious traditions) or minutely defined terminology, drown the analysis in a sea of references whose coherence is hard to grasp. Nevertheless, this is an important issue for Muslims living in the West, who need clear responses to their questions about their identity, culture, and civilization. What sense can be given to the shade of meaning between "Muslims in the West" and "Western Muslims"? Are they simply two ways of saying the same thing, or are they, more fundamentally, two very distinct realities?

What Is the Culture of Western Muslims?

Once again the analysis in part I will help us build our thinking about the central question of culture. To refer to Islam as such is therefore to refer first of all to a body of principles upon which are founded faith, spirituality, practice, and ethics. This core will necessarily be clothed in the forms of the various cultures in whose midst Muslims live. The Muslim women and men who emigrated from, for example, Pakistan, Algeria, Morocco, Turkey, or Guyana brought with them not only the memory of the universal principles of Islam but also, quite naturally, the way of life they followed in those countries. Moreover, to remain faithful to Islam meant, in the minds of first-generation immigrants, to perpetuate the customs of their countries of origin. They tried, without really being aware of it, to continue to be Pakistani Muslims in Britain or the United States, Moroccan or Algerian Muslims in France, Turkish Muslims in Germany, and so on. It is with the emergence of the second and third generations that problems appeared and the questions arose: parents who saw their children losing, or no longer recognizing themselves as part of, their Pakistani, Arab, or Turkish culture seemed to think that they were losing their religious identity at the same time. However, this was far from being the case: many young Muslims, by studying their religion, claimed total allegiance to Islam while distancing themselves from their cultures of origin.[1] At the same time, more and more converts to Islam, who find themselves having to choose between "becoming" Pakistani or "becoming" Arab rather than being Muslim, have slowly begun to be aware of this mistake: so there is a clear difference between Islam and the cultures of origin! This awareness and the birth of a new understanding of Islam marks the period of transition we are experiencing today, and it is inevitably difficult, even impossible, for parents of the first generation to cope with. For the younger generations, as for converts, it is a sign of hope, the way of salvation that has the potential to lead them to reconcile their Islamic principles with life in the West.

We have drawn attention in part I to the fact that a new environment may lead to a rereading of the sources with the aim of recovering a forgotten principle or discovering a horizon as yet unknown. This is what has happened with the presence of Muslims in the West. What we have tried to do in part I is a rereading and the formation of a body of reference drawn from the scriptural sources in light of Western realities. Indeed, what the latter have forced us to do is first of all to reevaluate our environment and the way we refer to it, but, more than that, also to define our Islamic identity by distinguishing it from the culture in which it is clothed in particular parts of the world. Thus, the elements that define our identity, perceived in the light of the Islamic principle of integration, appear to be very open and in constant interaction with society.

Sustained by their faith and on the basis of their understanding of the texts, Muslims must develop an understanding of the Western context that will make it possible for them to do what all Muslims have done throughout history: to integrate whatever there is in the culture[2] where they live that does not contradict what they are and what they believe. So, the universal and shared fundamentals of their Islamic identity will put on the trappings of a variety of cultures, which they should not fear or reject as long as they remain aware of the body of principles to which they must remain faithful. Their identity is determined by completely open, dynamic, interactive, and multiple factors. Depending on where they live, Muslims of immigrant background will be by culture French, Belgian, British, Spanish, or American, and, together with converts, whose role here will be crucial (because they have their roots in these cultures), they should settle on the spiritual and ethical modalities of a harmonious life through a real integration of the deep things of life. More broadly, this process will give birth to what we have called a European and American Islamic culture[3]—both respectful of the universal principles and sustained by the history, traditions, tastes, and styles of various Western countries. This exercise has already begun, but it remains complex and demands an awareness that is fed by the principles, an ability to analyze, an open mind, and a critical sense, as well as creativity. The challenges are many and weighty.

Isolation or Prohibition for Survival?

For the first generations of immigrants, the Western cultural universe was particularly disturbing. It appeared that no customs or tastes corresponded to those of their cultures of origin and, even worse, that there was hardly any respect for the traditional rules of Islamic morality. The prohibition (of alcohol and *riba*) was not recognized at all, and everything, or almost everything, seemed to be allowed in the name of freedom. The first and very natural reaction was to isolate themselves, either as individuals, as families, or as communities when they were able to organize themselves in a given place. It became a matter of living an almost parallel existence by protecting oneself and one's children from an environment that was considered morally and culturally dangerous. The equation, itself usually imported, was put in simple terms: less Western culture naturally equals more Islam.

With the arrival of the younger generations, the situation inevitably changed, but the state of mind remained the same: one had first and foremost to protect oneself. As well as imposing isolation, since the young were more and more in contact with the surrounding society, it became necessary to "prohibit." Everything that seemed more or less characteristic of the West in manners or style was considered dangerous, even unhealthy, and people contrived to forbid or avoid it as much as possible. Muslim families and organizations tried as best they could to find solutions, but it was a difficult situation, especially since there were numerous contradictions: for example, going out was forbidden, but almost free access to television was allowed (people felt themselves to be better protected from what was outside if they stayed at home); boys were allowed to try many kinds of activities that were forbidden to girls, while organizations usually provided alternative activities for boys only!

On the whole, the situation was quite bad and remains so: to be a Muslim man or woman in the West while trying to respect one's values and principles is not easy. To maintain a spiritual life, carry out the ritual obligations (prayer, *zakat*, and fasting), and keep to an ethical way of life is a daily test. All Muslims who are committed to their religion know this and experience it. People have often been advised that in order to remain themselves, they should distance themselves from society and be not only vigilant but even radical with regard to the prohibitions: some—a small minority—do practice this, while others, after repeated frustrated attempts, either remain deeply divided or have given up after failing to cut themselves off totally from society. What can be done? If we consider Western Islamic communities, we realize that they are all rather on the margins of society. There are numerous evidences for this quasi seclusion in their way of organizing themselves, their way of behaving, and even in the way in which they try to emerge from their isolation. People live within their own circle, and their very approach to inviting their fellow-citizens to meetings or conferences is inappropriate or even completely clumsy. They do not know how to go about it. It has to be said that they feel better in their isolation: in the end, this is the easiest and safest way. Confrontation with the other is dangerous and almost always constraining. We enjoy talk that affirms us in these feelings: in the mosque and at conferences and seminars, speakers who vigorously refer to the prohibitions, insist on "our essential difference," "our distinctiveness because of the excellence of our religion," "our necessary distance" find an audience that is emotionally receptive and supportive. To isolate oneself and forbid everything without half-measures is the first reaction of moral awareness when it faces a difficulty: this is initially the emotional reaction of a heart longing for peace. As such, it deserves our deep respect.

However, daily life is not as clear as our speeches, and even though the principles of Islam are essentially simple, our presence in the West reminds us that life is very complicated. The emotion that naturally results in distancing or rejection is not enough to solve a disturbing moral dilemma: sooner or later it becomes more disturbing and has to be confronted and appropriate solutions found. This is what all the new generations of Muslims born in the West tell us: we may well be satisfied with clear speeches that make no concessions, but around the mosques, after conferences, young people have school friends, listen to music, go to the cinema. So who is wrong—parents who delude themselves or young people who simply try to live in reality? It is a matter of urgency that these issues be faced and that we stop being incoherent and evasive. If the message of Islam is truly universal, if, as we keep claiming, one has to be able to find solutions appropriate for every time and society, then, in this area as in all others, Muslims must accept their responsibilities and put forward some alternatives.

There is still a long way to go, and so far the vast majority of Muslim social structures exist in completely parallel networks. In the United States and all the European countries, bookshops labeled "Islamic" stock only books written by Muslims (often selected according to the preference of the proprietor) and published by Muslims for a Muslim readership in a place patronized almost exclusively by Muslims. The universality of the message, its comprehensive nature, and the principle of integration are reduced and impoverished in this sad reality. In mosques and associations, activities are envisaged as being on the margins of society and conducted in a foreign language, a result of the unfortunate tendency to confuse the importance of learning Arabic in order to understand the Qur'an with the need to chant it in Arabic in order to remain Muslim. Cultural activities retain, imperceptibly, a pronounced Eastern flavor.

In order to protect young people, we often suggest leisure activities whose impact should be carefully considered. Offered almost exclusively to boys (why? In the name of which Islamic principle?), these activities are sometimes totally unrelated to the lived experience of young people, depending on their age, at school or even at university. We often reassure ourselves that we are providing protection by offering young people infantile activities and quickly persuading ourselves that young men and women of eighteen will generally be really pleased with things that the wider society offers to twelve- and thirteen-year-olds. The words of "Islamic" songs, the kinds of outings and games, even the organized discussions— all have the same orientation: the unnatural hope that adolescents will remain children, impervious to Western culture. The limits of their world should therefore comprise the house, the mosque or the local association, the "Islamic bookshop," and relationships with family and other young Muslims; they count themselves lucky if they can add "the Islamic school." This world "outside the world" is a fiction: the cultural environment, television, and their young contemporaries inevitably touch the hearts and minds of those who live in Europe or the United States, and the answer lies more in learning to manage this impact than in denying or rejecting it. The indications are that more and more parents and organizations have understood the meaning of these factors and are looking for new approaches. These initiatives are still few and isolated, but there is a good chance that with time the movement will grow and make it possible to reform our way of dealing with questions of culture and entertainment.

Reviving the Critical Mind and Creativity

In order to tackle the question of culture, the ulama referred to very systemized approaches through which one might consider on the one hand customs and entertainments (which were acceptable to the extent to which their practice respected Islamic principles) and on the other hand the arts, of which some were permitted and others of which were forbidden in themselves, apart from local considerations. We know the debates between scholars and the various schools of thought on the subjects of music, drawing, photography, and sculpture.[4] The distinction between forbidden and permissible art form is difficult to make in the West, where cultural expression often blends both types so that it is difficult to draw a line of demarcation between what is permitted and what is forbidden. So a more comprehensive approach is needed.

Our sources have taught us, as we saw in part I, that a Manichaean or dualistic approach should be avoided: what Muslims produce is "Islamic" and what comes from the non-Muslim West is "anti-Islamic." In the area of culture, as in every other, the criteria for evaluating an action, a production, or a custom are not to be found in the identity of its promoter or its origin but in its respect or lack of respect for the ethical principles we hold. This rule invites the mind to study, understand, and choose when it finds itself in a new environment, within a new culture. This is what Western Muslims are in need of today: a comprehensive vision and a selective approach.

Some scholars have used arguments taken from the Qur'an and the Sunna to forbid music and sometimes drawing and photography (and hence television and cinema). This is one of several opinions, and it must be respected. Others have permitted these arts, with the imposition of certain conditions concerning respect for ethical values. Those who follow the view of the former must effectively cut themselves off from the Western world, so much are music, photography, and television part of the daily way of life. The others, among whom I count myself,[5] must find a selective approach in these matters, as in others. Not everything produced in the West by way of literature, painting, music, television, and cinema is either of very high quality or very moral, but it is erroneous, and fundamentally false, to allow it to be thought that everything is perverted and useless. Honesty consists in being particular and not merging everything together. This is where the critical, selective approach comes into its own. French, English, American, German, and Spanish literatures, to name but a few, are immensely rich, and it is senseless to ignore them on the pretext that they are not "Islamic." The principle of integration has taught us to integrate into our identity and our culture everything humankind produces that is not in contradiction with a prohibition: we can find mountains of works that meet this criterion in the various literatures. It is impossible to be a European or American Muslim without integrating at least part of the world of that culture's imagination. It is not all of equal quality—we have to make a choice. But we must travel this road. So eventually "Islamic" bookshops will have to offer their customers new literary horizons: novels, short stories, poetry—but also works in the humanities and philosophy that feed and shape the mind, without its meaning that one "loses oneself."

The same approach should be followed with regard to music, cinema, and television programs. We can neither ignore the environment nor lose our critical awareness: we must always be discerning in the extraordinary volume of "culture" that bombards us every day. An ethic of consumption has to be observed, and there should be no unconscious sanctioning of musical or film productions that have become the products of a veritable industry whose promoters are without taste or scruples and whose only criterion for success is sales. Muslims are not the only critics of big-budget cinema, coarse musical productions, and "trash television": what is needed is to develop a critical eye, discover how to choose one's interests, and control one's inclinations toward the less worthy attractions. In the West, to educate oneself or another means to teach this critical approach, this active spirituality, this sense of control; it is undeniably difficult, but this is the effort, the spiritual *jihad*, that every person with moral awareness must take on in the West. It would be wrong to minimize either these realities or the detailed education they demand: to succeed in confronting the pressure of the world of television, music, and the cinema, with all their perverted and dehumanizing aspects, assumes not only a well-established ethic but also access to alternatives that themselves come to us through the most intelligent, dignified, and humane television, cinema, and musical productions. It is both a training and a struggle: we train ourselves to acquire a cultural and artistic eye and good taste, and we have to struggle to refuse being transformed into complacent, passive, docile consumers. It is sad to see what is more often the case—that those who are happiest to listen to the most violent and extreme speeches in the mosques about music and the cinema are often the first to spend their evening at home watching television programs or films that are completely lacking in intelligence or imagination, with hardly any awareness of the contradiction. It is one thing to anathematize in words and another to compromise in life.

The emotional management of our inner conflict is itself full of contradictions. Education toward a critical mind, toward the faculty of observing and understanding (the explicit as well as the implicit content of attitudes and messages), toward knowing how to make decisions in awareness and in full independence, is a necessary stage in the management of our relationship with culture and the arts. Self-isolation and complete prohibition are impossible, and, in my view, only selective development has some chance of success. The community of faith, in this Western world full of challenges, should pool its resources in order to fashion this new Muslim personality—a deep, intelligent spirituality, a critical and independent mind, a free, humble, determined will, increasingly confident in its choices. This development requires that we know our sources and know this environment from within, with its logic, its psychology, and its dynamics. In other words, it requires that we be here, that we really exist here, and that, out of the very heart of Western culture, we find the means to sustain ourselves, to outdo ourselves, and to become capable of making our own contribution.

We have to "rediscover," one might say, to use the famous expression of Rimbaud. And, while the critical work of selection we have referred to goes on, it is important that the talents of Muslim authors be expressed and that they produce original works inspired by their perceptions and their ethics but at the same time authentically "European" or "American" in quality, style, and taste. We should no longer import foreign works, thinking that the Oriental touch is the mark of the product's "Islamicness" or, on the other hand, imitate Western works while adding, with varying degrees of success, a sprinkling of phrases (often in Arabic) in order to "Islamize" them. We are in urgent need of artists who think for themselves, in their own language, with their own taste, and their own psychology. We are in need of creativity and new commitments. "God is beautiful and he loves beauty" says a well-known *hadith*, and Islamic art through the ages has expressed its excellence in various parts of the world. Today, Muslims are in the West; they are Americans and Europeans, and it is their responsibility to scrutinize the horizons of their imagination and breathe life into the arts that will wed their ethics harmoniously to their perception. In literature, music, and painting, as well as in cinema, the Way is open for experimenting with new modes of expression, new meanings, new colors, new words. We are still lacking in this creativity.

Reformist thinking has as a principle not to change Muslims of today into imitators of Muslims of yesterday. Faithful to the principles, they must find out how to live within their own time. In the same way, Muslims of today must not become imitators of the fashions of the day or be satisfied with the law of least resistance by contenting themselves with "Islamizing" whatever "goes" commercially. When this first stage of adaptation drags on, it is because laziness is overcoming us and we lack imagination. The indicators of this tendency to imitate are legion: in numerous Muslim gatherings, the bands, the varieties of music, and the types of presentation are pure reproductions of what one might see on television or at some young people's parties. The event has been "Islamized," that is to say, made permissible (*halal*), without any great concern for the implicit messages conveyed by this so-called substitute (*badil*) culture. For a party (exactly as at other parties *where-we-must-not-go*), we want bands with loud music, dim lighting, very up-to-the-minute performances, *because that is what young people want*. What is unconsciously reproduced is a kind of relation with consumerism and a focus on celebrity (the same as *there-where-we-must-not-go*), a relationship with night, with noise, with entertainment. Behind the entertainment that is being offered to people is a particular psychology of silence and noise, day and night, relation with oneself and with the other, which as a whole translates into a philosophy of existence. The message of Islam makes us attentive to silence, to the quality of what replaces or disturbs it. It also makes us aware that there is another way of facing night, by making way for silence in a sort of recollection. Ultimately, it guides our entertainment toward the exploration of that state in which one forgets the world without forgetting oneself, by remaining human and safeguarding one's dignity. These promptings should make it possible, even in the West, not to neglect the psychology that should underpin art and entertainment in the Islamic philosophy of life, not in order to isolate oneself or to forbid everything but, on the contrary, to commit oneself—to develop a critical mind, to make choices, to contribute, to renew, and always not to imitate either the past or the present. To be Western Muslims is to confront reality with all its challenges and, sustained every day by the "need of Him," to take on all our responsibilities.

CONCLUSION

Muslims in the West bear an enormous responsibility, and it falls to them to commit themselves to building their future. There is no doubt that some will continue to identify themselves over and against the West, as "the other," and to complain that in these places no one loves Islam or Muslims. They will thus maintain the unhealthy victim mentality, hoping that their salvation will come from scholars and thinkers in the East. But there are clear signs today, particularly among women, that things are changing and that more and more Muslims are aware of the challenges they have to confront. To remain Muslim in the West is a test of faith, of conscience, and of intelligence, but the only way to deal with it is to stand up and get involved—armed with the "need of Him," humility, and determination.

The reform movement that is in the process of being born has as its first requirement knowledge of the comprehensive message of Islam, its universal principles, and the tools available to help human beings to adapt themselves to their society as well as to change the world. All Muslims are invited first of all to this study, this initiation, this self-knowledge. Part I was intended as an introduction to this process, which must naturally continue to deepen and extend. At the same time, we must not short-change study of the Western world, the history of its societies and their institutions, cultures, and collective psychology. This is the route that must be traveled if we are to feel at home and apply in a positive way the Islamic principle of integrating all that does not contradict the prohibitions and making it our own. This reform movement requires, as we have said several times, a true intellectual revolution that will make it possible to be reconciled to the universality of Islamic values and to stop considering ourselves a marginalized minority, on the brink of adapting or integrating, and trying to do no more that protect ourselves from an environment we consider dangerous. In order to achieve this, Western Muslims need to free themselves of their double inferiority complex—in relation to the West (and the domination of its rationality and technology) on the one hand and in relation to the Muslim world (which alone seems to produce the great Arabic-speaking spirits of Islam who quote the texts with such ease) on the other. We shall have to liberate ourselves from these faults by developing a rich, positive, and participatory presence in the West that must contribute from within to debates about the universality of values, globalization, ethics, and the meaning of life in modern times.[1] In addition, it is time to be committed to forms of religious education that will encourage independence of mind and in-depth consideration of the application of Islamic principles in the West and the meaning of being a European or American Muslim. The foregoing pages make humble claim to opening the way to the first steps on this road, but there is still much to be achieved and many obstacles to be overcome. One of these is the reclamation by Muslims of complete political and financial independence: they must increasingly reject control, intervention, and surveillance by foreign states such as Western governments in order to be able to speak freely and credibly. Muslims increasingly have the means of doing this. This certainly does not mean that they should refuse to be in contact with the Islamic world for mutual advantage, but exchange is one thing and being under guardianship is another, here or anywhere else.

As citizens of states that recognize human rights, Muslims are no longer under the law of foreign states or former colonies and they should reject the status of subcitizens that is the product of a perverse internal neocolonialism. To regain confidence in oneself, one's values, one's role also means, in practice, reclaiming one's rights and respect. Through involvement in education reform, social and political participation, economic resistance, interreligious dialogue, and contributions to culture, people will be much more successful than if they persist in solitary confrontation and continual complaint. It is a struggle, a *jihad*—that goes without saying, but for principles, not against people, and if the people around one, willingly or unwillingly, forget the principles, the struggle consists in reminding them of those principles and making them apply them. In this way, the normalization of the Muslim presence will not be a trivialization: their presence, their contribution, their participation should make a difference, not because of their otherness but because of the singular richness they bring to their society.

Western Muslims will play a decisive role in the evolution of Islam worldwide because of the nature and complexity of the challenges they face, and in this their responsibility is doubly essential. By reflecting on their faith, their principles, and their identity within industrialized, secularized societies, they participate in the reflection the Muslim world must undertake on its relationship with the modern world, its order, and its disorder. Does the Islamic world have an alternative to offer? Does it have the means to implement new proposals? How should we engage in the debate between civilizations? Huntington's thesis on the "clash of civilizations" has been much criticized, and progressive, optimistic thinkers en masse have rejected this prophecy of doom. My many visits to the Muslim world and to European and American societies, especially after shocks like that of 11 September 2001, indicate that if the clash is not a reality, the ingredients that could lead to it are very present in current mentalities: on both sides, the lack of knowledge of the other (and of self), the acceptance of simplistic and absolute caricatures and final judgments, not to mention conflicting political and geostrategic interests, are objective features that could lead to the breakdown. In my view, the future dialogue between civilizations will not take place at the geopolitical frontiers between "the West" and "Islam" but rather, paradoxically, within European and American societies. Here again, Western Muslims will bear a heavy responsibility for demanding that the debate be opened and that it be conducted at a serious and deep level that requires listening to and exchanging with their fellow-citizens. They may be able to bring about the avoidance of a breakdown and the emergence of a path to fair dialogue and reconciliation.

This will not be easy. Prejudices, racism, and Islamophobia are tangible expressions of the hard reality of Western societies, and Muslims must not naively think that these will simply disappear as they become citizens settled in their societies. Increasingly, and for a considerable period, they will have to become accustomed to facing political security measures, discrimination, accusations of "double-talk," menacing, malevolent looks, and acts of surveillance and control.[2] Distrust is so great and suspicion so widespread that times of mutual trust seem still to be far away. But rather than complaining sadly, it seems to me that there is only one response to this state of affairs: to hold to one's convictions; express one's principles and hopes; make clear comments and criticisms; keep to one, open way of speaking (with Muslims and with one's fellow-citizens); participate in society for good in partnership with all human beings who, in conscience, reject a world without conscience; and, armed with one's faith and a critical mind, reject dualism and keep one's head by cultivating patience and long-suffering. If part II began with spirituality, it was to recall a priority: the effort and the process of spiritual initiation that lead us in our hearts toward the Transcendent are the best provisions for the journey. Through this teaching, we learn perseverance, which gives us the key to success: to stand firm in the face of people who trade in prejudice, who are responsible for oppression, and who spread hatred, while retaining the presence of mind to say, "Salam!" "Peace!" and not to give up one's efforts along the way, offering the brotherhood of one's soul and humanity to all people of conscience, from one's heart and in love, and inviting them to travel with one, training oneself to keep on resisting and learning how to be a friend, *faithfully*.

NOTES

Introduction

1. Leicester, U.K.: Islamic Foundation, 1999.

2. Particularly the science of the fundamental principles of the law and jurisprudence (*usul al-fiqh*).

3. In fact, my study as a whole also concerns very directly Muslims living in Muslim-majority societies. Many reflections and suggestions seem to me to be relevant and practical beyond the societies of America and Europe, and the movement toward reform in the latter will necessarily have an impact on the Muslim world.

4. They are also the means, it must be repeated, used to carry out surveillance of Muslim populations in the West. See my article "Les musulmans d'Europe pris en tenaille," *Le Monde Diplomatique* (June 2000); reprinted in *Manières de voir* (July–August 2002).

Chapter 1

1. This will be the subject of our discussions in the second part of this book.

2. It is unanimously understood among scholars that the Qur'an is the "revealed word" of God, but the word is not God.

3. "We are closer to him than his own jugular vein" (Qur'an 50:16). The "We" here is God, for whom three personal pronouns are used in the Qur'an— "I," "He," and "We"—in order to avoid any personalization that could unintentionally tend toward anthropomorphism.

4. Qur'an 24:41.

5. Qur'an 17:44.

6. As too are the "jinn" of the Islamic tradition—beings created from fire who, like human beings, can choose to accept or refuse to hold to faith in the Creator.

7. See my book *Islam, the West and the Challenges of Modernity*, Part III (Leicester, U.K.: Islamic Foundation, 2001).

8. Qur'an 42:11.

9. Ninety-nine names, and more, on the basis of the Qur'an and various traditions.

10. We may refer more specifically to the pre-Socratic tradition, as found specifically in Parmenides, with the dualistic proposition "Being is, nonbeing is not."

11. An interesting passage in the Qur'an speaks of beings who lose awareness completely as being more lost than animals. Consciousness, when it atrophies to the point of prompting the human being only by means of the same instinct as the animals possess, is dehumanized. It is consciousness and control that define the humanity of humankind.

12. Thus, every action, provided it is in the context of the remembrance of God, is considered sacred. Every action that takes place in recollection becomes sacred and is charged with a spiritual dimension and an ethical quality, even the sexual act. In several traditions, the Prophet (PBUH) reminded his Companions: "When you greet someone, it is a *sadaqa* [a giving of alms that brings one nearer to God]. When you give, it is a *sadaqa*. When you smile at your brother, it is a *sadaqa*. And when you have relations with your wife and you do it remembering God, that too is a *sadaqa*." This last astonished his Companions, who questioned him about how one could be rewarded for satisfying a desire. To which he replied: "If it were done illegally, would it not be a sin? So if it is done legally, one therefore deserves a reward" (*hadith* reported by Muslim).

13. Qur'an 17:15.

14. Qur'an 2:286.

15. Qur'an 7:172.

16. Qur'an 30:30. The best known Qur'anic commentators and ulama expert in various Islamic sciences have given diverse interpretations of the idea of *fitra*: some have spoken of "human nature," others of "natural religion," and many have translated it as "Islam." It is possible to find one point that is common to all these readings: in the Muslim understanding, the natural order is a witness to the *submission* of all the elements to the Creator (*submission* being the first meaning of *Islam*); humankind participates in this order, and people's natural desire for God extends and deepens in them this submission of the universe. Order is to nature what *fitra* is to the human being—the fundamental (natural) expression of the recognition of the Creator, of acceptance and of submission (Islam). This harmony expresses the original, essential Islam, which is confirmed and elaborated, as to worship and social affairs, by the Revelation to the seventh century. This is how "There is no change in God's creation. This is the unchangeable religion" is to be understood.

17. *Hadith* reported by al-Bukhari and Muslim.

18. We will return to this idea in part II, on interreligious dialogue.

19. Qur'an 41:53.

20. Qur'an 35:28.

21. The orthodox Islamic tradition has strongly emphasized this dynamic, this movement toward the beginning. The very word *Sharia* means "the way to the spring." However, it is in the experience of looking inward and of the "mystical way" that one naturally finds the strongest expression of this journey, which is a return. Paolo Coelho, in his *Alchemist*, is clearly inspired by these teachings: the answer to the purpose of the quest is always at the starting point of the journey, the initiation.

22. Qur'an 8:24.

23. Qur'an 6:165.

24. We refer here to the ecology that is born of the awareness of possible disasters caused by our insane consumption of the universe. The ecology that is born of the spiritual tradition establishes an awareness of limitations based on ethical principals, rather than on the wish to prevent disasters. It is an ecology of management, not an ecology of protection, a little in the sense intuited by Proudhon, in his well-known book *What Is Property?* when he speaks of humankind as a manager on the earth and not an owner. If the two ecologies share the same understanding of what the limits are, there is nevertheless a considerable difference between them: ecology based on principle requires management on both the global and individual levels in accord with the principles of respect for creation, while an ecology of limitation often concentrates on excesses and their consequences without always establishing clearly the connection between the incoherences of the system as a whole and the particular part played by individual consumption.

25. See *Islam, the West and the Challenges of Modernity*, Part II.

26. We shall come back later to this notion (see the first chapter of part II).

27. It is the Sunna that often lays down the precise details of practice. The Sunna, or traditions reported about the Prophet, is the collection of what Muhammad said or did or approved in his lifetime. The collection of these traditions and the verification of their contents are the sole object of a science (the science of *hadith*): the criteria are today very rigorously defined and make it possible to classify the texts by degree of authenticity. The traditions confirm, make explicit, and, more rarely, complete the Qur'anic obligations, prohibitions, and recommendations that are the first source.

28. See *To Be a European Muslim*, table, "Typology and Classification of the Islamic Sciences," in Part I, "Birth of the Islamic Sciences," ed. Islamic Foundation (Leicester, U.K.: Islamic Foundation, 1999).

29. We shall come back to these elements later in part I.

30. Some Christian and humanist authors think that an evolution of Islam will be possible when Muslims have developed a historical-critical reading of the Qur'an. Apart from the fact that, for Muslims, the Qur'anic text is the divine word (and that this is one of the pillars of their faith), it must be said that calling into question the divine origin of the message in order to achieve a complete humanization and historicization of the revealed Word does not in itself guarantee a reading free of dogmatism. Marx has been read dogmatically, and the Bible still is. The problem lies not in the divine nature of the origin of

the text but in the way it is read. One may read the Qur'an in the conviction that it is the Word of God without in the least minimizing the amount of human reasoning that must be invested in order for the Text to become accessible.

31. There may certainly be a relation between a way of reading the Qur'an and a political position, but this is not always the case, and in any case it does not follow an infallible logic. For example, the traditionalists, on the religious level, do not strongly support reactionary or dictatorial political regimes, just as liberal rationalists do not always quote the Qur'an in support of a state based on law and democracy. If distinctions of order and method are not clearly established here, a confusion will exist that may have serious consequences.

32. We shall return later to this question of unity and diversity on the cultural plane (see section 3).

33. Belonging to this broad trend does not imply that the various groups agree with each other; on the contrary, their dependence on one school of legal thought sometimes exacerbates tendencies to exclude and reject other schools within this broad band. Historical and doctrinal contentions may provoke fierce conflicts between Deobandis and Barelwis. The latter also oppose, on the doctrinal plane, the adherents of the Tabligh-i Jamaat, whose school of thought is based on a recognition of other scholastic loyalties, with their principle of action being to avoid controversy and concentrate on the essentials of religious practice.

34. In the Muslim world, these movements do not usually participate in politics. In a Muslim-majority country, they recognize the authority of the powers that be and do not stand in opposition. They are to be considered, to use the terminology of political science, conservatives. Nevertheless, certain trends within Scholastic traditionalism have displayed, in certain situations of social turmoil, a determined political engagement. This has usually been particular to a specific time and circumstance (in Pakistan, India, Turkey, and some parts of Africa). The case of the Taliban in Afghanistan is significant, for, in the opinion of the experts, there was nothing to make it likely that these students would become politically active in this way: they were encouraged and invited to it by Pakistan (with the support of the United States and Saudi Arabia).

35. In the Muslim world, this trend is found among ulama with a high reputation in the Islamic sciences (particularly the *hadith* sciences, such as al-Albani, Ibn Uthaymin, and Ibn Baz, who were internationally recognized and respected for their scientific rigor and for the breadth of their knowledge). On the political plane they display the same conservative attitude as the traditionalists: they recognize the authority of the ruling power, whatever it may be without dispute, provided that it is Islamic, and they refuse to use such terms as election, parliament, or democracy, because they were not used in the Qur'an or by the Prophet. By their refusal to be involved in the political arena, they often inadvertently serve to legitimate the powers that be, which are not disturbed by their literalism or entrenched position so long as they do not have adverse political implications.

36. See the third chapter of part I.

37. In the Muslim world, legalist *salafi* reformist movements are involved in the political arena and are usually in opposition. The majority of them support the idea of Islamic societies that respect Islamic terms of reference (particularly on the social and political level, the rule of law, political pluralism, parliamentarianism, and elections by universal suffrage), without implying subservience to the Western model. Their principle is to play the game of institutional legality. They are almost everywhere, though in different degrees, subjected to imprisonment, torture, and persecution. The positions of various groups differ with their histories and the societies in which they are active.

38. These movements exist in the Muslim world and are almost everywhere made up of very small groups. They are at the forefront of media attention because of their violent and spectacular actions. In Algeria, a section of the FIS went over to this type of stance after the suspension of the electoral process and the subsequent repression. Very marginal networks are built up transnationally, completely on the fringes of Muslim communities in the West.

39. Some rationalists or liberals have asked me to note that they refuse, as they say, to connect the development of their religious position to colonial influence alone. They state that they link themselves with the historical Islamic tradition of Mutazilism, which in effect proposed, or at least some of its thinkers did, a development that, even if it did not lead to the same conclusions as those of contemporary rationalists, provided a very open framework and way of reading the scriptural sources. This statement is welcome and completely legitimate: it requires a very serious and certainly fascinating historical study of the intellectual filiations at work in contemporary debates.

40. The liberal reformists are a minority in the Muslim world and are to be found both in power and in opposition (usually on the Left). They find much sympathy in the West and are often presented as the only true democrats in the Muslim countries. The reason for this is largely the fact that the articulation of their discourse is immediately audible to Western ears because they accept the frames of reference known in the North. The soundness of their democratic stance remains to be proved, however, since some reformists labeled "liberals" do not hesitate to support dictatorial regimes, as in Syria and Tunisia, or "eradicators" (a wing of the ruling military junta) in Algeria. As they see it, the struggle against the "fundamentalists" justifies alliances with despots.

41. These Sufi circles are almost completely apolitical in the West, and this is also their distinctive trait in the Muslim world. However, this last remark is relative, for the Sufi *turuq* have often been, as in the former Soviet Union or in Turkey, bastions of fierce political resistance to colonial occupiers or oppressors. Sufis were often supporters of the so-called *parallel* Islam, refusing allegiance to the ruling power in order to defend an authentic and independent faith removed from the compromises accepted by some religious dignitaries in the pay of the authorities and representatives of official Islam.

42. This is the approach I have defended earlier and that may be discerned in the sweep of the various trends of thought.

43. Behind the smokescreen of very open ideas about women, the reality is less rosy: a man may contract a temporary marriage with a woman without telling her that this is his intention (the marriage may last only a few days since this was the *intention*, even though unexpressed, of the "husband"), and adultery with a woman "unbeliever" is considered only a minor sin because she is not a Muslim. In reality, the entire discourse about ethics and social behavior is based on this distinction between "Muslims" (only the *Ahbash*) and others (the *kuffar*, understood by the members of this sect as "unbelievers" in the worst possible sense). The founder, al-Harari (who lived in Lebanon till his death in 2001), pronounced judicial opinions (*fatawa*) for his disciples in which he maintained that lying, stealing, and even killing a *kafir*, an unbeliever, are minor sins.

44. Their eruption on the Lebanese scene has caused some damage: they were behind some violent brawls and some killings in mosques. Not recognizing scholars of other parties as Muslims, since they are explicitly *kuffar*, they have gone as far as to eliminate them even if they were recognized scholars. Some of their leaders, members of the Lebanese parliament, have frequently praised the [late] Syrian president Hafez al-Asad and did not hesitate to describe him as a "saint" at the time of the accidental death of his eldest son. The tested strategy of Hafez al-Asad is well-known—to rely on sectarian groups, in the forefront of which is his own clan, the Alawites, to cause divisions and sow trouble among his opponents. The significant financial resources available to the *Ahbash* in the West are due to foreign support from Lebanon and, without the shadow of a doubt, from the Syrian regime.

Chapter 2

1. The mere fact that I have referred to this notion has caused some researchers to cast doubt on my works. In so doing, they do not take into account how I define it, or how I propose we should approach the subject. They simply, and often maliciously, "surf" the very negative images that are widespread among the general public in order to dismiss any approach to it, without taking the time to study it or discuss its principles, its logic, and the perspectives it may have to offer.

2. Is this not an innovative original, or at least self-contradictory, phrase?

3. There has been much discussion of the question "Who is a Muslim?" as much because scholars have differed in their opinions as out of the need to discuss the sectarian approaches of some movements that claim that they alone are the true "Muslims." In my view, all the women and men are Muslims who see themselves as such and have pronounced the *shahada*, which is the decisive factor in belonging to Islam. The question of practice and behavior falls within the responsibility of those who accept the consequences without this calling into question their being recognized as "Muslim." This is the opinion of many scholars, including al-Shafii. We are here interested more particularly, and almost naturally, in the women and men who are concerned about faithfulness

in their practice and daily life because it is for them especially that life in the West is sometimes a problem and often a challenge.

4. Attempts have often been made to oppose the intimate "mystical Way" (Sufism) to the "legal Way" (the *Sharia*). In the redefinition of concepts that is proposed here, this opposition becomes meaningless: the intimate "mystical way" is at the heart (it is the heart) of the "path toward the spring." Spirituality is the first requirement of faithfulness. There is no faithfulness without spirituality.

5. Upon reading the Texts, one discovers that these prohibitions are not numerous, even though in some areas they are very precise.

6. It is sometimes useful to remind certain intellectuals in the West of these truths when they forget that, although the principles of democracy are identical, the models of democracy in Europe and also in the United States vary widely. Often they demand that the Muslim world adhere to a particular model of democracy, while the heart of the debate lies in discovering whether or not Muslims oppose democratic principles. As far as the model is concerned, each society should be free to find one that is most appropriate to its history, its culture, and its collective psychology.

7. This explains the differences between the ways of life of Muslims in Europe, Africa, and Asia and on the continent of America. Their creed and the body of principles they hold to are the same (this is what is meant by *one* Islam, one and the same religion), but their cultures differ and are integrated into their way of being in the world in so far as this does not run counter to an accepted boundary. It is with regard to this cultural aspect that one may speak of an African, Asian, American, or European Islam, without having to use the plural when referring to "Islam": the universality of the latter accommodates the diversity of the former.

8. Some traditionalist and literalist trends do not make this differentiation: to follow the Prophet means to dress like him. The essence of the principle is subsumed into its historical application. The difference of approach in this is the most easily observed expression of the divergence between these trends and the reformist school.

9. This recalls the humility of origin of which we have spoken in the first chapter.

10. *Istislah* is the tenth form of the root *sa-lua*, which is also the root of *maslaha*.

11. Abu Hamid al-Ghazali, *Al-mustasfa min ilm al-usul* (Baghdad: Muthanna, 1970).

12. Cf. *Al-mustasfa min ilm al-usul*, vol. 1, pp. 286–87. See also Muhammad Khalid Masud's interesting book, *Shatibi's Philosophy of Islamic Law* (Islamabad: Islamic Research Institute, 1995), pp. 139–40.

13. Apart from the ulama of the Zahirite school, who did not even recognize the concept of *maqasid*.

14. *Al-masali al-daruriyya* are requirements upon which people's lives depend, as well as the protection of the meaning of their worship of God. Later some ulama added *al-ird* (honor).

15. *Al-masali al-hajiyya* are requirements related to difficult situations. We find in this category rules concerning, for example, the sick and the old and dispensations (*rukhas*) related to prayer and fasting.

16. *Al-masali al-tahsiniyya* may deal with, for example, cleanliness and moral virtues, which may lead to an improvement in religious practice and be a means of attaining what is desirable.

17. Thus considered that there was no room for speaking of *istislah*, since the *Sharia* itself and all its injunctions were founded on *al-masali*, which represent both the content and the objective of the revealed laws.

18. Al-Shatabi explains, in his analysis in *Al-Itisam*, that the two sources of Islam are the Qur'an and the Sunna, whose injunctions are based on *al-maslaha* (he agrees on this point with Ibn Hazm); but he is clear that we have to refer to our reason when the texts contain no indication (according to al-Shatibi, this was once done by means of *ijma* or *qiyas*). So, when the texts are silent, *al-maslaha* is the point of reference and acts as an independent source in light of the Qur'an and the Sunna.

19. This was the view of al-Ghazali, who, by subordinating the method of reasoning based on *al-maslaha* to *qiyas*, linked the sources in order to avoid a purely rational formulation that might be remote from any reference to the sources.

20. The meaning of *mursala* has been discussed by numerous scholars, and it would be pedantic and unprofitable to discuss it here. The classification "undetermined" gives the meaning generally admitted and legally appropriate.

21. Subhi Rajab al-Mahmasani, *Falsafat at-tashri fil-islam* (Leiden: Brill, 1961), p. 117. Cited by Mohammad Hashim Kamali, *Principles of Islamic Jurisprudence* (Cambridge: Islamic Texts Society, 1991), p. 276.

22. Such was the case when some ulama wanted to justify usury and bank interest (*riba*) in the name of the common good. There can be no *maslaha mursala* here because this matter is the subject of clear and indisputable directions in the Qur'an (*qati al-thubut wa-qati al-dalala*—indisputable with regard to both transmission and meaning) and the Sunna (*zanni al-thubut wa-qati al-dalala*—conjectural with regard to transmission and indisputable with regard to meaning).

23. There are numerous other secondary conditions (for example, the *maslaha* must be reasonable (*maqula*) according to Malik, and indispensable (*daruriyya*) according to al-Ghazali. For more details and deeper analyses, see the specialized works already referred to by al-Shatibi (*Al-Itisam*), Khallaf, Hassab Allah, and Kamali. We shall come back to this discussion when dealing with economy in the second part of this book.

24. Yusuf al-Qaradawi, *Al-Ijtihad al-muasir, bayna al-indibat wa-al-infirat* (Cairo: Dar al-tawzi wa-al-nashr al-islamiyya, 1993), pp. 66–77.

25. Qur'an 7:157.

26. Qur'an 10:57.

27. Qur'an 2:219.

28. Ibn al-Qayyim al-Jawziyya, *Ilam al-muwaqqiin an rabb al-alamin*, vol. 3 (Cairo, n.d.), p. 1.

29. We shall deal with various levels of "clarity" when we study the notion of *ijtihad*.

30. The vast majority of the ulama agree in saying that there can be no *ijtihad* (and hence no *maslaha*, no *qiyas*, no *istihisan*, and no need for *ijma*) as far as religious practice (*al-ibadat*) is concerned, for its judgments and modalities are known to us through Revelation and must be applied as they were revealed to the Prophet and taught and explained by him. Similarly, when there are clear and detailed injunctions (only a few judgments in fact meet these criteria), they must be applied (though of course without neglecting a vision of the whole body of objectives of Islamic law and the social situation, as we have explained).

31. Qur'an 2:185

32. Muhammad Khalid Masud, *Shatibi's Philosophy of Islamic Law*, p. 367.

33. Muhammad Hashim Kamali, *Principles of Islamic Jurisprudence*, p. 366.

34. Muhammad Hamidullah, *The Emergence of Islam*, ed. and trans. Afzal Iqbal (Islamabad: Islamic Research Institute, 1993), p. 97.

35. There are various opinions among the ulama as to the number of these verses and *ahadith*. For example, al-Ghazali and Ibn al-Arabi counted five hundred verses, while Abd al-Wahhab Khallaf has listed about two hundred and twenty-eight. Al-Shawkani, however, believed that such calculations were not reliable and definitive, since some verses can be variously interpreted according to the scholar and the context. One could say the same about the *ahadith al-ahkam*, even if Ibn Hanbal is supposed to have said that there are about one thousand two hundred *ahadith* in this category. Cf. al-Shawkani, *Al-qawl al-mufid fi al-ijtihad wa-al-taqlid*, ch. 2 (Cairo, 1975); and Abd al-Wahhab Khallaf, *Ilm usul al-fiqh* (Kuwait: Dar al-galam, 1978).

36. There are many other detailed classifications in the area of *ijtihad*, which are beyond the scope of this work. They are known by specialists in *usul al-fiqh* and are the subject of discussions and controversies among the ulama. An example is the "divisibility of *ijtihad*" (*al-tajza*), about which pages and pages of argument have been written. It is a very theoretical, and in fact secondary, issue. We shall tackle the question of *ijtihad fardi* (individual) and *jamai* (collective) later.

37. Al-Shatibi, *al-muwafaqat fi usul al-sharia*, new ed., vol. 4 (Lebanon: Dar al-marifa, 1996), ch. "The conditions for *ijtihad*," pp. 477ff., passim.

38. This is what al-Shatibi himself calls the second quality: having said that the first is the objective, he adds that "the second is the instrument" (ibid., vol. 4, p. 478).

39. Al-Shatibi, for example, was very demanding in this particular; he thought that no one could attain the true level of *ijtihad* without a deep knowledge of Arabic (ibid., vol. 4, pp. 590ff.).

40. This recognition must also come from other scholars and from the Muslim community.

41. The ulama have set down various conditions for the *mujtahid mutlaq* (absolute) and the *mujtahid muqayyad* (limited) who are content to deduce judgments within the framework of a specific juridical school. The condi-

tions required for the latter are certainly less demanding, and added to them are knowledge of the rules of deduction related to the juridical school in question.

42. For a detailed analysis of these historical reasons, see Muhammad Iqbal, *The Reconstruction of Islamic Thought* (Lahore: Ashraf, 1951), pp. 149–52.

43. We shall return to this issue in the next section.

44. Al-Shatibi, *Al-muwafaqat fi usul al-sharia*, vol. 4, pp. 595–602.

45. The ulama have often used the words *mujtahid* and *mufti* synonymously. However, the two functions are not exactly the same either in nature or in degree, even if the areas they cover do overlap. The *mujtahid* works on the sources and tries to deduce legal judgments from them, while the *mufti* must give specific answers to questioners (whether this is an individual or a community) and so works downstream from the *mujtahid*. *Mufti* must have most of the qualities referred to earlier, unless their *fatawa* are restricted to a specific subject area (*juzi*). We shall deal with the various levels of *fatwa* later.

46. In this explanation, al-Shatibi identifies the *mufti* with the *mujtahid*.

47. Al-Shatibi, *Al-muwafaqat fi usul al-sharia*, vol. 4, pp. 595–96.

48. Qur'an 21:79.

49. Al-Shafii, *Al-risala* (Cairo: al-Amiriyya, 1926), p. 128.

50. Cf. *Fatawa* of the European Council for research and fatwa, English translation, Islamic Foundation of Dublin, 2001.

51. Yusuf al-Qardawi, *Fi fiqh al-aqalliyyat al-muslima* (On Law and the Jurisprudence of Muslim Minorities) (Cairo: Dar al-Shuruq, 2001) (in Arabic).

52. This position is entirely understandable since he does not live in the West and his reflections accompanied the first stages in the establishment of Muslims in northern societies.

53. This approach is also necessary in all majority-Muslim countries, as they are nowadays all in contact with Western culture.

54. For this see my preface of *Recueil de fatwas*, Tawhid edition (Lyon: Tawhid, 2000), pp. 9–19, as well as the commentaries of the *fatwas*.

55. Critical and fruitful discussions with the anthropologist Abd al-Halim Herbert have fed and inspired the discussion developed in this section.

56. See *To Be a European Muslim*, Part I, "The Birth of the Islamic Sciences."

57. This is not to deny some possibilities of harmonization but rather to remember that the Qur'an is first and foremost a moral message and that the obsessive desire to show links between contemporary science and Qur'anic teachings tends to become very unhealthy and may even lead to serious reversals in conviction: the scientific truths of today may be considered erroneous tomorrow.

58. The "Islamic" sciences, as they are traditionally called, each have a methodology dependent on the areas of study of the revealed Book. All the other sciences also have varieties of methodologies differentiated on the basis of the object of study in the "open book" (the universe)—the book of nature.

59. We have chosen to include the most familiar sciences because the size of the table makes it impossible to mention them all.

Chapter 3

1. The notion of *dar al-harb* occurs twice, or rather three times in two *hadiths* whose authenticity is debatable (*mursal*). They can be used as rules only in very precise circumstances.

2. Between 6 AH (*Sulh al-Hudaybiyya*) and the death of the Prophet in 10 AH.

3. Also called *dar al-adl* (abode of justice) or *dar al-tawhid* (abode of belief in the oneness of God).

4. In so saying, al-Dusuqi established a distinction between Muslims whose presence and numbers were effectively an expression of the idea of the "ownership of the land" (*al-milkiyya lil-muslimin*) and rulers who might be non-Muslims. See the study by Chaykh Manna al-Qattan, *Iqamat al-muslim fi balad ghayr islami* (Muslim Residence in a Non-Muslim Country) (Paris: Fondation islamique pour l'information, 1993).

5. Also called *dar al-shirk* (abode of idolatry/polytheism) as opposed to *dar al-tawhid*, or *dar al-kufr* (abode of nonacceptance of Islam).

6. See *Al-usus al-shariyya lil-alaqat bayna al-muslimin wa-ghayr al-muslimin* (The Islamic Principles concerning Relations between Muslims and Non-Muslims), ed. L'Union des Organisations islamiques en France (UOIF) (Paris: UOIF, 1987), pp. 104–5.

7. See al-Qattan, *Iqamat al-muslim fi balad ghayr islami* (Muslim Residence in a Non-Muslim Country), pp. 7ff.

8. This debate is important because the ulama have often used it to try to define the fundamental principle (*al-asl*) governing a Muslim's place of residence. Once *dar al-islam* is defined, the principle (*al-asl*) seems to be that Muslims should live there except in very specific circumstances. The difficult of defining the various areas is, of course, connected with the other difficulty of deciding what is *al-asl*: this is precisely the issue we are dealing with in this study.

9. We shall define in the next section what we consider to be the foundations of Muslim identity.

10. After the events of 11 September 2001, the situation has somewhat deteriorated in the United States: the civil rights of numerous citizens or residents of the Muslim faith have been clearly flouted. The same is true in some European countries where "security reasons" legitimize all kinds of interventions irrespective of the law. These are the situations that tend to confirm in the mind of Muslims that they are not at home and that there is no willingness to consider them as such.

11. For a more detailed exposition of each of these rights, see *To Be a European Muslim*, Part II.

12. See the three different positions of the scholars in detail in *To Be a European Muslim*, Part II.

13. *Dar al-dawa* signifies a place for "inviting people to God," presenting what Islam is, and spreading its message.

14. Faysal Al-Mawlawi, *Al-usus al-shariyya lil-alaquat bayna al-muslimin wa-ghayr al-muslimin* (Paris: UOIF, 1987), p. 104.

15. The notion of *dawa* is often understood as the expression of the inherent Islamic inclination to proselytize and its desire to convert. However, the notion conveys rather the idea of presenting and expressing the message of Islam, because conversion, which must be a free act, is a matter entirely between God and the human heart. See part II, chapter 9 of this book, "Interreligious Dialogue."

16. Qur'an 2:143.

17. Qur'an 2:3.

18. Qur'an 17:34.

19. Qur'an 23:8.

20. Qur'an 16:90.

21. Which may sometimes appear to be a process of Westernization.

22. Al-Mawlawi, p. 104.

23. Qur'an 20:14.

24. *Hadith* reported by Bukhari and Muslim.

25. *Hadith* reported by Ibn Majah.

26. Qur'an 26:214.

27. Qur'an 6:164.

28. *Hadith* reported by al-Bayhaqi.

29. We shall return to this whole area in part II.

30. This means that the Muslim also recognizes all the previous messengers and books revealed by God throughout history.

31. Qur'an 17:22–24.

32. Qur'an 31:15.

33. *Hadith* reported by Muslim.

34. Qur'an 4:135.

35. We shall return to this important point of Muslim belonging when we deal with the question of *umma*.

36. Qur'an 1:5–6.

37. *Hadith* reported by Bukhari and Muslim.

38. Qur'an 49:10.

39. *Hadith* reported by Ahmad and Abu Dawud.

40. It may be spent abroad if all the local needs are met or if there is an exceptional and vital need (see part II).

41. Qur'an 2:143.

42. *Hadith* reported by Bukhari.

43. *Hadith* reported by Bukhari.

44. *Hadith* reported by Bukhari and Muslim.

45. Qur'an 5:8.

46. Eight verses in *surat al-Nisa* (Women) command the Prophet to acquit a Jew who was innocent and to condemn in his place the guilty party, who was a Muslim.

47. Qur'an 17:34.

48. Qur'an 23:8.

49. Qur'an 8:72.

50. It must be noted that freedom of worship is a sacred right in Islam that must be protected and defended whatever the religion of those who are persecuted. This is not the subject dealt with by this verse, but it is clearly the message of Islam in general.

51. *Hadith* reported by Muslim.

52. al-Mawlawi, op. cit., p. 101.

53. This is the meaning of the *hadith* of the Prophet: "Muslims are bound by their conditions [those of the agreements they have accepted]," reported by Bukhari.

54. Some Muslims state that it is illegitimate to pronounce an oath of this kind because it is similar to making an alliance, though the Prophet declared in a *hadith* reported by Muslim, Abu Dawud, and al-Tirmidhi: "There is no alliance [*hilf*] in Islam; whoever concludes an alliance is as if he were in the time of *jahiliyya*, and Islam will only cause him a difficulty." However, as Manna al-Qattan notes, the alliance of which this *hadith* speaks is one concluded against Islam and its teachings, and not one that respects them and is made to do good (e.g., to help the needy, exchange experiences, or protect the oppressed). He recalls that the Prophet, who had been present at the *hilf al-fudul* in his youth, said one day that if such an alliance had been proposed again, he would have agreed.

55. Qur'an 12:33.

56. This may well happen in the case of clear injustice committed by a group, as the Qur'an points out in 49:9: "If two groups of believers are fighting, reestablish peace between them; and if one group commits aggression against the other, fight the aggressor until he conforms with the command of God; if he conforms, reestablish peace between them with justice and be fair; for truly God loves those who are fair." Again, it is the principle of justice above all that must be taken as the criterion.

57. This is exactly what happened when the U.S. government decided to bomb Afghanistan after the atrocities of 11 September 2001. Some American Muslim citizens took it upon themselves to ask whether they could be involved in this bombing operation. Some scholars replied that loyalty toward their country allowed them, Islamically, to take part in the conflict. Other authorities replied in the negative. In the end, it is the individual conscience that must make the final decision; if one considers that bombing the Afghan people was just, involvement was Islamically consistent; but if, after analysis, this retaliatory operation was considered unjust, the conscience clause should have been invoked. This process of reflection and the debate that should have accompanied it were unfortunately vitiated in the United States: Muslim citizens were under such pressure to prove their patriotism and their true allegiance that simply to pose the question of the legitimacy of bombing Afghanistan was in itself already proof of culpable hesitancy. The emotiveness is understandable, but dangerous when pressure stifles a human being's ability to question his conscience.

58. See *Recueil de fatwas*.

Chapter 4

1. Among these are the two *fatwa* councils (American and European) already referred to.

2. See, for example, the recent books of Katherine Bullock, *Rethinking Muslim Women and the Veil: Challenging Historical and Modern Stereotypes* (London: International Institute of Islamic Thought, 2002), and Asma Lamrabet, *Musulmane tout simplement* (Lyon: Tawhid, 2002). There are so many other old and recent contributions impossible to mention here.

3. This does not refer to the same categories of people in the United States and Europe. In the latter, it is Muslims of migrant descent who most often have a lower social profile. This is the exact opposite of the situation in the United States, where it is above all the "native Americans," including Afro-Americans, who live in difficult conditions. Urban politics are also different: in Europe, with France as the archetype, the suburbs where people on modest salaries live are on the outskirts of the towns; in the United States, the most critical areas are near the centers, the "inner cities," and the areas for wealthier people are outside the towns.

4. I owe it to my various discussions with Professor Felice Dassetto that I have considered this question more widely and recognized the relevance of his critical views regarding the undifferentiated use of the concept of "Muslim minority."

5. We shall return to this analysis later.

6. *Hadith* reported by Bukhari and Muslim.

7. Some self-criticism may in fact be intended to please one's critic or the surrounding society, rather than being well-founded. There is nothing more pernicious than being self-critical simply to reassure others in what may be their very simplistic convictions. One thus maintains the worst defects of both sides—the humiliation of the dominated and the arrogance of the dominant—to no profit.

8. In conversation about the national team in football or basketball or any other sport, one is forced to recognize, by looking at the list of team members, how mixed the national identity has become.

Chapter 5

1. It seems clear today that the obsession of some people (Muslims and non-Muslims) with promoting Sufism springs less from a real interest in the spiritual aspects of Sufi teaching than from the belief that it is the best way of combating the "communitarian" form of orthodox Islam from the inside in order to encourage individual initiation into an Islam that then becomes restricted in the private sphere. In other words, this is about using one strand of Islam to take Islam along the way to secularization. Apart from the fact that this project seems bound to fail and that the Sufism it encourages is often void of substance, if not an actual deception, it remains to discover whether reform can be achieved by this intellectual strategy. We think not, and the sum purpose

of this book is to propose an alternative, still looking to the inner life, but taking care to be faithful to both the Islamic tradition and its highest mystical expressions.

2. Qur'an 91:7–10.

3. Qur'an 49:7.

4. Qur'an 12:53.

5. Qur'an 3:14.

6. *Jihad* is often spoken of as if it were a call to war. In fact, on the intimate level, as on the level of war rightly so-called, *jihad* is the management of a state of conflict before going on to peace. We are looking at it here in the intimate context, and it is the same in a war situation: legitimate defense in the face of aggression (which gives the meaning of *jihad* in the sense of *qital*) is in fact resistance that must lead to a harmonious, just, and peaceful solution. See my *Jihad, violence, guerre et paix en islam* (Lyon: Tawhid, 2002).

7. On this subject, see the excellent work of Malik Badri, *On Contemplation: An Islamic Psychospiritual Study* (London: IIIT, 2000).

8. Qur'an 55:5.

9. It is noteworthy that the word translated as "verse," as biblical verses, especially verses of the Psalms, are called, has a completely different meaning in Arabic: the Arabic *ayat* clearly means "signs," and the two books reflect each other and form a true spiritual correspondence.

10. Qur'an 3:190.

11. This division between public and private space, which is put before Muslims in a quite obsessive way by some people as if it were an insurmountable problem lying in the way of their settling in Western societies, is a false problem. It expresses, in fact, the division our societies set up between the dogmatic or doctrinal and rational order on the one hand and religious and public authority on the other. It has never been a question of forbidding citizens to be nourished and inspired by the teachings of their religious traditions and to draw on them to guide their public behavior or to determine their civil choices. This would be inconceivable and basically impossible. If we recall the presentation made in part I, we see that the "comprehensive character" of the message of Islam touches on every area of life but does not confuse the categories of things. If, in addition, we remember that there is no institutional clerical religious authority, we can be open to a quite different vision of the question of private and public for Muslims. From the beginning and at the very heart of Islam, the relation between spirituality and reason has been a "relation of inspiration." The heart must be always trying to remind reason of its fragility, of "the need of Him," of the need not to forget Him. The strength of this influence depends on people's concern that this flame live in them. There is no doubt that the environment exercises a crucial role and that it is difficult in a society focused on consumerism, performance, and individualism, so this really is the heart of the work on the self, the *jihad al-nafs*, to which all Muslims are called.

12. Muslims would do well not to rush into formulaic arguments on this point: they often concentrate simply on the way an animal is slaughtered and

not on the way it is treated during its life before the ritual slaughter. It must be said repeatedly that Islamic teachings on respect for animal life are clear. The way in which sheep and other animals are treated is unacceptable, and farms where care is taken to allow animals to grow naturally and with respect are in fact more *Islamic* than is the simple application of formal rules for sacrifice.

Chapter 6

1. All Muslims should, as we shall see, acquire a minimum of knowledge in order to be able to assume their responsibility to be free and independent before God. We do not mean here that they should be able to determine *maslaha*, exercise *ijtihad*, or pronounce *fatawa*, which are the prerogative of specialists who have studied specific Islamic sciences and mastered the subject. The use of these legal instruments is extremely sensitive and is not accessible to everyone.

2. For example, most Islamic schools in Britain are for girls, and the main concern is not to provide a comprehensive, coherent, in-depth education but above all to protect them from society. The school program often finishes at the lower secondary level, and girls find themselves forced to give up studying.

3. Some Muslims who defend every Islamic school project unconditionally say that the "framework of an Islamic life" for the children is alone sufficient justification for the creation of this type of school. We know today that the behavior of children in the West is more influenced by the social environment in the broad sense (television and group fashions) than by the atmosphere that pervades the school. Without minimizing the latter, it is clear that its influence is less decisive than we used to believe.

4. No education is complete without the involvement of parents. Some people speak very glibly, often too glibly, these days of the abdication of parents who are no longer concerned with their children. Things are more complex than that, and the life some parents lead simply forces them to deal with the most urgent things, and sometimes just to "survive." Ways must nevertheless be found to involve parents in one way or another. Even in Islamic schools already functioning, we find that the lack of participation on the part of mothers and fathers is catastrophic, even counterproductive, to the point of making Islamic education itself ineffective. The complementary approach cannot be a way of cutting down on parental involvement, first and above all in the various types of contact possible in the public school system.

5. This kind of involvement can and often should be carried out in partnership with non-Muslim groups.

6. We shall return later to the question of culture.

7. The question of Arabic language learning is also crucial. The way in which it is taught in most mosques and Muslim organizations is often catastrophic and calculated to repel young people irreversibly. Some people think it is possible to produce Arabic speakers in the midst of the West but use inappropriate methods, while others have no method at all and often, year after

year, keep putting the children through the same programs, which are never fully assimilated. The results in both cases are depressing. We should be more modest and have more realistic objectives when it comes to learning classical Arabic: to have access to the basic texts (including the ability to read the Qur'an), to understand a simple passage (to let children hear the language), and to master the basic elements of speech and writing. It is most important to find ways of giving a taste for the language and awaking a desire to learn it; in other words, of giving the Arabic language value in young people's minds. Later, if the desire remains, it will be up to the young woman or man to make the necessary effort to master the language more completely. Some organizations, notably in France with the *Ecole de la réussite*, have succeeded in this area by establishing themselves professionally and producing a very serious program. They are the exception, and their example deserves to be studied and exported.

8. Some associations offer very interesting and effective programs of cultural and/or humanitarian visits, which develop a fresh relationship with history and the world.

9. It is not essential to involve the local political authorities, who often tend to be suspicious when it comes to activities linked to Islam. Working in the city and establishing contacts with various partners is, in the short term, the best way of explaining our intentions and showing the open nature of our involvement.

10. *Hadith* reported by Bayhaqi.

11. See on this subject the very interesting research of Margot Badran and especially her article "Towards Islamic Feminisms," in *Hermeneutics and Honor* (Cambridge, Mass.: Harvard University Press, 1999). After in-depth studies of the speeches of Muslim militants in the Islamic world and in the West, she suggests that, today, only a feminism anchored in Islamic tradition has some chance of success and is in the process of fostering a profound and real reform from inside Islam.

12. See the preface by Françoise Germain-Robin in *L'Islam en questions* (Paris: Actes Sud, 2000). In the thinking of Muslims, "feminism" often means "Westernization" or colonialism. A clear definition of the concept and its pitfalls is then imposed.

13. The fact that they are converts means that they are not always credible among Muslims, who see them as being Western-influenced. This is perhaps why they often educate themselves all the more seriously and rigorously in order to base their position on a solid juridical foundation. In the medium to long term, the legitimacy of the thesis cannot fail to be recognized (so well is it founded on serious and rigorous study).

14. See the works of Nilüfer Göle and Ziba Mir-Hosseini (among others), who demonstrate similar and very dynamic trends in the Muslim world.

Chapter 7

1. See on this subject the first Actes du Colloque des musulmans de l'espace francophone (CIMEF), *Musulmans francophone* (Lyon: Tawhid, 2001). The ideas

on secularism that were presented and discussed, and that also concern Muslims in Africa, explain and insist on these distinctions.

2. We shall return to this point later.

3. This is a frequent accusation. One of the points on which we are sometimes suspected of "double talk" is that we accept the secularization of society in the West, but we do not promote it, and we even oppose it, in the East. Reading between the lines, people see this as an expression of duplicity and, in discussions that agree to accept secularism, a simple stratagem designed to deceive our audience. What we have against these critics, who reach very quick conclusions, is that they confuse social orders with histories. We have already shown that the principle of "separation" was born in the West in the course of a history that was essentially about Christianity and that made possible the birth of secularism and democracy. However, we propose that the principle of "distinction" should allow Muslim societies to evolve toward an open political system based on very demanding pluralist principles. The scriptural sources inspire us with four fundamental principles in this area: the rule of law, equality of citizenship, the principle of universal suffrage, and the establishment of rules that enable change or removal of the people in power (to avoid having people "democratically" elected for life). It is for Muslim states to think of a model that would be faithful to these principles and at the same time take into account the specifics of their history and culture. The principles are universal, but not the models. Anyone who travels in Europe and the United States realizes that the general democratic principles that underpin the various systems are the same, but the models and systems vary with the countries, their history, and even their collective psychology. Why should it be otherwise for Muslim countries? The four principles previously stated are actually those on which democracy is based: it is for each Muslim majority society to choose its model and to have its specific qualities respected, as Britain, France, and the United States, to name only the most typical, require of all the other nations in the world.

4. Qur'an 13:11.

5. Qur'an 28:77.

6. *Hadith* reported by Bukhari.

7. Qur'an 16:90.

8. Qur'an 4:135.

9. Qur'an 51:19.

10. Qur'an 3:92.

11. Many Westerners are therefore mistaken about Muslims' motives. It is true that some do in fact twist their commitment by using social action to "bring people into Islam." These deviations should be recognized, and it should be made clear that the meaning of the call to Islam (*dawa*) that one finds in the Qur'an consists not in using people's needs and problems in order to deceive them about our intentions but rather in the expression of wisdom, good counsel, and worthy ideas. It is these last three qualities that identify the *call* as being simply the living testimony (*shahid*) borne by the Muslim man or woman.

12. For a presentation of these schools of thought, see the section "Typology of Trends of Thought" in chapter 1, "Encounter with the Universal."

13. For a discussion of these concepts and their acceptance, see my book *Islam, the West and the Challenges of Modernity*, Part II; *Shura or Democracy?* (Leicester, U.K.: Islamic Foundation, 2000).

14. We shall return to the question of economics in the next chapter.

15. These models are almost always based on the situation at the time of the Prophet, or a given period in history, or on the theoretical construction of an order where all would be perfect on the basis of an imagined application of revealed principles. See the discussion in part I.

16. We have already seen this in the United States during the presidential elections in November 2000, when the African American community decided, as a result of tradition or thoughtful choice, to vote for Gore, while second-generation immigrant Muslims preferred Bush. The former were sensitive to the domestic policy of the future president, while the latter were often more narrowly interested in international policy, particularly with regard to Palestine.

17. Following the Qur'an, "Develop an awareness of God as far as you are able" (64:16); "God does not require of anyone more than he can bear" (2:286); and the *hadith* "When I command you to do something, do it as much as you can" (Bukhari and Muslim).

18. Following the rule of the foundations of law and jurisprudence (*usul al-fiqh*) that stipulates that one must choose the least evil option. Compare too the Qur'anic story of Moses, whose brother Aaron chose the evil of the people's disobedience rather than the greater evil of causing them to be divided.

19. According the Qur'anic verse "God wants things to be easy for you, not difficult" (2:185) and the sound tradition "Make things easy, not difficult: spread good news, don't drive people away" (Bukhari and Muslim).

20. Following the example of the commands related to alcohol and financial interest, which were revealed in three and four stages, respectively.

21. See the whole of *sura* 12 and the story of Joseph, "Yusuf," especially v. 55: "Appoint me guardian of the storehouses. Surely I am a good guardian and of good understanding."

22. We refer here to human rights. For a discussion of the question of the rights of man, see *Islam, the West and the Challenges of Modernity*, Part I.

23. Some even come to make speeches at the mosque before or after Friday prayers.

24. *Hadith* reported by Hakim.

25. This question has been the subject of intense debate between literalist and reformist scholars: for the former giving power over a Muslim to non-Muslims is out of the question because it amounts to according them authority or establishing an alliance with them that, in their view, is forbidden in numerous verses. Among others, they quote: "O you who bear the faith, do not take as allies deniers rather than believers [Muslims]" (4:144). The interpretations the reformists give to such verses, including this one, is different: the context of Revelation makes it clear that it is a question of not establishing, in a situation of conflict, an alliance with non-Muslims who could become

enemies and, in those circumstances, act against Muslims. They also refer to the history of Muslims societies, in which political responsibilities were very early delegated to non-Muslims.

Chapter 8

1. That is, wherever the five essential objectives of the Way are protected: religion, the integrity of the person, reason, familial relations, and possessions.

2. If the word *dar* (dwelling) is perfectly appropriate to designate geographical frontiers, the word *alam* (world) is more apt for describing a categorization based on fields of activity (as for example in "the world of economics").

3. To continue to assess the "Islamic" character of a society on the sole criterion of the practice of particular laws or ways of life (as in the petromonarchies) is a partial and reductionary approach. To forget economic management and the integration of the country into the global capitalist system is illogical. This approach may point us to the areas of life where we think it may be easier to feel Muslim and live our faith in everyday matters. But this is not always the case, and this assessment, as far as our subject is concerned, is very inadequate.

4. See Qur'an 2:278–79.

5. This is the case with numerous Turkish and Pakistani individuals and organizations (of the Hanafi school) that, following this advice, have had no hesitation in making use of credit and interest to advance their affairs and business enterprises (in Britain, Germany, and France).

6. Qur'an 76:8–9.

7. Qur'an 2:261.

8. Qur'an 2:265.

9. Qur'an 17:29.

10. Qur'an 25:67.

11. Qur'an 59:9.

12. Qur'an 9:34–35.

13. Qur'an 2:271.

14. Qur'an 2:264.

15. To continue speaking of civil rights as an idealized abstraction remote from the logic of economic alienation is mistaken, and even manipulative. This fragmented approach to the actuality of industrialization gives the lie to the actual powers and prerogatives of citizens in society.

16. Qur'an 2:284.

17. Qur'an 31:20.

18. Qur'an 4:32.

19. *Hadith* reported by Muslim.

20. Hamid Algabid, *Les Banques islamiques* (Paris: Econimisa, 1990), p. 43.

21. Qur'an 30:39.

22. Qur'an 4:160–62.

23. Qur'an 3:130.

24. Qur'an 2: 275–81.

25. Qur'an 34:34.

26. On the basis of the instructions given by the Prophet to Muadh when he sent him to Yemen and asked him to tell the rich that they should pay a tax to be returned to *their* poor, making it clear that he meant the poor of their own society. *Hadith* reported by Ibn Abbas.

27. "House of goods" or "house of endowments"; these are to encourage Muslims to pay their dues regularly to institutions that specialize in managing them for the purposes designated for various types of goods (e.g., *zakat*, donations, legacies).

28. Constraining necessity may sometimes make what is forbidden permissible according to an established rule of the foundations of law and jurisprudence: "Constraining necessity allows recourse to what is forbidden."

29. For details see Yusuf al-Qaradawi, *Fi fiqh al-aqalliyyat al-muslima*, pp. 154–91.

30. They have long permitted the Hanafis to engage in economic activity with interest in important projects that are especially profitable today.

31. For these categories, see part I.

32. For the sense and details of each of these concepts, see part I.

33. On this subject see the very substantial study by Yusuf al-Qaradawi, *Fiqh al-zakat* (The understanding and legislation of *zakat*), 2 vols (Beirut: Muassasat al-Risala, 1986) (Arabic) and also, by the same author and recently translated into French by Salah Basalamah, *Le Rôle de la* zakat *dans l'assainissement des problèmes économiques* (Paris: AIEF, 2002).

34. Both through existing associations and by creating new ones completely dedicated to this work of planning and local intervention (such as already exist in the United States and Europe).

35. In this regard, we may point out that, presaging the renaissance of "civil rights," Islam demands recognition of the "economic right" to be free and autonomous. The latter protects human beings, the former gives them room to act, but one could not exist without the protection of the other. So the economic jungle killed political rights. This is what the objectives of the "Way" teach us and it is confirmed by our industrialized societies.

36. The whole of the presentation, the summary document, and the *fatwa* were published in 1966 in the journal *Al-Muslimun*, edited by Said Ramadan in Geneva (tenth bound volume).

37. Some traditional banks today are even offering "Islamic" management, which allows so-called Islamic transactions. These allow the investor to recover in one way or another the income from interest that was voluntarily "excluded." The outward appearance of respect for Muslim ethics ill conceals the reality of the desire for profit.

Chapter 9

1. Although it must be pointed out that more and more dialogue initiatives are aimed at the local level and in the United States and Europe unite believers from various religions.

2. Qur'an 2:38.

3. Qur'an 6:35.

4. Qur'an 10:99.

5. Qur'an 5:48.

6. The Qur'an confirms this in a clear general rule: "No compulsion in religion" (2:256).

7. Qur'an 2:251.

8. Qur'an 22:40.

9. Qur'an 49:13.

10. Read and understood globally, these Qur'anic references bring together all the dimensions of "difference" among human beings: tribe, nation, race, religion.

11. Qur'an 29:46.

12. It does not mean that it would be impossible to dialog with pantheistic spirituality or Buddhism, but its ground and its focus would naturally be more essentially directed toward common moral values and ethical commitment.

13. Qur'an 3:64.

14. In the mind of Muslims, the Qur'an confirms, completes, and corrects the messages that came before it, and in this Muslims hold the same position that Christians hold toward the Jews. It is a position that is in itself perfectly coherent: to believe in a Book that comes later necessarily assumes that one considers that there is a deficiency or distortion in the former.

15. Qur'an 3: 2–3.

16. Qur'an 16:125.

17. Qur'an 29:46.

18. Qur'an 5:82.

19. Qur'an 60:8.

20. Whether one translates this as "they are miscreants who . . ." or "they are infidels who . . ." depends on the sense one gives to *kafara*. We shall return to this.

21. Qur'an 5:17.

22. Qur'an 98:1. We find the same senses here: "who have done wickedly" or "who are infidels."

23. Qur'an 3:19.

24. Qur'an 3:85.

25. Qur'an 2:120.

26. Qur'an 3:28.

27. See part I.

28. Qur'an 2:34.

29. Qur'an 2: 131.

30. Qur'an 2:62.

31. On the strength of an opinion attributed to Ibn Abbas reported in al-Tabari's commentary (*tafsir*). It was said to be abrogated by 3:85, already referred to.

32. After the revelation of the last message, those who had knowledge beforehand would be judged according to their sincerity in the search for truth.

Only God is the judge of this, and no human being can declare another's destiny, or his own.

33. The concept of "milla" used in this verse to express the idea of religion conveys the idea of "people"s community of faith," a sense of belonging, much more than the word "din," which is "religion" or "concept and way of life" per se.

34. In Qur'anic usage, the word *mumin* (bearer of faith) usually means *Muslim*.

35. Qur'an 60:9.

36. Qur'an 16:125.

37. Qur'an 2:143.

38. As I see it, interreligious debate cannot take place by way of a debate on theological questions. We often witness a choice between extremes: either the discussion is completely theological, or the theological aspect is totally ignored and people behave as if the cause of the problem were understood. Both approaches are, in my view, defective and illusory.

Chapter 10

1. I do not believe it is a question of belittling, even despising, the culture of origin. It is a source of wealth, a powerful aspect of the plural character of the identity of the children of immigrants, and they must be taught to live it as it is, to be inspired by and proud of it. Our intention here is to put an end to the confusion between religious principles and culture. Respect for religious principles is not the same as preserving the richness of a culture of origin.

2. We refer to "Western" culture generally in order to clarify the principle, but it is clear that the French, American, British, German, and Swedish cultures are not the same. This work of integration must take place in each country, and Muslims will naturally take on different cultural features. Differences are already apparent among American, French, British, and Belgian Muslims, for example.

3. See *To Be a European Muslim*, Part III.

4. A summary of the arguments can be found in *To Be a European Muslim*, Part II.

5. For two basic reasons: first, on the basis of the arguments put forward by the two parties, and second, because it is juridically preferable (*min bab al-tarji*) as a way of dealing with the realities of life in the West.

Conclusion

1. This book has sketched out the global vision. The nature of involvement is a function of the realities and the factors that Muslims must take into account.

2. These acts are expressed in various ways: through surveillance by the security services of the various states and through collaboration with governments in countries of origin. Control also takes multiple forms: the obsession

with "Muslim representation" on the national level is one of its manifestations. We are pressed to find a spokesperson for Muslims lest something should emerge not to the liking of the authorities. It is true that Muslim representation is important, but it is not a priority to the extent that all the legitimate processes of representation based on popular choice, election, and respect for diversity and independence should be overridden. The obsession with control in some governments has no concern for the betrayal of democratic principles. But in the end it is for Muslims to find out how to differentiate between "being represented" and "being controlled."

GLOSSARY

Ahkam, plur. of hukm: rulings, values, prescriptions, commandments, judgments, laws stemming from Islamic law.

Aqida: faith and all the matters related to the six pillars of *al-iman* (God, his names, his attributes, the angels, the prophets, the day of Judgment, and predestination). In general, it studies what is beyond sensory perception. It does not exactly cover the sphere of theology or that of Christian dogmatics, despite what some orientalists attempted to suggest. Neither does it correspond to the sphere of philosophy, understood in the sense of Western philosophy.

Asl, plur. usul: root, origin, source, foundation.

Ayah, plur. ayat: sign, indication, but also verse.

Dalala: meaning, implication.

Dalil: proof, indication, evidence, scriptural support, and source.

Dhahir: manifest, apparent. The literal meaning of the text.

Dhanni: inexplicit, leaving room for conjecture as to its origin and/or allowing scope to interpretation as to its meaning.

Faqih, fuqaha: literally, "who understands deeply." Generally defines the jurist who masters the sciences of law and jurisprudence, but this title is sometimes used for scholars of very diverse abilities. By referring to etymology, one may apply this term to individuals who possess great religious knowledge, without thinking of a particular field of specialization. In the language of specialists, the term rather refers to those who are conversant with legal matters without necessarily being competent to develop and

253

formulate specific and/or new legal rulings. Their knowledge may relate to one particular school or to several, they may know the views expressed about a given legal issue, they may for instance know the points on which scholars disagree, they may also express one or several already formulated legal rulings, but this is generally where their competence stops. The *mujtahid* or *mufti* are generally acknowledged *fuqaha*, but a respected *faqih* is not necessarily a *mujtahid* or a *mufti*.

Far, plur. furu: branch, subdivision, secondary element as opposed to roots, foundations (*usul*). It also means a new case in the practice of *qiyas*.

Fard ayn: personal, individual duty or obligation.

Fard kafai (kifaya): collective obligation. If part of the community takes care of it and fulfils such an obligation, the rest is relieved of it.

Fatwa, plur. fatawa: specific legal ruling: it can be a mere reminder of a prescription explicitly stated by the sources, or else a scholar's development on the basis of an inexplicit text, or in the case of a specific situation for which there is no scriptural source.

Fiqh: Islamic law and jurisprudence. It comprises two general sections that are based on different and opposed methodological approaches: *al-ibadat*, worship, where only what is prescribed is permitted; and *al-muamalat*, social affairs, where everything is permitted except what is explicitly forbidden.

Hadith, plur. ahadith: reported and authenticated traditions about what the Prophet said, did, or approved.

Hukm taklifi: restrictive law defining rights and obligations. It is based on human responsibility.

Ijma: consensus of opinion, in the sense of unanimous or majority opinion.

Ijtihad: literally "effort," it has become a technical term meaning the effort accomplished by a jurist, either to extract a law or a ruling from unexplicit scriptural sources or to formulate a specific legal opinion in the absence of texts of reference.

Illa: the actual cause of a specific ruling. It makes it possible to understand a ruling through its cause and thus opens the way to elaborating other rulings through analogy or extension.

Imam, plur. aimma: literally, "the one who is placed at the front." Applies to any person, specifically trained or not, who directs prayer or officiates during Friday sermons. More particularly, this term is used to qualify a scholar who has historically left his mark on the development of Islamic sciences and knowledge, especially in the field of law and jurisprudence. One thus speaks of the "great *imams (aimma)*" when thinking of Abu Hanifa, Malik, al-Shafii Ibn Hanbal, or Jafar al-Sadiq, for instance. This may express the recognition of the community as a whole or sometimes, more specifically, of the circle, the school of thought, or organization in which the said scholar may have been involved.

Istihsan: judging something good, it is in fact the application of "legal preference."

Istinbat: both inductive and deductive extraction of the implicit or hidden meaning of a given text. More broadly, it means extracting, pointing out the laws and rulings specified by a scriptural source.

Istishab: presumption of continuity of what was previously prescribed.

Istislah: consideration linked to general interest.

Jumhur: majority trend, when referring to the majority opinion among the conflicting views of scholars; this does not affect the validity of a minority opinion if it is justified.

Kalam: literally "speech." In *ilm al-kalam*, it is linked to Islamic philosophy but also concerns fields that, according to the Western repartition of domains, involve theology or dogmatics. This science is, in several aspects, situated at the intersection of these three spheres.

Madhhab, plur. madhahib: juridical school.

Makruh: abhorred.

Mandub (or mustahab): recommended.

Maqasid, sing. maqsud: objectives, aims, finalities.

Maslaha: consideration of public interest.

Mubah: permitted.

Mufti: some scholars have often made undifferentiated use of the terms "*mujtahid*" and "*mufti*," as for instance al-Shatibi (whom we mentioned in the second chapter of the first part). The link indeed seems natural, since the practice of *ijtihad* is necessary to the formulation of a *fatwa* (same root as *mufti*). A *mufti* (man or woman) is therefore someone who formulates specific legal opinions on the basis of inexplicit texts or in the absence of specific texts. Three slight specificities were pointed out by scholars to justify the differences in denominations and functions. The *mufti* is clearly at the disposal of the community or of individuals; his function is to *answer* questions; and these questions direct his reflection; this is not the case for the *mujtahid* (man or woman), who is not necessarily asked questions and who can work upstream. More than the *mujtahid*, since he works downstream and interacts more directly with his environment, the *mufti* must know the people and society he lives among; this is also required of the *mujtahid*, but less expressly. Lastly, some have noted a mere institutional difference: the *mufti* is a *mujtahid* who has been employed by the state or who serves a specific institution to formulate legal rulings and direct the administration of affairs. The *mufti* is thus simply a *mujtahid* who has become a civil servant. The same distinctions exist among scholars regarding the *mufti mutlaq* and the *mufti muqayyad*.

Mujtahid: a scholar working on scriptural sources in order to infer or extract judgments and legal rulings. He is recognized as competent to practice *ijtihad* (same Arabic root, *ja-ha-da*) on inexplicit texts or in the absence of specific texts. Numerous qualities are required to reach this level of competence: (1) knowledge of the Arabic language; (2) knowledge of Qur'an and *hadith* sciences; (3) deep knowledge of the objectives *(maqasid)* of the *Sharia*; (4) knowledge of the questions on which there was a consensus: that makes it necessary to know the substance of the works on secondary questions *(furu)*; (5) knowledge of the principle of analogical reasoning *(qiyas)* and its methodology; (6) knowledge of the historical, social, and political context; that is, the situation of people living around him *(ahwal an-nas)*; (7) recognition by others of his competence, honesty, reliability, and uprightness (see the detailed analysis in the second chapter of part I). Scholars have distinguished two types of *mujtahid*, for whom the required competence criteria are different:

1. *Mujtahid al-mutlaq* (absolute): One who extracts legal rulings and opinions directly from the sources and beyond all specific school criteria. His recognized knowledge of texts and methodological principles enables him to formulate views that do not necessarily refer to juridical schools and their rules.
2. *Mujtahid al-muqayyad* (limited): One who simply extracts prescriptions within the framework of a specific juridical school. The conditions required for this are of course less demanding; they also include the knowledge of the deduction rules linked to the juridical school to which the *mujtahid al-muqayyad* belongs or refers.

Mukallaf: one who has reached the age of puberty and who is in full possession of one's mental faculties.

Muqayyad: limited, restricted, defined, determined, circumscribed. This also qualifies a *mujtahid* who formulates legal rulings within a specific juridical school.

Mutlaq: absolute, unrestricted. Also qualifies a mujtahid who is competent to formulate legal rulings beyond juridical schools, directly from the sources.

Qati: clear-cut, explicit, definite, leaving no scope for speculation as to its interpretation.

Rukhsa, rukhas: alleviations in the practice or implementation of prescriptions due, for example, to age, illness, travel, poverty, or social conditions.

Rukn, plur. arkan: pillar, fundamental principle.

Sahih: authentic, meeting specific authentication criteria.

Shahada: the profession of faith and its testimony through the formulation, with the heart and intelligence, of "I bear witness that there is no god but God and that Muhammad is His prophet." It is the foundation, the axis, and the determination of *"being a Muslim."*

Sharia: There is no one single definition of the concept of *Sharia*. Scholars have generally circumscribed its meaning from the standpoint of their own sphere of specialization. Starting from the broadest to the most restricted acceptations, we may present the definitions as follows:

1. *Sharia*, on the basis of the root of the word, means "the way," "the path leading to the source," and outlines a global conception of creation, existence, and death and the way of life it entails, stemming from a normative reading and an understanding of scriptural sources. It determines *"how to be a Muslim."*
2. *Sharia*, for the *usuliyyun* and jurists, is the corpus of general principles of Islamic law extracted form its two fundamental sources, the Qur'an and the Sunna, but also using the other main sources *(al-ijma and al-qiyas)* and secondary ones *(al-istihsan, al-istislah, al-istishab, al-urf)*.

Shart, plur. shurut: condition, sometimes criterion.

Sheikh, plur. shuyukh: literally "old": generally qualifies persons who have a degree in one branch or another of Islamic sciences. It is also very broadly used to express students' respect or recognition of a teacher's abilities, even if the teacher does not have an official degree. One can note some obvious instances of excess in this respect. In mystical paths and circles, the *sheikh* is the initiating master who guides and accompanies the *murid* (the initiate in quest of knowledge) on the path to knowledge and elevation.

Shura: consultation.

Takhsis: restriction from a general to a specific meaning.

Taklif: responsibility, obligation.

Taqlid: imitation. In legal matters, it means the blind imitation of one's predecessors without questioning, assessing, checking, or criticizing their legal opinions.

Tasawwuf: Sufism. It is in fact a science, the science of mysticism, which has a specific framework, norms, and a technical and specialized vocabulary. It requires an initiation. Synthetically, it comprises the studies of different scholars or schools concerning the stages and states that allow intimate progress toward God. It is the dimension of *al-haqiqa*, of truth, of ultimate spiritual Reality, that only the nearest can know.

Tawhid: faith in the unity of God.

Tawil: interpretation, specifically in the sciences of faith: allegorical or metaphorical interpretation.

Tazkiyyah (*al-nafs*): effort of spiritual purification, initiation to spiritual elevation.

Ulama, sing. Alim: literally, "the one who knows." A scholar in a broad sense, who may be specialized in one particular branch of Islamic sciences. It can today refer to those who have graduated from a university with a degree in a field related to Islamic sciences (the term *mawlana* is also used to express the idea of "scholar" or *sheikh*).

Umma: community of faith, spiritual community, uniting all Muslim men and women throughout the world in their attachment to Islam.

Usul al-fiqh: The fundamental principles of Islamic law: it expounds the principles and methodology by means of which the rules of law and jurisprudence are inferred and extracted from their sources. It involves the study and formulation of rules of interpretation, obligation, and prohibition, global principles, *ijtihad (ijma, qiyas)*, and so on.

Usuli, plur. usuliyyun: a scholar conversant with the knowledge of the fundamental principles of Islamic law. Such scholars work on the Qur'an and Sunna and must master the juridical instruments and know the principles and methodology by means of which the rules of law and jurisprudence are inferred and extracted from their sources. They study rules of interpretation and the fields related to obligation and prohibition, as well as general orientation rules. The principles of implementation of *ijtihad, ijma* or *qiyas* also fall within their province, although this does not mean they are competent to implement them themselves. Their knowledge is first of all essentially theoretical. A *mujtahid* or a *mufti* necessarily masters the field of knowledge and competence of an *usul* scholar, but such scholars are not immediately nor necessarily *mujtahid* or a *mufti* since their knowledge may be only theoretical, merely enabling them to identify the instruments of extraction and deduction without being competent to make use of them.

Wajib: obligation, often used as a synonym of *fard* except by Hanafi jurists.

INDEX

Council on Islamic Education (CIE), 135
"couscous de l'amitié," 155
covenant, original, 16–17, 19–20, 31
creation, story of, 16
creativity, 219–23
creed, 56, 115
critical interpretation. See *ijtihad*
cultural alternative, 24, 214–23, 251nn1,2,5
cultures of origin, 215, 251n1

dar al-ahd, 66–67, 69, 72
dar al-dawa, 72–75, 239n13
dar al-harb, 27, 63–77, 239nn1,5,10,12
  economic resistance and, 175–77, 190–91, 196–97
dar al-islam, 63–67, 69–70, 72, 239nn3,4,8
  economic resistance and, 175–76
Dassetto, Felice, 242n4
David, 50
dawa, 73–74, 205, 208, 240n15, 246n11
deficits, 105–9, 242n7
democracy, 158–59, 164, 172, 233n40, 235n6, 246n3
Deobandis, 24, 196, 232n33
development cooperatives, 173, 199
dialogical monologue, 33
dialogue, 5, 106, 124–25, 157–58, 166–67, 200–213, 226
dictatorships, 111, 164, 171–72, 233n40
difference. *See* diversity; Otherness
discretion, 180–81
discrimination
  dar al-harb and, 71
  immigrant populations and, 147
  interreligious dialogue and, 212
  Islamic education and, 134
  Islamophobia as, 6–7, 154, 226
  social commitment and, 153–54, 156
  women and, 139, 141, 143, 217
"Divers-Cité," 156
diversity
  cultural alternative and, 214
  dar al-harb and, 68
  as deficit, 105–6

interreligious dialogue and, 202–4, 210, 250n10
Revelation and, 21
Sharia and, 32, 235n7
social commitment and, 158
divorce, 140–41, 143
double discourse, 29
dress codes, 24, 25, 27, 36, 235n8
dualistic vision, 5
  cultural alternative and, 219
  dar al-islam vs. *dar al-harb*, 64–68, 75–76, *fig. 3.1*
  Islamic education and, 127
  Islamic sciences and, 58
  Otherness and, 5–6, 52, 54
  principle of integration and, 52–54, 115
  tawhid and, 14–17, 230n10
al-Dusuqi, 65, 239n4
dysfunctions, societal, 143, 147, 153–55, 167, 189–90

Ecole de la réussite, 244–45n7
ecology, 19, 156, 182–83, 231n24
economic resistance, 174–99, 248n15
education, Islamic
  belonging to *umma* and, 99, 100–101
  cultural alternative and, 221
  dar al-harb and, 71
  interreligious dialogue and, 211–12
  isolationism and, 107
  Muslim identity and, 81–82
  reform of, 126–43
  social commitment and, 150
efforts. *See jihads*
egoism, 180, 183
elections, 159, 164–65, 170–71, 247nn16,23,25
Eliade, Mircea, 16
emotions, 108, 117–25, 241n57
eradicators (Algeria), 233n40
essential principles. *See* universal principles
ethics
  consumption and, 123–25
  cultural alternative and, 215–16, 220

historical models, 36, 133, 160,
235n6, 246–47nn3,15
Hizb al-Tahrir movement, 27
home ownership, 190–91, 195, 199
housing, 150, 190–91
Hudaybiyya, peace of, 63, 92, 239n2
human intelligence, 22, 34, 36–37,
80–81
humanism, 56, 111, 124
human nature, 14–19
human rights. *See* rights
humility
"need of Him" and, 18, 20–21, 31,
122–25, 138, 224
Sharia and, 37, 235n9
Huntington, Samuel P., 226

Iblis, 205
Ibn Abbas, 250n31
Ibn al-Arabi, 237n35
Ibn al-Qayyim al-Jawziyya, 42, 44,
46
Ibn Baz, 232n35
Ibn Hanbal, 237n35
Ibn Hazm, 38, 193, 236n18
Ibn Hisham, 64
Ibn Taymiyya, 65
Ibn Uthaymin, 232n35
idolatry, 18, 19, 120–21, 180
ijtihad, 21–22, 43–48, 115,
237nn30,35
Ahbash and, 30
conditions of, 46–48, 237–
38nn36,38–41
cultural alternative and, 219–23
economic resistance and, 192, 197
fatawa and, 48
Islamic education and, 244n1
Muslim identity and, 83
political participation and, 159–60,
163
principle of integration and, 51–
52, 54
salafi reformism and, 26, 28–29
scholastic traditionalism and, 24–
25
women and, 141–42
Ilam al-wuwaqqiin an rabb al-alamin
(Ibn al-Qayyim al-Jawziyya), 46
immigrant populations
assets of, 103–5

contributions of, 111
cultural alternative and, 215–16,
251n1
deficits of, 105–6, 242n3
economic resistance and, 195
Islamic education and, 126, 135
Muslim identity and, 78
political participation and, 171,
172
principle of integration and, 52
social commitment and, 147
independence, 6, 229n4
individualism, 28, 29, 243n11
inheritance, 38, 95, 183
inner-city schools, 132
inspiration, 145, 147
insurance, obligatory, 95, 195
integration into Western society
cultural alternative and, 214, 216,
218, 220, 251n2
economic resistance and, 191, 199
liberal reformism and, 27, 224
political participation and, 171–73
principle of, 51–55, 115, 139
Sharia and, 34
interest, financial. See *riba*
International Institute of Islamic
Thought (IIIT), 58
internationalism, 68, 173
International Monetary Fund, 172,
174
interreligious dialogue, 200–213,
249–51nn1,12,38
Interreligious Platform (Geneva), 212
intracommunal dialogue, 106, 209–
10
islam, 206
Islamic associations
Islamic education and, 137,
245nn8,9
political participation and, 165,
167, 173
social commitment and, 146, 153–
58
women's emancipation and, 142
Islamic Benevolent Association, 29,
234nn43,44
Islamic economics, 182–88
Islamic identity. *See* Muslim identity
Islamic schools. *See* private schools,
Islamic

Islamic sciences, 21
  dar al-harb and, 69
  interreligious dialogue and, 205
  salafi literalism and, 25
  Sharia and, 55–61, *figs. 2.1,2,*
    238nn57–59
  as source, 4, 229n2
"Islamization of knowledge," 58
Islamophobia, 6–7, 154, 226
isolationism, 107, 154, 168, 216–19,
  221
istislah, 38, 235nn10,17
Al-Itisam (al-Shatabi), 236n18

Jazara rebels, 26
Jesus, 187
Jews, 146, 151, 169, 186, 203–7,
  210, 250–51nn14,33
jihad al-nafs, 119, 120, 243n11
jihads, 27, 113–14, 120, 221, 225,
  243n6
jinn, 229n6
Joseph, 98, 164, 247n21
jugular vein, 12, 229n3
jurisprudence. See *fiqh*
justice
  belonging to *umma* and, 89–92,
    94, 98, 100, 240–41nn46,56
  economic resistance and, 179–80,
    184, 186–87, 194
  interreligious dialogue and, 204
  path toward (see *Sharia*)
  political participation and, 161,
    163–64, 168, 170
  social commitment and, 151–53,
    156
al-Juwayni, 39

Kaba, 115
kafara, 205, 250nn20,21
Kamali, Hashim, 43, 44, 236n23
Kant, Immanuel, 53
Khallaf, Abd al-Wahhab, 44, 236–
  37nn23,35
al-Khattab, Umar ibn, 195
kuffar, 16, 30, 205–6, 234nn43,44

laicism. *See* secularization
Latinos, 195
Latouche, Serge, 5
law. See *fiqh*

League of Human Rights, 156
League of Scholars of Sharia, 190–
  91, 196, 199
legal opinions. See *fatawa*
liberal reformism, 27–29, *fig. 1.1,*
  224, 233nn39,40
  cultural alternative and, 222
  economic resistance and, 191
  political participation and, 159–60,
    247n25
liberation of self, 119–22
literalists. *See salafi* literalism; *salafi*
  political literalism
living faith, 70–71
lobbying, 169
longing for the Transcendent. *See*
  fitra
loyalty, 93–96, 146–47, 191

madrasas, 126
Al-Mahajirun movement, 27
al-Mahmasani, Subhi Rajab, 41
Malik, Imam, 38, 236n23
Maliki school, 38, 40, 65, 192
Manichean approach. *See* dualistic
  vision
Mansuri, Shabbir, 135
marriage contracts, 95, 100–101,
  139–41
Marx, Karl, 231–32n30
masalih mursala, 42–43
maslaha, 38–43, 115, 235–37nn10,14–
  19,22,23,30
  belonging to *umma* and, 99
  economic resistance and, 192, 196–
    98
  fatawa and, 49
  Islamic education and, 244n1
  Muslim identity and, 83
  political participation and, 161
  principle of integration and, 51,
    54
maslaha al-mursala, 40–41, 161,
  236nn20,22
al-Mawardi, 193
al-Mawlawi, Faysal, 66, 72, 73, 75,
  94
Mecca, 89, 92, 188
Meccan period, 72–73
media coverage, 174, 233n38
Medina, 35–36, 91–92

microcredits, 193
minority thinking, 53–55, 107–8,
    154, 156, 165, 242n4
Mir-Hosseini, Ziba, 245n14
monopolies, 183–84, 186, 188
monotheism, 203, 211, 250n12
Moses, 247n18
Muadh, 43, 248–49n26
Muhammad, W. D., 104
Muhammad Ali, 98
mujtahid, 46–50, 237–38nn38–
    41,45,46
Murids (Senegal), 28
Muslim, 207, 251n34
Muslim American Society, 104
Muslim associations. *See* Islamic
    associations
Muslim Brothers, 26
Muslim identity, 69–70, 77–85, *fig.*
    3.3, 115, 239n9
    action and participation, 82–85
    belonging to *umma* and, 86–93,
        100
    cultural alternative and, 216, 220
    education and transmission, 81
    faith, practice, and spirituality, 79
    Islamic education and, 130–31
    Sharia and, 33, 234–35n3
    understanding of texts and
        context, 80–81
    women and, 105
Muslim-majority societies, 4, 53–54,
    176, 232n34, 238nn52,53
Muslim minority, 6, 53–55, 68, 107–
    8, 242n4
"Muslim personality," 4
Al-mustasfa min ilm al-usul (al-
    Ghazali), 39
Al-mutamad fi usul al-fiqh (Abu al-
    Husayn al-Basri), 39, 46
Mutazilism, 39, 233n39
mysticism, 34, 115, 119, 125, 235n4

Nahda movement, 26
names of the Transcendent, 13,
    230n9
Nanutfi, Qasim, 196
Naqshbandis, 28
national identity, 93–96, 111, 242n8
natural religion, 206
nature, 12–13, 16, 121–22

necessity, 159–60, 176, 190, 198,
    249n28
need, 159–60, 176, 183, 190, 193
"need of Him," 7, 13–14, 18, 20, 31,
    224
    cultural alternative and, 222
    Islamic education and, 129, 138
    spirituality and, 122–23, 243n11
neoliberal capitalist system. *See*
    capitalist system
Noah, 187

oaths, 96, 241n54
oneness of God. See *tawhid*
*On Law and the Jurisprudence of
    Muslim Minorities* (al-Qaradawi),
    53, 238n52
Organization of African Unity, 66
Organization of Islamic Conference
    (OCI), 185
original sin, 16
Otherness, 224
    deficits and, 107, 124
    dualistic vision and, 5–6, 52, 54
    in Islamic education, 128, 138
    political participation and, 168
    social commitment and, 147, 158

pantheism, 250n12
paradigm shifts, 135
parallel Islam, 123, 130–31, 134, 217–
    18, 233n41
parents, 87–88, 135, 143, 244n4
Parmenides, 230n10
partnerships, 155–56
Pascal, Blaise, 17
patriotic allegiance. *See* loyalty
Peasant Confederation, 173
periphery. *See* center/periphery
persecution, 92, 233n37, 240n50
petromonarchies, 175, 248n3
pilgrimage, 89, 115, 120, 181
pledge, 81, 93
pluralism, 5–6
    dar al-harb and, 68, 76
    interreligious dialogue and, 200,
        209
    Islamic education and, 135
    Muslim contributions to, 111
    Sharia and, 32
    social commitment and, 158